Understanding Attitude in
Intercultural Virtual Communication

Advances in CALL Research and Practice
Series Editor: Greg Kessler, Ohio University

This series is published in cooperation with the Computer Assisted Language Instruction Consortium (CALICO). Each Spring just prior to the CALICO annual conference the series publishes one volume comprised of original studies on a specific topic.

Published:
2016
Landmarks in CALL Research
Edited by Greg Kessler

2017
Learner Autonomy and Web 2.0
Edited by Marco Cappellini, Tim Lewis, and Annick Rivens Mompean

2018
Assessment Across Online Language Education
Edited by Stephanie Link and Jinrong Li

2019
Engaging Language Learners through CALL
Edited by Nike Arnold and Lara Ducate

Understanding Attitude in Intercultural Virtual Communication

Edited by Ana Oskoz and Margarita Vinagre

SHEFFIELD UK   BRISTOL CT

Published by Equinox Publishing Ltd.

UK: Office 415, The Workstation, 15 Paternoster Row, Sheffield, South Yorkshire S1 2BX
USA: ISD, 70 Enterprise Drive, Bristol, CT 06010

www.equinoxpub.com

First published 2020

© Ana Oskoz, Margarita Vinagre and contributors 2020

All rights reserved. No part of this publication may be reproduced or transmitted in any form or by any means, electronic or mechanical, including photocopying, recording or any information storage or retrieval system, without prior permission in writing from the publishers.

British Library Cataloguing-in-Publication Data
A catalogue record for this book is available from the British Library.

ISBN-13   978 1 78179 937 6   (paperback)
ISBN-13   978 1 78179 938 3   (ePDF)

Library of Congress Cataloging-in-Publication Data
Names: Oskoz, Ana, editor. | Vinagre Laranjeira, Margarita, editor.
Title: Understanding attitude in intercultural virtual communication / edited by Ana Oskoz and Margarita Vinagre.
Description: Sheffield, South Yorkshire ; Bristol, CT : Equinox Publishing Ltd, 2020. | Series: Advances in CALL research and practice | Includes bibliographical references and index. | Summary: "Understanding Attitude in Intercultural Virtual Communication focuses on attitude, the 'willingness to explore, learn and participate in online networks, collaborate with others, share ideas, knowledge, media and contribute to the collective construction of knowledge' (Helm & Guth, 2010, p. 81) in telecollaborative encounters. Recent studies have suggested that, to ensure successful virtual collaboration, interpersonal factors such as identity, rapport and trust are essential and the development of these factors relies heavily on the attitudinal dimension and how participants chose to reflect it in their interaction (Oskoz & Gimeno-Sanz, in press; Vinagre & Corral, 2018; Vinagre & Corral, forthcoming). In telecollaboration, research on the participants' use of attitudinal resources has been mostly content-based and Byram's (1997) model of intercultural competence the approach most widely used for analysis. More recently, studies have looked at attitude from a linguistic perspective, and frameworks such as appraisal (Martin & White, 2005) that examine L2 learners' attitudes and ideological positions have been employed. Despite these efforts, research in this field is still scarce and this volume aims to further explore this topic by gathering contributions in which a variety of approaches and perspectives have been taken to investigate attitude in virtual communication"-- Provided by publisher.
Identifiers: LCCN 2019034721 (print) | LCCN 2019034722 (ebook) | ISBN 9781781799376 (paperback) | ISBN 9781781799383 (ebook)
Subjects: LCSH: Language and languages--Computer-assisted instruction. | Intercultural communication. | Teaching teams. | Language teachers--Attitudes. | Language teachers--Training of. | Internet in education--Social aspects.
Classification: LCC P53.28 .U48 2020 (print) | LCC P53.28 (ebook) | DDC 418.0071--dc23
LC record available at https://lccn.loc.gov/2019034721
LC ebook record available at https://lccn.loc.gov/2019034722

Typeset by S.J.I. Services, New Delhi, India

Contents

	Introduction *Ana Oskoz and Margarita Vinagre*	1
1	Reconsidering Attitude as a Relational and Negotiated Sociocognitive Construct *Zsuzsanna I. Abrams*	9
2	Intercultural Virtual Communication and Novice Learners: Attitudes, Perception, and Beliefs *Liudmila Klimanova and Valentina Vinokurova*	30
3	Exploring Attitude in Bilingual Virtual Exchanges: A Linguistic Perspective *Margarita Vinagre and Ana Oskoz*	64
4	Linguistic and Non-Linguistic Choices and Attitudes in an East-West Telecollaboration *Carolin Fuchs, Tsz Yan Lo, and Sneha Thapa*	92
5	Understanding L2 Teachers' Attitudes via Their Uses of Multimodal Resources in Telecollaboration *Meei-Ling Liaw and Sabrina Priego*	117
6	What's with the Attitude? Exploring Attitudinal Resources in Telecollaboration for Teacher Education *D. Joseph Cunningham and Marianna Ryshina-Pankova*	144
7	Researching Emotions and Attitude through Student Teachers' Reflections on Virtual Exchange *Francesca Helm and Alice Baroni*	166
	Index	196

Introduction

Ana Oskoz and Margarita Vinagre

There is no question about the increasing presence in our classrooms of telecollaborative encounters or virtual exchanges, the practice "of sustained, technology-enabled, people-to-people activities in which constructive communication and interaction takes place between individuals or groups who are geographically separated and/or from different cultural backgrounds, with the support of educators or facilitators" (Evolve, 2019: para. 1). In its beginnings, the emphasis of telecollaborative encounters was placed on the development of learners' cultural knowledge and intercultural awareness (Schenker, 2012). Today, pedagogical and empirical research in virtual exchanges have also focused on second language (L2) learning (Chun, 2011; O'Dowd & Lewis, 2016), the presence of different technology-based modes, and their impact on participants' literacies (Fuchs, Hauck, & Müller-Hartmann, 2012) and teacher preparation (Vinagre, 2015).

Among the studies that explored the development of intercultural competence in the foreign language classroom, we find that many have followed Byram's (1997) model of Intercultural Communicative Competence (ICC) and adopted his definition of intercultural competence understood as "the ability to relate to and communicate with people who speak a different language and live in a different cultural context" (p. 1). According to Byram, successful intercultural communication depends on the speaker's ability to manage relationships with others, accept various perspectives and ideas of the world, and mediate between them. Specific skills, attitudes, and knowledge that shape his model of ICC are required to achieve these objectives.

In virtual exchange, studies that have applied Byram's (1997) proposal to assess the presence of intercultural competence are also abundant (Belz, 2003; O'Dowd, 2003; Elola & Oskoz, 2008; Schenker, 2012; Vinagre, 2016). Yet, few have focused on its attitudinal component given the difficulty its analysis poses for researchers. Vogt (2006) even refers to the impossibility of assessing this component in virtual exchange. However, attitude is particularly relevant for virtual intercultural learning, since, unlike other components of Byram's model, it is both a necessary prerequisite and an anticipated outcome of intercultural competence. Hence, an early analytic focus on attitude may serve practical purposes as well as theoretical ones, for practitioners and participants engaged in virtual exchange (Belz, 2003). Following Belz's and Vogt's call, we envisioned this book as a contribution to the exploration of attitude in telecollaborative encounters.

Overall, in tellecollaborative studies, attitude has been defined as the "willingness to explore, learn and participate in online networks, collaborate with others, share ideas, knowledge, media and contribute to the collective construction of knowledge" (Helm & Guth, 2010: 81). In this context, we were aware that, while Byram's (1997) model has been the most widely employed to assess attitude to date, other frameworks, such as appraisal (Martin & White, 2005; White, 2015) or Bennet's (1993, 2011, 2017) developmental model of intercultural sensitivity, could be as valid to examine L2 learners' attitudes and ideological positions in their online discussions. In fact, the seven chapters that compose this volume provide different approaches to the analysis of attitude, focusing both on L2 learners and trainee teachers. We have also become aware that, while Byram's (1997) framework is still prevalent in telecollaborative work, current research either combines his model with other proposals or applies entirely new models to the analysis of attitude. For example, taking as a starting point Gardner & Lambert's (1972) socio-educational model of motivation and attitude, Bennett's (1993, 2011, 2017) developmental model of intercultural sensitivity, and Byram's (1997) model, in Chapter 1, Abrams redefines the concept of attitude as a relational and dynamic experience. After examining the benefits of telecollaboration to help develop positive attitudes toward the target culture, she also highlights the challenges of telecollaboration since, for many reasons that include differences in communication styles among others, it can have the opposite effect. Her contribution points out that most current research has focused on the individual learner, who is supposed to be open to new experiences and beliefs, rather than on the role that interlocutors might play in shaping their listeners' attitudes. That is, previous research has ignored the role that social context, people, tasks, and technological tools have in L2 learners' attitudes in virtual interaction. In order to address one of these issues, Abrams provides us with guidelines pertaining to task design in telecollaboration, including timing, content, and format, that can enhance the maintenance or development of attitudes (understood as openness, curiosity, acceptance, engagement, and interest) during telecollaborative projects.

Another example of how Byram's (1997) model is combined or supported by other proposals is provided in Chapter 4 by Fuchs, Yan Lo, and Thapa. These authors connect Byram's (1997) model to Breen & Littlejohn's

(2000) proposal in order to analyze attitudes in virtual negotiation. In their study, graduate students from Hong Kong collaborated with student teachers in Germany to complete three sequential tasks using different technological tools (Facebook, Google Docs, Wix). Following an ethnographic approach to data analysis and using a triangulation of instruments that included content from discussions and post-project questionnaires, their findings indicate that, regardless of task performance, participants made both linguistic and non-linguistic choices that facilitated team negotiations, such as using accommodating propositions, emoticons, or constructive communication styles. According to the authors, these constructive communication styles were reflective of students' positive attitudes toward each other and the exchange. In contrast, frequent L1 use or aggressive communication styles led to participants' negative attitudes towards each other and frustration with the project.

Within the context of student-teacher training, in Chapter 5, Liaw and Priego contend that the effects of telecollaboration cannot be properly understood without a sound understanding of how multimodality, the use of different modes in an integrated manner to communicate meaning, affects teachers' attitudes or abilities to "decenter" (Byram, 1997) from pre-existing notions of language learning and teaching. The analyses of the multimodal ensembles (i.e., Google Docs discussions, joint reflections, and finalized collages) created by pre- and in-service teachers in Taiwan and Canada engaged in a telecollaborative encounter, reveal the participants' ability to decenter from their individual pre-conceptions of language teaching. That is, participating in multimodal designs can provide teachers with opportunities for intercultural dialoguing of pedagogical issues and allow for epistemological and cultural decentering.

Other proposals for the analysis of attitude in virtual interaction, in particular focusing on learners' perceptions, can be found in Chapters 2 and 7. In Chapter 2, Klimanova and Vinokurova examine the significance that novice L2 learners give to their telecollaborative encounters. In particular, they examine L2 learners' attitudes, perceptions, and beliefs, and willingness to explore, learn, and participate in online social networks as platforms for intercultural learning, using their target language as a primary means of communication. Conducting both quantitative and qualitative analyses of the pre- and post-project questionnaires designed for their project, Klimanova and Vinokurova found that at beginners' language levels, learners were already excited about participating in telecollaborative encounters. Yet, as suggested by Abrams, as the communication progresses, learners' attitudes change. Reminding us of Abram's contribution, Klimanova and Vinokurova suggest that learners' identities and their language affiliations in combination with the task type and choice of communicative tools might also influence learners' evolving attitudes and perceptions.

Within a European context, Helm and Baroni, in Chapter 7, explore learners' emotions, which as the authors pose, are fundamental since emotions influence attitudes such as curiosity and "openness" to other perspectives and ways of knowing as well as the acquisition of knowledge and skills. In the context of the EVALUATE project, a large-scale policy experimentation funded by the European Commission, the authors analyzed one part of the dataset produced by participants in this project. Adopting a content analysis based on principles of grounded theory (Charmaz, 2005; 2006) as their primary methodological approach and supported by sentiment analysis using the LIWC software, Helm and Baroni drew on the participants' reflective journals to explore their emotional responses in virtual exchanges. They identified some general trends regarding the "emotional journey" of participants in virtual exchange and studied the impact of its challenges on participants and the ways in which they engaged with difference. Helm and Baroni found that most participants' attitudes oriented towards similarity in order to facilitate task completion while they avoided the risks of critical episodes and very few displayed evidence of curiosity and interest in exploring cultural diversity or divergences in opinion.

In the literature on virtual exchange, most of the studies that assess intercultural competence have relied on analyst-sensitive content analyses of interaction. According to Belz (2003), content-based interpretations of virtual interaction should be expanded by adding Hallidayan-based linguistic analyses that would "broaden the investigative focus on *what* learners say to include *how* they say it" (p. 69, emphasis in the original). As Belz continues (p. 70), the absence of linguistically-grounded examinations of intercultural communication in VE "is somewhat surprising, since advocates of intercultural learning in FLL&T tend to ground their attention to this concept in social semiotic accounts of language (e.g., Halliday, 1978)." Yet, despite this call more than a decade ago, research that provides linguistic analyses of intercultural interaction, and in particular analyses of attitude, is still scant.

In order to address this gap, Chapters 3 and 6 apply a systemic functional approach (appraisal) to analyze how students deploy attitude in virtual exchange from a linguistic perspective. Overall, the appraisal framework developed by Martin (2000), Martin & Rose (2003), and Martin & White (2005) provides a systematic account of language resources to express emotions and attitudes (attitude), the sources of evaluation and the play of voices within and across texts (engagement), as well as the amplification of both attitude and the degree of engagement (graduation). As mentioned above, these chapters are concerned with attitude, which refers to the meanings by which speakers indicate either a positive or negative assessment of people, places, things, happenings, and states of affairs.

With the intent of examining the extent to which the appraisal framework would be a reliable approach to examine L2 learners' virtual exchange interactions, in Chapter 3, Vinagre and Oskoz present the findings from two unrelated telecollaborative encounters, which involved different tasks, technological tools, number of participants, and project duration. The results of their study suggest that, despite the differences in project design, there were observable cultural discourse patterns between the participants from two universities in Spain and two universities in the United States. For example, the Spanish students tended to use more judgment markers while their American counterparts favored appreciation markers. Yet, despite these similarities across both studies in terms of the attitudinal markers employed by members of the same cultural background, the results also provided further support for the idea that participants in virtual exchanges adopted and integrated each other's pragma-linguistic discourse patterns. That is, when working together, participants from different cultural backgrounds created a common space through the use of similar attitudinal markers that helped them continue their intercultural dialogue. The resulting pragma-linguistic hybridity might be linked to the nature of the tasks and topics, social presence, and length of collaboration.

In Chapter 6, Cunningham and Ryshina-Pankova expand the application of the appraisal model to the analysis of pre-service teachers' interactions gathered over a 10-week exchange. In particular, they examined the attitudinal resources used by graduate student-teachers in the US and in Germany as materials developers in a teacher education course. Similar to Liaw and Priego, Cunningham and Ryshina-Pankova understand that the selection of pedagogical texts and the development of related teaching materials can be characterized by an extended negotiation with a common goal. The results of their study illustrate that, through a process of dialogic mediation, student-teachers express their attitudes when developing specific pedagogical materials during the synchronous audiovisual interaction. Yet, they do so differently depending on whether they are selecting a text, focusing on quality, complexity, cultural significance, and impact on learners' factors, or discussing the tasks, which learners evaluated in terms of their originality and complexity. Taken together, the findings from the two studies presented in Chapters 3 and 6 suggest that appraisal is an effective linguistic approach that can provide rich insights into the complexities of attitude in virtual interaction, and that, when used together with content-based approaches, can provide an "additional and revelatory 'analytic cut' (Layder, 1993: 108) into the rampantly complex and multi-layered social action of telecollaborative language study" (Belz, 2003: 69).

We hope that this volume will be useful for researchers and practitioners who may wish to explore attitude in their telecollaborative encounters. What we have learned from working on this volume is that, despite all the years since Belz's (2003) and Vogt's (2006) calls, attitude remains a slippery concept to grasp, and its assessment complex. As research in virtual exchange moves forward, we need to search for theoretical frameworks and methodological approaches that help us delve into participants' attitudes in the ever-growing multimodal telecollaborative world.

References

Belz, J. A. (2003). Linguistic perspectives on the development of intercultural competence in telecollaboration. *Language Learning & Technology*, 7(2), 68–99.

Bennett, M. J. (1993). Towards ethnorelativism: A developmental model of intercultural sensitivity. In M. Paige (ed.), *Education for the Intercultural Experience*. Yarmouth, ME: Intercultural Press.

Bennett, M. J. (2011). A developmental model of intercultural sensitivity. Hillsboro, OR: The Intercultural Development Research Institute. http://www.idrinstitute.org/allegati/IDRI_t_Pubblicazioni/47/FILE_Documento_Bennett_DMIS_12pp_quotes_rev_2011.pdf.

Bennett, M. J. (2017). Development model of intercultural sensitivity. In Y. Kim (ed.), *International Encyclopedia of Intercultural Communication*. New Jersey: Wiley. https://doi.org/10.1002/9781118783665.ieicc0182

Breen, M. P., & Littlejohn, A. (2000). The significance of negotiation. In M. P. Breen & A. Littlejohn (eds.), *Classroom Decision-making: Negotiation and Process Syllabuses in Practice* (pp. 5–38). Cambridge: Cambridge University Press.

Byram, M. (1997). *Teaching and Assessing Intercultural Communicative Competence*. Clevedon: Multilingual Matters.

Charmaz, K. (2005). Grounded theory in the 21st century: A qualitative method for advancing social justice research. *Handbook of Qualitative Research*, 3, 507–535.

Charmaz, K. (2006). *Constructing Grounded Theory: A Practical Guide through Qualitative Analysis*. London: Sage.

Chun, D. (2011). Developing intercultural communicative competence through online exchanges. *CALICO Journal*, 28(2), 392–419. https://doi.org/10.11139/cj.28.2.392-419

Elola, I., & Oskoz, A. (2008). Blogging: Fostering intercultural competence development in foreign language and study abroad contexts. *Foreign Language Annals*, 41(3), 421–444. https://doi.org/10.1111/j.1944-9720.2008.tb03307.x

Evolve. (2019). https://evolve-erasmus.eu/about-evolve/what-is-virtual-exchange/.
Fuchs, C., Hauck, M., & Müller-Hartmann, A. (2012). Promoting learner autonomy through multiliteracy skills development in cross-institutional exchanges. *Language Learning & Technology*, 16(3), 82–102.
Gardner, R. C., & Lambert, W. E. (1972). *Attitudes and Motivation in Second Language Learning*. Rowley, MA: Newbury House.
Halliday, M. A. K. (1978). *Language as Social Semiotic: The Social Interpretation of Language and Meaning*. London: Edward Arnold.
Helm, F., & Guth, S. (2010). The multifarious goals of Telecollaboration 2.0: Theoretical and practical implications. In S. Guth & F. Helm (eds.), *Telecollaboration 2.0: Language, Literacy and Intercultural Learning in the 21st Century* (pp. 69–106). Bern: Peter Lang.
Layder, D. (1993). *New Strategies in Social Research*. Cambridge, England: Polity Press.
Martin, J. R. (2000). Beyond exchange: Appraisal systems in English. In S. Hunston and G. Thompson (eds.), *Evaluation in Text: Authorial Stance and the Construction of Discourse* (pp. 142–175). Oxford: Oxford University Press.
Martin, J. R., & Rose, D. (2003). *Working with Discourse: Meaning beyond the Clause*. London: Continuum.
Martin J. R., & White, P. R. R. (2005). *The Language of Evaluation: Appraisal in English*. London and New York: Palgrave. https://doi.org/10.1057/9780230511910
O'Dowd R. (2003). Understanding the "other side": Intercultural learning in a Spanish-English e-mail exchange. *Language Learning & Technology*, 7(2), 118–144.
O'Dowd, R., & Lewis, T. (eds.) (2016). *Online Intercultural Exchange*. New York, NY: Routledge.
Schenker, T. (2012). Intercultural competence and cultural learning through telecollaboration. *CALICO Journal*, 29(3), 449–470. https://doi.org/10.11139/cj.29.3.449-470
Vinagre, M. (2015). Training teachers for virtual collaboration: A case study. *British Journal of Educational Technology*, 47(4), 787–802. https://doi.org/10.1111/bjet.12363
Vinagre, M. (2016). Promoting intercultural competence in culture and language studies: Outcomes of an international collaborative project. In E. Martín-Monje, I. Elorza, & B. García Riaza (eds.), *Technological Advances in Specialized Linguistic Domains: Practical Applications and Mobility* (pp. 23–35). London: Routledge.
Vogt, K. (2006). Can You Measure Attitudinal Factors in Intercultural Communication? *ReCALL*, 18(2): 153–173. https://doi.org/10.1017/S095834400600022X
White, P. (2015). Appraisal theory. In K. Tracy, C. Ilie, & T. Sandel (eds.), *The International Encyclopedia of Language and Social Interaction* (pp. 1–7). Hoboken (New Jersey): John Wiley & Sons, Inc.

About the Authors

Ana Oskoz is Professor of Spanish and Applied Linguistics at the University of Maryland, Baltimore County (UMBC). Her research interests include different aspects of online learning and telecollaboration, with a special focus on the development of second language digital literacies and intercultural communicative competence. Her publications have appeared in professional journals including *Foreign Language Annals*, *ReCALL*, and *Language Learning & Technology*. She is co-editor of *CALICO Journal*.

Margarita Vinagre is an Associate Professor at Autónoma University of Madrid where she teaches Educational Technologies and English Language and Linguistics. Her main research interests are the integration of technologies in the foreign language classroom, computer-mediated communication, and the implementation of intercultural exchanges for the development of linguistic and generic competences. She has published widely on these topics and is currently the coordinator of the VELCOME project on the integration of virtual exchange for key competence development in higher education, with twenty participating researchers from five countries.

1 Reconsidering Attitude as a Relational and Negotiated Sociocognitive Construct

Zsuzsanna I. Abrams

1 Introduction

Byram's (1997) seminal work on intercultural communication identified the essential components of intercultural competence as (1) attitude, (2) knowledge about social groups, (3) skills of interpreting and relating, (4) skills of discovery and interaction, and (5) critical cultural awareness. The present volume focuses specifically on the first component, *attitudes* – defined as curiosity and openness towards other cultures and regarding one's own (Byram, 1997; Lee, 2018; Schenker, 2012) – and how its development can be fostered by telecollaborative projects.

Ideally, telecollaborative projects bring about linguistic, cultural, and affective gains, including improved attitudes toward the L2 and its speakers (Guth & Helm, 2010, 2012; Lee & Markey, 2014; Lin, Warschauer, & Blake, 2016; O'Dowd & Lewis, 2016; Schenker, 2012; Vurdien & Puranen, 2018a, b). However, some exchanges yield less optimal outcomes, when misunderstandings hinder openness and curiosity toward another culture or when negative attitudes prevent intercultural communication (Lee, 2018; O'Dowd & Ritter, 2006; Schenker, 2012; Ware, 2005; Ware & Kramsch, 2005). Clearly, attitude is an essential component of telecollaboration, but its role is as yet under-investigated.

After briefly contextualizing intercultural communication, the present chapter reviews research on telecollaboration and explores the construct of attitude, reconceptualizing it as a relational and dynamic experience, shaped by the interactants and the pedagogical context in which they participate. After articulating this hypothesis, informed by sociocognitive theory (Atkinson, 2011), the chapter offers guidelines for pedagogical design that foster the development of positive attitudes as relational skills contributing to intercultural communicative competence.

2 Intercultural Communication

Byram's book entitled *Teaching and Assessing Intercultural Communicative Competence* (1997) has come to serve as the foundation for decades-long investigations into the role of intercultural communicative competence (ICC) in second/foreign language (L2) pedagogy: what ICC entails, how to teach it, and what might be ideal conditions for developing ICC. At the heart of Byram's model lies the intercultural speaker,

> a learner with the ability to see and manage the relationships between themselves and their own cultural beliefs, behaviours and meanings, as expressed in a foreign language, and those of their interlocutors, expressed in the same language – or even a combination of languages – which may be interlocutors' native language, or not. (Byram, 1997: 12).

In order to become intercultural speakers, who operate across, beyond, and within diverse languages or language varieties, successfully navigating diverse linguistic and cultural repertoires, learners need to develop a range of knowledge and skills:

1. *attitudes*: experiencing curiosity, openness, and a willingness to learn about other cultures and one's own;
2. *knowledge*: seeking to understand the products, beliefs, values, and practices of social groups, while reflecting on one's own, and explore processes of societal and individual interactions;
3. *skills of interpreting and relating*: interpreting documents or events from another culture, seeking to understand them, while relating them to documents or events from one's own cultural context;
4. *skills of discovery and interaction*: acquiring new knowledge of another culture and its practices, as well as implementing knowledge, attitudes, and skills in real-time interactions;
5. *critical cultural awareness*: evaluating perspectives, practices and products in one's own and another culture critically, based on clearly articulated criteria (Wagner & Byram, 2017).

As learners work towards developing these skills and gaining relevant knowledge pertaining to the L2 and the cultural contexts in which that language is spoken, Byram argues, they can also engage in critical reflection about their own linguistic and cultural practices. In other words, the challenges we struggle with as L2 learners, both linguistically and culturally, can help us explore the assumptions underlying our own practices. However, we can only take advantage of these opportunities if we remain curious and open to new information about culturally situated beliefs, behaviors, and practices.

In fact, Bennett (1993, 2011, 2017) outlined a developmental model of intercultural sensitivity, which requires an attitude of openness towards other cultures and people in particular. Progression entails moving from ethnocentrism as the first stage to ethnorelativism (see below), although individuals do not necessarily progress through all steps; they may skip some or reach a higher step and backslide.

	Stages	Descriptions
Ethnocentrism	*Denial of difference*	Simplistic, unreflective view of one's own culture, little or no knowledge about another culture; cultural differences are viewed as inferior compared to one's own (superior) culture
	Defense against difference	Viewing others in terms of "us" versus "them"; exaggerating positives of one's own culture, possibly denigrating the other culture; reliance on (usually negative) stereotypes regarding others (for self-protection); simplistic cultural categories
	Minimization of difference	Self-perception as being culturally sensitive; may prevent actual engagement with one's own and others' cultures, since "we are all the same"; "one's own worldview [is] central to the reality of everyone" (Bennett, 2011: 5)
Ethnorelativism	*Acceptance of difference*	Recognition that different social contexts have distinct patterns of beliefs, behaviors and practices; acceptance does not reflect positive or negative valuation of "the other," but merely a perception of difference; elaborated cultural categories situated in appropriate cultural contexts; self-reflection and cultural self-awareness
	Adaptation to difference	Conscious shifts in perspectives and behavior to suit situationally appropriate expectations; ability to *apply* acceptance and practice cognitive and affective empathy; cultural categories become flexible and permeable
	Integration of difference	The individual makes "a significant, sustained effort to become fully competent in new cultures"; may feel comfortable in both cultures or never quite "at home" in either; can access "a wide repertoire of cultural perspectives and behaviors" (Bennett, 2011: 11)

Ethnocentrism reflects an attitude whereby one's own culture (norms, beliefs, etc.) is seen as the right way to live. At the other end of the continuum, individuals know how to interpret and create meaning within particular cultural contexts (O'Dowd, 2003), and moderate their affective and cognitive responses to other people or cultural phenomena without relying on their "own culture as normative benchmark" (Oetzel, 2009: 101). Telecollaboration has been viewed as a promising pedagogical tool for improving the skills and attitudes outlined in Byram's model of intercultural communicative competence and encouraging learners' progress along Bennett's continuum of intercultural sensitivity.

3 Telecollaboration

Guth & Helm (2010: 14) define telecollaboration as an "exchange between people of different cultural/national backgrounds, set up in an institutional context with the aim of developing both language skills and intercultural communicative competence through structured tasks," while O'Dowd (2013: 47) highlights the virtual nature of interaction "between classes of foreign language learners in geographically distant locations." In telecollaborative exchanges, learners have to deploy linguistic, cultural, and multimedia skills to interact successfully with their peers and attend "to the real world in all its linguistic and cultural complexity" (Kramsch, 2009: 166).

These virtual partnerships may last from a few weeks (e.g., Ware, 2003) to a year (O'Dowd, 2003), and implement synchronous (i.e., in real-time) or asynchronous (i.e., delayed) communication. Telecollaboration can utilize Web 1.0 (e.g., email, discussion boards) or Web 2.0 (e.g., social media, podcasts, video-mediated communication, blogs) technologies, with the latter offering more opportunities for multimodal communication, which may be more appealing to learners (Hampel & Stickler 2012; Lee, 2018; Lee & Markey 2014; Puranen & Vurdien, 2016; Vurdien & Puranen, 2018a, b). Although they are challenging to organize, telecollaborative projects can provide excellent opportunities for L1/L2 users – on both sides of the exchange – to practice real-world communication and language use.

3.1 Benefits of Telecollaboration – a focus on attitude

Telecollaborative projects have yielded *linguistic* and *pragmatic gains* (Chun, 2011; Guth & Helm, 2010; O'Dowd & Lewis, 2016; Ware & O'Dowd, 2008) *cultural knowledge* (Chen & Shu, 2016; Lee & Markey, 2014; Schenker, 2012), as well as *affective benefits*, including increased levels of learner motivation and autonomy (Canto, Jauregi, & Bergh, 2013; Lin et al., 2016; Vurdien & Puranen, 2018a).

Supporting such positive outcomes for telecollaboration, Lee's (2018) study described a multimodal project between advanced learners of Spanish in the US and of English in Spain, with the objectives to improve learners' intercultural skills, linguistic accuracy, and pragmatic awareness. These objectives were met successfully, as the US students "showed curiosity about the target culture, and ... became more conscious of their personal beliefs and attitudes about their culture by discussing various points in reference to cultural products, practices and perspectives" with their Spanish peers (Lee, 2018: 316).

Echoing such positive findings, in a six-week study between American and German students, who exchanged email messages twice a week, Schenker (2012) found that participants improved on several aspects of Byram's (1997, 2009) model of intercultural communicative competence. They learned about other social groups, their beliefs, practices, and products; they exhibited skills of interpreting, relating, discovery, and interaction; and students also demonstrated critical cultural awareness. Intriguingly, however, the pre- and post-telecollaboration surveys indicated no growth in learners' attitudes, a finding the author attributed to "the fact that the students' interest in cultural learning was already at a very high level before the exchange took place" (Schenker, 2012: 460). This finding also confirms earlier claims by Godwin-Jones (2003) that L2 learners tend to be highly motivated to learn about other cultures.

In a related vein, Lee & Markey (2014) found that a positive attitude towards members of the other culture played an important role in a semester-long study between students in Spain and the US. The authors found that telecollaboration (1) created a cohesive learning community that fostered linguistic improvements, as native speakers of each language provided L2 learners with valuable feedback, (2) promoted technological literacy, and (3) established rapport within the group, promoting openness and curiosity, evinced by the many questions participants on both sides asked their interlocutors.

Such positive reports regarding the affective benefits of telecollaboration abound, as Avgousti (2018) found in her systematic review of recent research. Specifically, she noted that telecollaboration allows students to:

1. let go of negative attitudes towards the other culture,
2. explore and revise their preconceptions about that culture, which they usually base on images presented by popular media,

3. become more interested in and reflective about their own cultures, and
4. realize that their interlocutors do not represent national stereotypes, but rather reflect individual cultural variation and identities, reducing or eliminating cultural generalizations.

These positive outcomes are worth striving for and can be reached, if the challenges that telecollaborative projects sometimes encounter are addressed adequately.

3.2 Challenges of Telecollaboration

Less optimal outcomes in telecollaboration manifest particularly in the form of intercultural misunderstandings (Lee, 2018; O'Dowd & Ritter, 2006; Schenker, 2012; Ware, 2005; Ware & Kramsch, 2005). In an early study on telecollaboration, for example, Ware (2005) found that students of English in Northern Germany and of German in the US encountered regular communicative mishaps during their online interactions, in spite of their advanced proficiency in their respective L2s. The author attributed these problems to "the different socially and culturally situated attitudes, beliefs, and expectations that informed students' communicative choices in the online discourse" (Ware, 2005: 64). Differing views about the value of L2 learning, how L2s are taught at the partner institutions, and lack of (or differing) experience with CALL may contribute to communicative tensions (Ware, 2005), as does learners' unfamiliarity with aspects of language that convey speakers' attitude (e.g., intonation, pragmatic cues to soften criticism). In fact, the online nature of telecollaboration and the inherent lack of face-to-face opportunities to resolve conflict often make it challenging to engage in discussions that foster deep cultural reflection. In severe cases, instead of helping foster intercultural communication, miscommunication may reinforce or create new negative attitudes in the learners towards their interlocutors and the culture they represent.

In a related study, Ware & Kramsch (2005) reported on missed communication between a German (Marie) and a US student (Rob), who participated in a three-week telecollaborative project based on a language and culture survey conducted prior to the project. Unfortunately, the participants' interaction took a negative turn and led to Rob withdrawing from the communicative process entirely. This failure occurred after Rob described his previous experiences in Germany, which seemingly influenced his subsequent attitude towards his partner's comments. Their miscommunication was exacerbated by divergent interactional styles, which prevented effective negotiations of social meaning (as opposed to cognitive meaning), when Marie framed her response as a "little history lesson" (Ware & Kramsch, 2005: 195) and called Rob out for "sulking" (p. 197).

O'Dowd (2003), who analyzed interactions between university students in Spain and the UK, reported similar findings. His participants, who were studying each other's language as their respective L2s, completed ten tasks in pairs, ranging from introductions at the beginning, to discussions about moral values and sexuality in both countries at the end. While many participants proceeded to have successful conversations about the various topics, some dyads were unsuccessful, and their participation suffered due to their partner's (real or perceived) lack of acceptance of their specific points. Some participants found linguistic limitations to lead to attitudinal difficulties, when they could not articulate their ideas effectively in the L2, and their responses were viewed as impolite instead of just limited by language proficiency. Ultimately, O'Dowd concluded that telecollaboration can lead to important gains regarding intercultural communicative skills and knowledge, but that "some students simply confirmed their negative attitudes towards the target culture" instead of growing from the experience (O'Dowd, 2003: 137).

Scholarship has attributed difficulties in telecollaboration to a variety of causes. Lee (2018), for example, points to differing communication styles and stereotypes that can lead to intercultural misunderstandings. Additionally, discussing personal feelings or opinions may be challenging even for linguistically competent individuals, as they negotiate meaning not as a cognitive language learning activity but as an interpersonal process (Bennett & Bennett, 2004). Another related challenge can be the mismatch between textbook language that L2 learners typically acquire (abstract, objective, factual information), versus the real-world language they need for relating "subjective and personalized accounts" about themselves, their families, likes and dislikes, and opinions about controversial topics (Vurdien & Puranen, 2018a: 242).

Whether positive or negative, learners' affective experiences with telecollaboration impacts their attitude, which is the emotional gateway to developing skills and gaining knowledge for effective intercultural communication.

4 Attitude in L2 Research

Most studies on telecollaboration adopt Byram's (1997) definition of attitude:

curiosity and *openness* ... readiness to *suspend disbelief and judgement* with respect *to others' meanings, beliefs and behaviours*. There also needs to be a willingness to suspend belief *in one's own meanings and behaviours*, and to analyse them *from the viewpoint of the others* with whom one is engaging (p. 34; emphasis mine).

Attitude is a component of social competence, alongside "the will and the skill to interact with others, involving motivation ... self-confidence, empathy and the ability to handle social situations" (Byram, 1997: 10). This construct has been adopted in applied linguistics research as follows (emphases mine):

- *respect* for cultural diversity and complexity (Meng, Zhu, & Cao, 2017);
- increasing *sensitivity* towards another culture and its members, and the *ability to accommodate cultural differences* (Chen & Starosta, 2000);
- *interest* in international issues, living and working in another country, *being open* to interaction with members of an intercultural community (Yashima, 2002);
- *ability to interact* with members of another culture, with a *positive motivation* towards them, also with *self-confidence* and *empathy* (van Ek, 1986);
- *appreciation of* the "*cultural products* associated with the particular L2 and conveyed by the media; e.g. films, TV programs, magazines and pop music" (Dörnyei, 2009: 26);
- "great *interest in* American partners with regard to their various daily life experiences" (Jin, 2015: 43);
- "the ability to put oneself into another's shoes – is indispensable to motivate students *to fully engage* in the process of negotiation of meaning during online exchanges" (Lee, 2018: 317);
- *curiosity, tolerance* and a *positive orientation* towards members of another culture (Vurdien & Puranen, 2018b);
- *appreciation* of "the *value of experiencing another culture* besides their own" (Carlorosi et al., 2008: 177).

These interpretations reflect Gardner and Lambert's (1972) research on attitude in L2 learning, according to which attitude is a component of motivation, and is comprised of affective, cognitive, and behavioral components (Gardner, 2006; Liaw, 2002; Liaw, Huang, & Chen, 2007).

1. *the affective component* refers to emotions or feelings (including anxiety, confidence, and enjoyment) about certain people, events or objects, often stated as "I like …" or "I don't like …" (e.g., "I really like to travel" or "I don't like argumentative people");
2. *the cognitive component* includes beliefs and thoughts about persons, events, or objects; beliefs and thoughts can pertain to real or perceived usefulness, such as believing that learning other languages increases one's chances of finding a well-paying job or that one is a "good" or "bad" language learner;
3. *the behavioral component* entails what we intend to do or actually do about people, events or objects (e.g., withdraw from a conversation or study abroad).

Gardner & Lambert's (1972) socio-educational model was revolutionary, because it acknowledged "The seemingly simple idea that intergroup attitudes and motives matter in language learning … with a focus on attitudes, affect, intergroup relationships and motives" (McIntyre, Mackinnon, & Clément, 2009: 43–44). According to this model, an individual's interest in learning about another culture, the desire to interact with members of that speech community, and favorable attitudes toward the community constitute *integrativeness* or openness to cultural identification (Gardner, 2006; McIntyre et al., 2009). Integratively motivated individuals want "to learn the other language … because of a genuine interest in communicating with members of the other language" and they have "a favourable attitude toward the language learning situation" (Gardner, 2006: 12). Thus, in addition to learners' interest in the L2 and its cultural contexts, the learning environment (pedagogical tasks, the instructor, interactional partners, etc.) shapes attitude as well.

Additionally, research shows that learners' experience with computer assisted/mediated L2 learning (CALL) impacts attitude. Ware (2005), for example, observed that the German students, who were newcomers to CALL, were excited by its novelty, while the American students, who used it regularly, just wanted to get to work; this discrepancy caused tension and disappointment among the participants. Recent research (Oz, Demirezen, & Pourfeiz, 2015) confirms this observation and shows strong relationships connecting attitude, CALL and L2 learning: (1) participants with a positive attitude towards CALL are more likely to stay on task and invest time in their online activities, (2) learners' experience (skill and enjoyment) with general computer use is strongly related to their attitude toward CALL activities, and (3) learners' attitude towards the L2 significantly impacts their attitude towards CALL. Other studies similarly reiterate the importance of familiarity with technology, attitude towards the task, and learners' willingness to communicate with their L2 interactants (Dooly, 2011, 2016, 2018; Lee & Markey, 2014).

While Gardner & Lambert's (1972) model recognizes the social context, attitude in research on telecollaboration is still seen primarily as a personal responsibility and process. This perspective merits reconsideration, in light of recent developments in second language acquisition research.

5 Attitude as a Relational, Socially Negotiated Construct

Some aspects of attitude are relatively constant across situations, such as experience with CALL or personal characteristics (e.g., introversion/extraversion). Other aspects of attitude, in contrast, are more malleable and are influenced by the specific social context. In other words, attitude is a complex affective construct that varies across situations and interlocutors, using social cues to negotiate interpersonal relationships dynamically and in the local context. When we communicate with others, we co-construct interactions: my question is followed by a response and possibly a check to make sure I understood my interlocutor. When I produce my next utterance, I try to ensure that not only the content of my message is conveyed accurately, but also that the appropriate affect is communicated, encouraging a desired interaction or redirecting (or stopping) conversations that are objectionable. Similarly, attitude is negotiated. If I am welcoming towards another person and express positive attitudes (e.g., interest) in her culture, she is more likely to reciprocate. If I seem like I am attacking her beliefs and values (the affective aspect of attitude), she may become hostile in return or at the very least defensive.

Yet, in spite of Gardner's socio-educational model of motivation, integrativeness, and attitude and Byram's (1997) model of intercultural communication, there is a notable lack of attention to the role of interpersonal work in studying attitude in ICC research. That is, the onus is placed systematically on the individual to develop positive attitudes towards the L2, members of the L2 culture(s), and the specific tasks to be completed. With some exceptions (e.g., Lee, 2018; O'Dowd, 2003; O'Dowd & Ritter, 2006; Ware, 2003; Ware & Kramsch, 2005), there is little discussion of the role that interlocutors (including instructor/s and classmates) might play in shaping learners' attitudes, and even in those studies, the effect of the interlocutor's beliefs, emotions, and behaviors are not elaborated on. Instead, learners are expected to be open to new experiences, question their beliefs, study evidence from multiple perspectives, and develop language skills that allow them to engage in intercultural communication effectively as a life-long endeavor. This is a rather cognitive view of attitude, seen as an *individual* variable that *the learner brings to the learning process,* and does not adequately reflect the *relational* nature of attitude, or current thinking in L2 learning, which recognizes the importance of the social context (Atkinson, 2011).

Expanding from earlier notions of cognitivist and sociocultural approaches to second language acquisition, sociocognitive theory posits that L2 learning draws on both cognitive and social processes (Canale & Swain, 1980; Toth & Davin, 2016; Young, 2009). Accordingly, individual cognition, social relationships, and the broader social context are integrated, and learning is dynamic and adaptive (Atkinson, 2011). A sociocognitively informed L2 pedagogy focuses on context-sensitive language use and reflects the symbolic complexity of real-world language, including both interpretive and productive uses of the L2 in interpersonal communication (Toth & Davin, 2016). In this paradigm, other people, the social context, the task, and technological tools all play a significant role not only in the development of L2 skills and learners' ability to participate meaningfully in L2 speech communities, but also of the attitudes they form towards all four (interlocutors, social context, tasks, and technology).

To provide an example of the complexity and context-dependence of attitude, I include a vignette about a group of American students who studied in Germany a few summers ago.

> A curious, excited group of students from the US, with approximately intermediate-low to intermediate-high proficiency in German, shared a couple of courses with students from a German university and spent a considerable amount of time interacting with this group outside of class as well. Amongst themselves, they were politically quite engaged and articulated complex thoughts about US politics (espousing different political affiliations). About two weeks into the program, several American students expressed frustration about not being able to "discuss" politics, as they felt that the German students did not really listen to their perspectives, but rather "interrogated" them about who they voted for, why, and how the US could have possibly elected a particular president. For the remaining time, the American students continued to participate in discussions about literature and history, went out for beer or ice cream and enjoyed excursions with their German counterparts; thus, they continued practicing German and learning about cultural practices, beliefs, and products during their sojourn. However, with very few exceptions, these students stopped discussing politics with the German students, surprisingly, especially the students who had not voted for the president to whom the German students objected, because they felt that they should not have to defend themselves.

As this example demonstrates, attitude is not static: it varies across activities and depends on the behaviors and attitudes of one's interlocutors in specific situations. In other words, attitude is shaped in collaboration with others; it is relational. Therefore, in order to reflect the dynamic nature and complexity of attitude, discussions of it should be expanded to make the social context more salient. While telecollaboration is inherently social and interpersonal, both tasks and subsequent analyses need to emphasize and make explicit the *co-construction* of attitude. This can be accomplished by including tasks that explicitly discuss and reflect on learners' attitude (and affect more broadly) during telecollaboration. That is, during the initial stages of a telecollaborative project, participants could discuss their views about the tasks, their courses, the telecollaborative project, or other concerns they have regarding the L2, its use, and the cultural contexts in which it is spoken (including addressing stereotypes head-on). Discussions should also explore potential sources of tension, such as divergent conflict styles (cf. https://www.ucalgary.ca/ssc/files/ssc/intercultural-conflict-styles-general.pdf). The contextual, social, relational aspects of the project also need to be acknowledged in subsequent research analyses. If we adopt a broader, socially focused lens for designing telecollaborative projects, we might be able to reduce some of the challenges discussed in Section 3.2. In the next section, we propose possible considerations for tasks that highlight learners' attitude during telecollaborative projects.

6 Task Design in Telecollaboration: Reconceptualizing Attitude as a Relational Construct

Telecollaboration creates an environment in which participants are both present and absent (Kramsch, 2009), and in which interpersonal aspects of communication – such as tone, facial expressions, and gestures – are often either absent (without video) or delayed and therefore unidirectional at any given time (Jim, 2015; Satar, 2016; Vurdien & Puranen, 2018a). In spite of these limitations, telecollaborative exchanges must and can encourage the sustained exchange of ideas across cultural boundaries and support learners' positive attitudes towards both the tasks and their collaborators. This can be achieved by including tasks that explicitly address the attitudinal component of Byram's model, either in class or during telecollaborative projects with the L2 interactants; this is a worthwhile investment of time, given the crucial role that affect plays in successful L2 learning (cf. Gardner, 2006; McIntyre et al., 2009).

These discussions should acknowledge the *relational* aspects of attitude, namely, that attitude:

- does not merely reside in the learner, independent of others or the context (societal, interpersonal, or educational),
- is not static, but changes over time and across situations, and
- is influenced both by the perceptions and behaviors of the individual, and by the reactions, behaviors and attitudes of his or her interlocutors.

Based on the studies reviewed in this chapter, and considering attitude as pertaining to L2 learning, the L2 community/social context, tasks, and technology, a few guidelines emerge that can facilitate the maintenance or development of positive attitudes – openness, curiosity, acceptance, engagement, interest – and help learners progress towards Bennett's (1993, 2011, 2017) model of intercultural sensitivity in telecollaboration. These guidelines pertain to the timing, content, and format of telecollaborative tasks.

6.1 Time

Timing is an important consideration in effective task design, both in terms of learners' overall progress and individual telecollaborative projects. From a long-term perspective, learners' L2 proficiency must be considered in topic selection. Beginning learners, for example, are not likely to be able to discuss abortion or same-sex marriage in depth in the L2; they cannot yet express sufficient nuance to put forward their views effectively, while sustaining interpersonal relationships. In terms of individual projects, tasks should also be selected carefully for the amount of time available (e.g., do not discuss contentious topics if you only have a week). Providing insufficient time for task completion may engender negative attitudes towards the task, which may impact learners' attitude towards their interlocutors (Vurdien & Puranen, 2018a, b). When designing tasks, instructors should also take into consideration that learners may find the sheer amount of reading daunting, which may limit genuine communication (Ware, 2005); therefore, instructors should include enough time to complete each task, possibly adjusting timelines during the project.

A crucial aspect of task-design is allowing ample time for participants to establish interpersonal relationships, to build trust, raise learners' level of self-confidence and comfort levels, all pre-requisites for honest discussions about more challenging topics (Lee, 2018; Lin et al., 2016). Such requisite trust can be fostered by sequencing tasks in a way that allows for a careful progression towards opinion exchange, starting with an interpersonal task, for example, followed by information gap tasks using source texts (readings, videos), a collaborative creative writing task (e.g., a movie scene with appropriate L1/L2 use), and closing with a debate-style interaction. This progression can build learners' self-confidence and empathy as well, prior to engaging with more delicate topics.

6.2 Task Content

In addition to considerations of time, several content-oriented strategies have emerged from research. First, it is helpful to select discussion topics and tasks with student input, to increase their level of interest and engagement (Lee & Markey, 2014). Not surprisingly, students seem very interested in language use, such as dialects, slang, and other colloquial expressions; such relatively non-controversial topics can foster communication in addition to fostering curiosity and positive attitudes (Lee & Markey, 2014; O'Dowd, 2003). Controversial topics should not be avoided, as they can stimulate learners' interest, but they can be difficult to negotiate in an L2 with the limited social context that asynchronous or infrequent tasks provide. To mitigate this problem, it might be useful to address the lack of affect in asynchronous (and to a lesser degree in synchronous) online communication explicitly. It can be equally helpful to discuss how to

- handle sensitive topics politely and with consideration,
- express agreement and disagreement in pragmatically appropriate ways in the L2,
- ask follow-up questions of an interlocutor (signaling interest),
- maintain the floor or take turns (useful for sustaining successful interactions during synchronous telecollaboration),
- assume misunderstanding instead of criticism, and
- treat miscommunication as such (i.e., communicative mishaps), without ascribing negative intent to one's partner(s).

Moreover, learners should know how to redirect an unwanted conversation effectively without shutting down lines of communication. In addition to mitigating potential conflict this way, learning how to handle sensitive topics may protect learners' privacy (Vurdien & Puranen, 2018a). Explicit discussions regarding the affective, cognitive and behavioral components of attitude (Gardner & Lambert, 1972), and that attitude is dynamic and relational, might also help sustain telecollaborative relationships.

Some task content is unplanned and may take the form of critical incidents (Brookfield, 2017; Tripp, 2012). Instead of treating these as a threat to the telecollaborative effort, they can be deployed to draw learners' attention to linguistic, discursive, and social differences that can lead to a "deeper negotiation of social and cultural meanings, let alone worldviews" (Malinowski & Kramsch, 2014: 175). It is important not to use these incidents as essentialized reflections of the other culture (Avgousti, 2018; Dooly, 2011), however, to avoid confirming or creating new, negative stereotypes. In order to benefit from positive and negative experiences in telecollaboration (Müller-Hartmann & O'Dowd, 2017), learners need support and guidance from their instructors, as they navigate divergent communication and conflict styles with their interlocutors. Pre-, during- and post-telecollaboration tasks should interrogate learners' pre-existing prejudices (positive or negative) and experiences with the L2 and the L2 community, as well as other attitudinal issues. By monitoring exchanges, instructors can help learners identify and manage critical incidents or problems and help repair communication with their peers (Lee, 2018). There should also be opportunities during the telecollaborative project to discuss such incidents in the classroom, both to raise learners' awareness of them and to make them explicit learning opportunities for the entire classroom community. To ensure that critical incidents are productive for developing intercultural communicative competence, tasks should help learners identify *both* differences and similarities between their cultures' beliefs, practices, and behaviors and recognize *intra*cultural (within the same culture) variation across different situations (Vurdien & Puranen, 2018a).

6.3 Task Format

The last set of the guidelines pertains to task formatting, including group constellation and task structure. Regarding the former point, using small-group interactions (instead of dyads) allows multiple voices to weigh in and interpret the interaction, task, or project (and reduce stress from absentee partners). Such an arrangement further supports the idea that perspectives vary intraculturally. Encouraging the examination of intracultural variation this way helps learners view members of the other culture as individuals, rather than representatives of stereotypes and overgeneralized perceptions. Additionally, a peer-evaluation component might help foster accountability, so that all students work equally in their assigned teams (Arnold, Ducate, & Kost, 2009), thus reducing resentment among participants, while simultaneously increasing learners' positive attitude towards their interlocutors and the task. Video-mediated communication, either synchronously (if feasible timewise) or asynchronously, and other multimodal tasks may similarly foster a sense of community among participants and increase their positive relational attitudes (Hampel & Stickler 2012; Lee, 2018; Lee & Markey 2014; Puranen & Vurdien, 2016; Vurdien & Puranen, 2018a, b), because multimodality "is a critical predictor for [learners'] perceived enjoyment" (Liaw et al., 2007: 1076).

Just as importantly, learners need sufficient digital literacy skills to manage tasks (Dooly, 2016, 2018; Fuchs, Hauck, & Müller-Hartmann, 2012; Lee, 2018). Discussing learners' familiarity with and attitude towards computers, computer-literacy, and new communication tools explicitly may help reduce their frustration with technology; instructors should not just assume that learners know how to use the tools or are comfortable with them (see Liaw, 2002; Liaw et al., 2007; Oz et al., 2015).

7 Conclusion

In their discussion of the requirements of intercultural citizenship, Byram & Wagner (2018), citing Huber & Reynolds (2014), describe several characteristics that enable individuals

1. to understand and respect members of cultures that differ from the speaker's cultural affiliations,
2. to interact and communicate appropriately and effectively with members of other cultures in a respectful manner,
3. to develop positive relationships with members of other cultures, and
4. to take advantage of interactions with people from different cultures in order to understand their own cultural affiliations better.

These goals can be achieved if, in addition to skills and knowledge development, L2 pedagogy also fosters the development of positive attitudes towards the L2 and its speakers, an essential component of intercultural communicative competence and intercultural citizenship. Prior to participating in the L2 speech communities in real-world settings (Byram, 1997), classroom tasks can provide learners with opportunities for engaging, maintaining, or improving their attitudes vis-à-vis the L2 and its speakers.

Telecollaboration, in particular, can open invaluable avenues for interacting with members of the L2-community, increasing learners' linguistic skills, cultural knowledge, and affective connections to the L2 and its speakers. However, collaborative projects must be designed carefully, in order to diminish potential pitfalls, whereby students retain or even reinforce stereotypical views of and negative attitudes towards another culture (O'Dowd, 2003; Vurdien & Puranen, 2018a). Tasks that explicitly address the relational nature of attitude – that it is shaped not only by the individual, but also by the learning context – can help enhance the benefits of telecollaboration and minimize its challenges. Moreover, during pedagogical implementation, instructors should consider learners' attitude towards the L2 (and language learning in general), the other participants in the exchange, as well as the tasks and technological tools selected for the project, since all of these components contribute in dynamic ways to learners' enjoyment of telecollaboration, and therefore its success.

References

Arnold, N., Ducate, L., & Kost, C. (2009). Collaborative writing in wikis: Insights from culture projects in German classes. In L. Lomicka & G. Lord (eds.), *The Next Generation: Social Networking and Online Collaboration in Foreign Language Learning* (pp. 115–144). San Marcos, TX: CALICO.

Atkinson, D. (2011). A sociocognitive approach to second language acquisition: How mind, body and world work together in learning additional languages. In D. Atkinson (ed.), *Alternative Approaches to Second Language Acquisition* (pp. 143–166). New York, NY: Routledge. https://doi.org/10.4324/9780203830932

Avgousti, M. I. (2018). Intercultural communicative competence and online exchanges: A systematic review. *Computer Assisted Language Learning*, 31(8), 819–853. https://doi.org/10.1080/09588221.2018.1455713

Bennett, M. J. (1993). Towards ethnorelativism: A development model of intercultural sensitivity. In R. M. Paige (ed.), *Education for the Intercultural Experience* (pp. 21–71). Yarmouth, ME: Intercultural Press.

Bennett, M. J. (2011). A developmental model of intercultural sensitivity. Downloaded on February 27, 2019 from https://www.idrinstitute.org/wp-content/uploads/2018/02/FILE_Documento_Bennett_DMIS_12pp_quotes_rev_2011.pdf.

Bennett, M. J. (2017). Development model of intercultural sensitivity. In Y. Y. Kim (ed.), *International Encyclopedia of Intercultural Communication*. Hoboken, NJ: John Wiley & Sons. https://doi.org/10.1002/9781118783665.ieicc0182

Bennett, J. M., & Bennett, M. J. (2004). *Developing Intercultural Competence: A Reader*. Portland, OR: Intercultural Communication Institute.

Brookfield, S. (2017). *Becoming a Critically Reflective Teacher* (2nd ed.). San Francisco, CA: Jossey-Bass.

Byram, M. (1997). *Teaching and Assessing Iintercultural Communicative Competence*. Clevendon, UK: Multilingual Matters.

Byram, M. (2009). Intercultural competence in foreign languages: the intercultural speaker and the pedagogy of foreign language education. In D. K. Deardorff (ed.), *The Sage Handbook of Intercultural Competence*. Los Angeles, CA: Sage.

Byram, M., & Wagner, M. (2018). Making a difference: Language teaching for intercultural and international dialogue. *Foreign Language Annals*, 51, 140–151. https://doi.org/10.1111/flan.12319

Canale, M., & Swain, M. (1980). Theoretical bases of communicative approaches to second language teaching and testing. *Applied Linguistics*, 1, 1–47. https://doi.org/10.1093/applin/1.1.1

Canto, S., Jauregi, K., & van den Bergh, H. (2013). Integrating cross-cultural interaction through videocommunication and virtual worlds in foreign language teaching programs. Burden or added value? *ReCALL*, 25(1), 105–121. https://doi.org/10.1017/S0958344012000274

Carlorosi, S., Helm, F., Marini-Maio, N., & McMahon, K. K. (2008). Confronting new technologies: A cross-cultural telecollaborative project across the ocean. In E. Occhipinti (ed.), *New Approaches to Teaching Italian Language and Culture: Case Studies from an International Perspective*. Newcastle upon Tyne, UK: Cambridge Scholars Publishing.

Chen, J.-J., & Shu, C.-Y. (2016). Promoting cross-cultural understanding and language use in research oriented Internet-mediated intercultural exchange. *Computer Assisted Language Learning*, 29(2), 262–288. https://doi.org/10.1080/09588221.2014.937441

Chen, G. M., & Starosta, W. J. (2000). The development and validation of the intercultural communication sensitivity scale. *Human Communication*, 3, 1–15.

Chun, D. (2011). Developing intercultural communicative competence through online exchanges. *CALICO Journal*, 28(2), 392–419. https://doi.org/10.11139/cj.28.2.392-419

Dooly, M. A. (2011). Crossing the intercultural borders into 3rd space culture(s): Implications for teacher education in the twenty-first century. *Language and Intercultural Communication*, 11(4), 319–337. https://doi.org/10.1080/14708477.2011.599390

Dooly, M. (2016). "Please remove your avatar from my personal space": Competences of the telecollaboratively efficient person. In R. O'Dowd & T. Lewis (eds.), *Online Intercultural Exchange: Policy, Pedagogy, Practice* (pp. 192–208). London: Routledge.

Dooly, M. (2018). "I do which the question": Students' innovative use of technology resources in the language classroom. *Language Learning & Technology*, 22(1), 184–217.

Dörnyei, Z. (2009). The L2 Motivational Self System. In Z. Dörnyei & E. Ushioda (eds.), *Motivation, Language Identity and the L2 Self* (pp. 9–42). Tonawanda, NY: Multilingual Matters. https://doi.org/10.21832/9781847691293-003

Fuchs, C., Hauck, M., & Müller-Hartmann, A. (2012). Promoting learner autonomy through multiliteracy skills development in cross-institutional exchanges. *Language Learning & Technology*, 16(3), 82–102.

Gardner, R. C. (2006). Motivation and Second Language Acquisition. Paper given at Seminario Sobre Plurilingüismo: Las Aportaciones Del Centro Europeo de Lenguas Modernas de Graz, on December 15, 2006 at the

Universidad de Alcalá, Spain. Accessed November 30, 2018 at http://publish.uwo.ca/~gardner/docs/SPAINTALK.pdf.
Gardner, R. C., & Lambert, W. E. (1972). *Attitudes and Motivation in Second Language Learning*. Rowley, MA: Newbury House.
Godwin-Jones, R. (2003). Emerging technologies. Blogs and wikis: Environments for on-line collaboration. *Language Learning & Technology*, 7(2), 12–16.
Guth, S., & Helm, F. (2010). New trends and environments in telecollaboration. In S. Guth & F. Helm (eds.), *Telecollaboration 2.0: Language and Intercultural Learning in the 21st Century* (pp. 13–35). Bern, Switzerland: Peter Lang. https://doi.org/10.3726/978-3-0351-0013-6
Guth, S., & Helm, F. (2012). Developing multiliteracies in ELT through telecollaboration. *ELT Journal*, 66(1), 42–51. https://doi.org/10.1093/elt/ccr027
Hampel, R., & Stickler, U. (2012). The use of videoconferencing to support multimodal interaction in an online language classroom. *ReCALL*, 24(2), 116–137. https://doi.org/10.1017/S095834401200002X
Huber, J., & Reynolds, C. (eds.) (2014). Developing intercultural competence through education. Strasbourg: Council of Europe. Retrieved September 9, 2017, from https://book.coe.int/eur/en/pestalozzi-series/6968-pdf-dvelopper-lacomptence-interculturelle-par-l-ducation-srie-pestalozzi-n-3.html.
Jin, S. (2015). Using Facebook to promote Korean learners' intercultural competence. *Language Learning & Technology*, 19(3), 38–51.
Kramsch, C. (2009). *The Multilingual Subject*. Oxford: Oxford University Press.
Lee, L. (2018). Using Telecollaboration 2.0 to build intercultural communicative competence: A Spanish-American exchange. In D. Tafazoli, M. E. Gomez Parra, & C. A. Huertas-Abril (eds.), *Cross-Cultural Perspectives on Technology-Enhanced Language Learning: Advances in Educational Technologies and Instructional Design* (pp. 303–321). Hershey, PA: IGI Global. https://doi.org/10.4018/978-1-5225-5463-9.ch017
Lee, L., & Markey, A. (2014). A study of learners' perceptions of online intercultural exchange through Web 2.0 technologies. *ReCALL*, 26(3), 1–20. https://doi.org/10.1017/S0958344014000111
Liaw, S. S. (2002). An Internet survey for perceptions of computer and World Wide Web: relationship, prediction, and difference. *Computers in Human Behavior*, 18(1), 17–35. https://doi.org/10.1016/S0747-5632(01)00032-2
Liaw, S. S., Huang, H. M., & Chen, G. D. (2007). Surveying instructor and learner attitudes toward e-learning. *Computers and Education*, 49(4), 1066–1080. https://doi.org/10.1016/j.compedu.2006.01.001
Lin, C.-H., Warschauer, M., & Blake, R. (2016). Language learning through social networks: Perceptions and reality. *Language Learning & Technology*, 20(1), 124–147. Retrieved from http://llt.msu.edu/issues/february2016/linwarschauerblake.pdf. https://doi.org/10.1037/t64110-000
Malinowski, D., & Kramsch, C. (2014). The ambiguous world of heteroglossic computer-mediated language learning. In A. Blackledge & A. Creese (eds.), *Heteroglossia as Practice and Pedagogy* (Vol. 20) (pp. 155–178). Dordrecht, the Netherlands: Springer. https://doi.org/10.1007/978-94-007-7856-6_9
McIntyre, P. D., Mackinnon, S. P., & Clément, R. (2009). The baby, the bathwater, and the future of language learning motivation research. In Z. Dörnyei &

E. Ushioda (eds.), *Motivation, Language Identity and the L2 Self* (pp. 43–65). Tonawanda, NY: Multilingual Matters. https://doi.org/10.21832/9781847691293-004

Meng, Q., Zhu, C., & Cao, C. (2017). An exploratory study of Chinese university undergraduates' global competence: Effects of internationalisation at home and motivation. *Higher Education Quarterly*, 71(2), 159–181. https://doi.org/10.1111/hequ.12119

Müller-Hartmann, A., & O'Dowd, R. (2017). *A Training Manual on Telecollaboration for Teacher Trainers*. Retrieved from https://www.evaluateproject.eu/evlt-data/uploads/2017/09/Training-Manual_EVALUATE.pdf.

O'Dowd, R. (2003). Understanding the "Other Side": Intercultural learning in a Spanish-English e-mail exchange. *Language Learning & Technology*, 7(2), 118–144. Retrieved from https://scholarspace.manoa.hawaii.edu/bitstream/10125/25202/1/07_02_odowd.pdf.

O'Dowd, R. (2013). Telecollaborative networks in university higher education: Overcoming barriers to integration. *The Internet and Higher Education*, 18, 47–53. https://doi.org/10.1016/j.iheduc.2013.02.001

O'Dowd, R., & Ritter, M. (2006). Understanding and working with "failed communication" in telecollaborative exchanges. *CALICO Journal*, 23, 1–20.

O'Dowd, R., & Lewis, T. (eds.) (2016). *Online Intercultural Exchange*. New York, NY: Routledge. https://doi.org/10.4324/9781315678931

Oetzel, J. G. (2009). *Intercultural Communication: A Layered Approach*. Upper Saddle River, NJ: Pearson.

Oz, H., Demirezen, M., & Pourfeiz, J. (2015). Digital device ownership, computer literacy, and attitudes toward foreign and computer-assisted language learning. *Procedia – Social and Behavioral Sciences*, 186, 359–366. https://doi.org/10.1016/j.sbspro.2015.04.028

Puranen, P., & Vurdien, R. (2016). A Spanish-Finnish telecollaboration: Extending intercultural competence via videoconferencing. In S. Papadima-Sophocleous, L. Bradley, & S. Thouësny (eds.), *CALL Communities and Culture – Short Papers from EUROCALL 2016* (pp. 391–396). Research-publishing.net. https://doi.org/10.14705/rpnet.2016.eurocall2016.594

Satar, H. M. (2016). Meaning-making in online language learner interactions via desktop videoconferencing. *ReCALL*, 28(3), 305–325.

Schenker, T. (2012). Intercultural competence and cultural learning through telecollaboration. *CALICO Journal*, 29(3), 449–470. https://doi.org/10.11139/cj.29.3.449-470

Toth, P. D., & Davin, K. J. (2016). The sociocognitive imperative of L2 pedagogy. *The Modern Language Journal*, 16, 148–168. https://doi.org/10.1111/modl.12306

Tripp, D. (2012). *Critical Incidents in Teaching: Developing Professional Judgement*. London: Taylor & Francis Ltd. https://doi.org/10.4324/9780203802014

van Ek, J. (1986). *Objectives for Foreign Language Learning*. Vol. 1: Scope. Strasbourg: Council of Europe.

Vurdien, R., & Puranen, P. (2018a). Enhancing students' intercultural competence and learner autonomy via Facebook Telecollaboration. In B. B. Zou (ed.), *Handbook of Research on Integrating Technology into Contemporary*

Language Learning and Teaching (pp. 240–260). Hershey, PA: IGI Global. https://doi.org/10.4018/978-1-5225-5140-9.ch012

Vurdien, R., & Puranen, P. (2018b). Intercultural learning via videoconferencing. In D. Tafazoli, M. E. Gomez Parra, & C. A. Huertas-Abril (eds.), *Cross-Cultural Perspectives on Technology-Enhanced Language Learning: Advances in Educational Technologies and Instructional Design* (pp. 264–282). Hershey, PA: IGI Global. https://doi.org/10.4018/978-1-5225-5463-9.ch015

Wagner, M., & Byram, M. (2017). Intercultural citizenship. In Y. Y. Kim (ed.), *The International Encyclopedia of Intercultural Communication* (np). Hoboken, NJ: Wiley & Sons.

Ware, P. D. (2003). From involvement to engagement in online communicating: Promoting intercultural competence in foreign language education. Unpublished PhD Dissertation. University of California, Berkeley.

Ware, P. (2005). "Missed" communication in online communication: Tensions in a German-American telecollaboration. *Language Learning & Technology*, 9(2), 64–89. https://doi.org/10.1111/j.1540-4781.2005.00274.x

Ware, P., & Kramsch, C. (2005). Toward an intercultural stance: Teaching German and English through telecollaboration. *The Modern Language Journal*, 89(2), 190–205. https://doi.org/10.1111/j.1540-4781.2005.00274.x

Ware, P., & O'Dowd, R. (2008). Peer feedback on language form in telecollaboration. *Language Learning & Technology*, 12(1), 43–63.

Yashima, T. (2002). Willingness to communicate in a second language: The Japanese context. *Modern Language Journal*, 86(1), 54–66. https://doi.org/10.1111/1540-4781.00136

Young, R. F. (2009). *Discursive Practice in Language Learning and Teaching*. Malden, MA: Wiley–Blackwell.

About the Author

Zsuzsanna I. Abrams is Professor of Applied Linguistics and Multilingualism at the University of California Santa Cruz. Her research focuses on computer-mediated communication, computer-supported collaborative L2 writing, L2 pragmatic development, and language pedagogy. She applies her research to help learners develop the ability to use the L2 in real-world communicative situations by engaging them actively in analyzing authentic materials and interacting in the L2 as it is used by culturally complex communities of practice. Her research has been published in the *CALICO Journal*, *CALL*, and *Language Learning & Technology*, among other venues.

2 Intercultural Virtual Communication and Novice Learners: Attitudes, Perception, and Beliefs

Liudmila Klimanova and Valentina Vinokurova

1 Introduction

In the context of language learning, intercultural virtual exchange combines the deep impact of intercultural dialogue with the broad reach of digital technology in a technology-enabled practice of bringing together learners in geographically distant locations to exchange skills and knowledge and, more importantly, to develop intercultural competence through communication activities and collaborative tasks (Jager, Nissen, Helm, Baroni, & Rousset, 2019; O'Dowd, 2007, 2011). Since the 1990s, a variety of terms have been developed to describe various configurations that intercultural exchange can take, including telecollaboration (as a form of classroom-based language exchange) (Belz, 2003; Guth & Helm, 2010), e-Tandem reciprocal one-on-one language learning (Brammerts, 2001; Cziko, 2004; O'Rourke, 2007), e-Twinning as a form of virtual exchange engaging students in collaborative cross-institutional and cross-curricular international projects (Condruz-Bacescu, 2016; Dominga Miguela, 2007), and TRIDEM telecollaboration linking students from three distant parts of the world (Hauck, 2007; Hauck & Lewis, 2007). These terms describe various types of intercultural virtual exchange initially conceptualized as asynchronous modalities of communication with other second language (L2) learners and native speakers (NS) via emails. With the proliferation of social media and mobile technology, the format of intercultural virtual exchange has significantly expanded to include synchronous (i.e., in real time) interactions via online chat and video applications as well as multimodal communication involving combinations of media and mobile technologies for a more rich and dynamic exchange of languages and cultures among students in distant parts of the world. Intercultural virtual exchange has become a so-called "pillar of the intercultural turn in foreign language education" (Thorne, 2010) allowing language instructors, and more broadly educators, to engage their students in meaningful communication with members of other cultures and reflect on their own culture within the supportive context of their classroom. Moreover, more recently foreign language educators have turned their attention to the critical nature of intercultural exchange, moving away from what Kramsch (2014: 300) frames as a superficial surfing of diversity or "phatic exchanges that are no longer what communicative language pedagogy had in mind" to a collaborative dialog around a diverse range of critical topics and global issues in various parts of the world.

It goes without saying that these sophisticated types of intercultural communication require rather high (functional) levels of language ability or a shared native language allowing participants to engage in meaningful synchronous and asynchronous modalities of intercultural communication with each other and discuss complex topics and issues. It is not surprising that intercultural telecollaborative exchange has been widely used in foreign language instruction as a learning activity, targeting predominantly intermediate and advanced proficiency learners. With regard to beginning-level language learners, research and practice have been rather scarce, limited only to a handful of studies (e.g., Dunne, 2014; Schenker, 2015, 2018; Stepp-Greany, 2002). At the same time, with the help of Google Translate and immediate translation tools featured in most social networking sites, even a minimal proficiency in the target language can create a unique opportunity for beginning L2 learners to engage in extensive, and often linguistically sophisticated, intercultural conversations with target language speakers via digital communication tools and platforms (Klimanova & Bondarenko, 2018).

The present study aims at investigating the significance of such intercultural encounters for novice L2 learners, focusing specifically on their attitudes, perceptions, and beliefs about intercultural virtual exchange with other language learners and native speakers as a meaningful language learning activity. In particular, we analyze novice learners' willingness to explore, learn, and participate in online social networks as platforms for intercultural learning, and to collaborate with others, using their target language as a primary means of communication. More importantly, this study investigates the possibility of positively affecting learner attitudes towards intercultural virtual exchange as a form of intercultural learning early in their language studies (as early as the first semester of L2 study) with the purpose of preparing them for future intercultural exchanges. Along with attitudes, perceptions, and beliefs about intercultural exchange, we consider such factors as intercultural partner identity, format of exchange, participants' first and second language affiliations, types of anxiety associated with intercultural communication as a learning activity, and learning outcomes resulting from this experience, as expected and perceived by novice learners. Two contextual configurations – an exchange between unfamiliar novice L2 learners (cross-institutional) and an exchange between a group of novice L2 learners and native speakers (cross-cultural) – are examined as a potential factor that influences learners' perceptions of intercultural virtual exchange as a learning activity. The present study aims to answer the following research questions, following both quantitative (QUAN) and qualitative (QUAL) types of inquiry:

1. How do novice learners' perceptions of intercultural virtual exchange as a learning activity differ at the beginning and end of a two-week telecollaborative class project? (QUAN/QUAL)
2. To what extent do learners' attitudes, perceptions, and beliefs about intercultural virtual exchange, including such factors as learning gains, fears and doubts, satisfaction, etc. differ between cross-cultural and cross-institutional virtual exchange groups before and after the telecollaborative project? (QUAN/QUAL)
3. What specific attitudes and beliefs do novice L2 learners have about cross-institutional and cross-cultural telecollaborative language exchanges as a learning activity? (QUAL)
4. What fears and doubts do novice language learners have when they are asked to participate in intercultural communication in the target language? (QUAL)

2 Learner Attitudes, Perceptions, Beliefs, and Virtual Intercultural Communication

Learner attitudes are a universally abstract construct that has been the focus of language acquisition research since the 1970s (e.g., Bartley, 1970; Horwitz, 1988). As settled ways of thinking or feeling about something, learner attitudes are believed to be reflected in a learner's behavior and can relate to two targets: the learning/teaching process (attitudes towards the learning situation) and attitudes towards the target language community (attitudes as a component of intercultural competence) (Yashima, 2009). Investigating learners' attitudes, perceptions, and beliefs about intercultural communication is a matter of examining a variety of evidence, including non-observable or often self-reported data, as well as observable attributes that can manifest themselves in the types of reactions learners exhibit during an intercultural exchange. Broadly speaking, learner attitudes, perceptions, and beliefs can be linked to the learners themselves and their belief systems and to the interaction between the learner and the learning environment. Wesely (2012) describes three principal orientations in the literature on learner attitudes, perceptions, and beliefs: (1) studies of static and unchanging learner attitudes related to learner's demographic and identity characteristics ("trait" or "learner" studies); (2) studies of learners' attitudes as affected by their learning situation ("state" or "environmental" studies), and (3) studies focusing on the fluid, constantly negotiated nature of learner attitudes, perceptions, and beliefs that reflect learners' dynamic interaction with a learning environment ("dynamic" or "complexity" studies).

Attitudes are often examined together with learner perceptions, beliefs, and anxieties as underlying individual factors that determine learners' successes and failures (e.g., Williams & Burden, 1999). Perceptions are similar to attitudes and are often understood as how learners make sense of themselves and their learning environment. Learner beliefs, on the other hand, are deeply linked to learners' belief systems, and are "more overarching and pervasive than perceptions" (Wesely, 2012: 100). Belief systems may include the category of learner self-construct – what students think of themselves as language learners and of their potential capability to complete a task or execute the courses of action required to master a certain skill (Mills, Pajares, & Herron, 2007). Learner beliefs are experiential as they arise from learners' previous experiences with language learning; but also dynamic, socially constructed, paradoxical, changeable, and contextually situated (Barcelos, 2003).

Attitudes, perceptions, and beliefs inform students' motivation and may cause anxiety since motivation is closely connected to the affective characteristics of the learner (Dörnyei, 2003, 2009). Learner anxiety, including fears and apprehensions, is used as "a way to understand and contextualize learner attitudes, perceptions, and beliefs in a framework that is easily measured and understood" (Wesely, 2012: 100). Probably the most researched form of learner anxiety is an anxiety toward foreign language use, or foreign language anxiety, a unique type of anxiety that is situation-specific arising from the uniqueness of learning and using a second language (Horwitz, Horwitz, & Cope, 1986). Foreign language anxiety is fundamental to our understanding of how learners approach language tasks, their expectations for success and failure, and their desire to continue or abandon language learning (Horwitz, 2010). Also, research on L2 learners has shown that learner attitudes about themselves as L2 users and their learning abilities affect the level of anxiety associated with L2 use (Yan & Horwitz, 2008), enjoyment with the process of reading in L2 (Brantmeier, 2005), and achievement on proficiency measures (Mills et al., 2007). In her meta-analysis of the current research on learner attitudes, Wesely (2012) rightly points out that there is only a small body of work examining learner attitudes alone without connecting them to observable learning outcomes, or learner attitudes in relation to specific learning contexts and learner characteristics, with the exception of studies about heritage, gender, and first language affiliations.

Although there are only a handful of studies on the relation between learner attitudes and proficiency levels, a wide consensus is that low-level learners generally perceive authentic language learning tasks less favorably than advanced learners. The latter show more enthusiasm for engaging with target language use and intercultural encounters. An earlier study by Kern (1995), for example, found that beginning-level students tend to develop idealistic learning goals and narrowly defined perspectives on L2 learning. When comparing learner and teacher beliefs about effective foreign language teaching across levels and languages, Brown (2009) found that first-year L2 learners felt less strongly than second-year L2 learners that teachers should require them to use the target language starting from the first day of class. Novice learners expressed a stronger preference for discrete-point grammar instruction and explicit error correction as part of their learning experience. On the other hand, beginning-level learners of less-commonly taught languages (LCTL), such as Russian, for example, generally felt more strongly about the importance of L2 use outside of class than learners of commonly-taught languages, such as Spanish, French, German, etc. More generally, students who perceived higher target language use in class reported lower levels of anxiety about target language use (Levine, 2003). Brown (2009) concludes that learners' ideals and beliefs may change from their first to their second year of language instruction and that researchers should not assume that beginning-level learners have no preconceived beliefs about L2 use during the language learning process. Little is known, however, about how such novice learners perceive online social language use as a language learning activity.

Literature on computer-mediated communication is replete with studies delving into students' perceptions of various aspects of online L2 use (e.g., a meta-analysis by Çiftçi & Savaş, 2018). Most of these studies, however, are based on qualitative, often anecdotal, evidence focusing on the effects of intercultural communication on the development of L2 learners' linguistic and intercultural competences. In general terms, language learners believe that interaction with other speakers via social technological tools facilitates the acquisition of second language, particularly, L2 grammar and vocabulary; however, it is also a distraction from "real" language learning in the classroom and a source of intimidation and unnecessary stress (Chen &Yang, 2016; Kelly, 2018). The positive attitudes toward social online interaction are often attributed to learners' access to and ability to communicate with target language speakers (Kramsch, A'Ness, & Lam, 2000). Establishing a contact with native speaker communities was found to be intriguing and motivating for language learners (Lin, Warschauer, & Blake, 2016); however, sustaining such contact over time becomes problematic after the initial intrigue peters out (Chen, Shih, & Liu, 2015). When it comes to intercultural communication as part of a telecollaborative experience, participants often enjoy a contact with speakers of the target language and people from diverse cultures (e.g., Bueno-Alastuey & Kleban, 2016; Angelova & Zhao, 2016). Yet, individual learners' perceptions may contribute to the level of engagement and quality of their online communication (Hauck, 2010). Nonetheless, it is not clear how communicative contexts, learner variables, and learner beliefs shape the perceptions and attitudes of individual learners towards intercultural communication as a language learning activity. One of the few studies of the interaction between online intercultural contexts and learner attitudes was conducted by Yang (2018), who investigated L2 learners' perceptions of online pair activities and group discussion in e-Tandem learning, a form of language learning in which two learners of different native languages work together to help each other learn the other language. Her participants' perceptions of two interactional contexts as complementary or non-complementary for learning purposes had an impact on their participation and L2 use in intercultural e-Tandem partnerships.

Finally, learner attitudes, perceptions, and beliefs towards the intercultural component of telecollaborative exchange are typically outlined as learning objectives (Byram, 1997). Attitudes towards intercultural communication as an outcome of the interaction between the learners (participants) and the learning environment (the online exchange platform) are expressed through learners' (un)willingness to engage with otherness and to interpret familiar and unfamiliar cultural phenomena in both one's own and other cultures. In an attempt to measure attitudinal factors in intercultural communication, Vogt (2006) examined the instances of attitudinal factors in learners' observable interactional data, using Byram's classification of intercultural attitudes as a baseline. She concluded that it is impossible to quantify attitudinal data in computer-mediated intercultural communication. However, interactional data, interactional journals, or broadly, what learners say about intercultural communication, may allow the researcher to trace changes and developments in learners' attitudes, measure their perceptions of individual activities, and unveil their beliefs about learning language and culture via intercultural communication. The present chapter responds to this claim proposing a study of novice learners' attitudes, perceptions, and beliefs towards intercultural telecollaboration as a learning activity. The following factors are examined: (1) attitudes toward varied telecollaborative contexts; (2) attitudes towards partners' cultural and linguistic background; (3) perceptions of expectations and outcomes; (4) anxiety, associated with target language use, (social) technology, task difficulty and complexity, and intercultural contact, and (5) attitudes toward telecollaborative exchange as a learning activity at the beginning level of instruction. More specifically, we will examine attitudes, perceptions, and beliefs that beginning-level Russian learners have towards an opportunity to interact with target language speakers during a brief online intercultural exchange.

3 Methodology and Study Design

In this study, four groups of students (n = 70) – three intact elementary Russian sections (n = 56); and a group of Russian native speakers (n = 14) – from three partner universities participated in a telecollaborative project. By the start of the project the study participants in Russian (L2) sections had completed only eight weeks of college-level classroom instruction and, based on the number of contact hours (32–35 in each class), were approximately at Level A1.1 (CEFR Framework) or Novice Mid/Novice High (ACTFL Proficiency Scale). Although no formal evaluation was undertaken to ascertain the participants' proficiency level more accurately, it was assumed that all students from beginning Russian sections had no prior formal instruction in the target language. All but one participant indicated that they had never participated in an intercultural virtual exchange.

The unilingual cross-institutional exchange (Group #1) was organized between two groups of beginning Russian learners at two Canadian universities (Figure 1). The second partnership, bilingual and cross-cultural (Group #2), was organized between a group of Canadian students learning Russian and a group of Russian students learning French (Figure 2). A popular Russian social networking platform, *vkontakte* (VK, a Russia-based analog of Facebook), was used as a virtual medium for student tandem writing. Over the period of two weeks, learners completed several telecollaborative tasks that were differently configured from the perspective of "participation structure" defined as social factors such as the number and identity of participants in the online communication situation; the amount and rate of participation; the language affiliation of interlocutors; and the extent to which interlocutors chose to interact anonymously/pseudonymously as opposed to in their "real life" identities" (Herring, 2007) (Table 1).

Table 1. Language learning tasks (Groups #1 and #2)

Task	Type of virtual exchange task	Instructions
Task 1. Registration on VK	Non-communicative task	Register on vk.com and join project group page; Complete the entry questionnaire
Task 2. Introductions	Asynchronous, text-based, non-communicative	Post a short introduction on the group VK page; Complete Reflection Journal 1
Task 3. Questions	Asynchronous, text-based, communicative	Post a question (of any nature, for instance: Do you know what a *samovar* is? What do you like to do on Fridays? Do you like parties?) on the group VK page and post at least 5 answers to other students' questions; Complete Reflection Journal 2 (instructor and students together wrote a list of questions for the one-on-one interview)
Task 4. Partners	Asynchronous, text-based, communicative	Establish contact with assigned partner from the partner university; Post a basic greeting/introduction on your partner's wall (length: 5 sentences); Discuss with your partner (publicly, on the wall) when you would like to meet or Skype in order to conduct an interview with them; Complete Reflection Journal 3
Task 5. Interview	Synchronous, oral, communicative	Meet with your partner in person or over Skype, conduct the interview; Complete Reflection Journal 4
Task 6. Report	Non-communicative	Fill out the "Data Collection Form" with the information you will obtain from your partner (the forms were used in a class activity where students were asked to analyze their findings and create a visual infographic showing a typical profile of a Russian learner [Group #1] or a French learner [Group #2] based on the results of their interviews with tandem partners); Complete the exit questionnaire

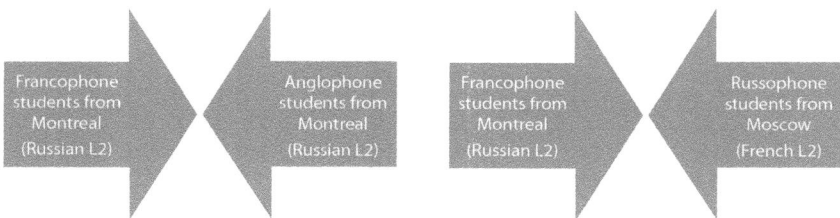

Figure 1. Group #1(L2 as a lingua franca)   **Figure 2.** Group #2 (e-Tandem model)

In this study, *intercultural virtual exchange* is defined broadly as a language learning activity that engages learners from different cultures (not necessarily target L2 cultures) and *telecollaborative project/activity* involves computer-mediated tasks that these learners complete during an intercultural virtual exchange. Based on these definitions, both exchanges can be classified as intercultural because all participants interacted with partners from another culture (locally or globally defined); however, the groups' participatory configuration varied. In Group #1, participants shared the same target language (Russian as L2 as a lingua franca), but most of them did not share the same native language. One group was represented by predominantly native English speakers in an English-speaking university, while the other group included beginning Russian learners in a French-speaking university whose native language was French. Both institutions were located in the bilingual region of the Quebec province in Canada where both English and French are used as a means of communication, with French given more symbolic power due to the province's unique sociopolitical and sociolinguistic context. It is also important to note that although the participants in Group #1 did not share the same native language, they represented two language majorities in Canada, sharing the same country affiliation as anglophone and francophone Canadians, but differing in their unique locally- and historically-sedimented backgrounds associated with French- and English-speaking cultures.

In Group #2, another group of beginning Russian L2 learners from a French-speaking institution participated in a similar interactional exchange; however, their intercultural partners were native speakers of Russian who were learning French at a higher educational establishment in Russia. The participants in these groups did not share their native language and were asked to engage in an e-Tandem-type of virtual exchange where they took turns interacting in pairs in their target language – Russian (L2) for the francophone Canadian group and French (L2) for the Russian group. All groups were made aware of the primary language affiliations of their exchange partners before the exchange started and more detailed instructions about each activity were given during a class session. Essentially for this group, the project was divided into two sequential parts: for the first two weeks, students communicated solely in Russian, and for the second two weeks, only in French.

3.1 The Questionnaire

Students' attitudes towards intercultural exchange in both projects were measured by the pre-project and post-project questionnaires, consisting of Likert-scale evaluative statements as well as open-ended questions about learners' expectations, fears, apprehensions, anticipated and perceived learning gains, and anticipated and perceived value of intercultural exchange as a learning activity (Appendix). While a number of rigorously validated attitude-related questionnaires have already been developed (e.g., Gardner's Attitude-Motivation Test Battery, 2004; or Horwitz's Foreign Language Classroom Anxiety Scale, Horwitz et al., 1986), none of them was applicable to the context of this study. Since the present study aimed at examining attitudes of learners not towards language or language learning in general, but towards a particular type of learning activity (i.e., an intercultural tele-collaborative project), project-specific questionnaires were developed to serve this purpose. The entry questionnaire contained prompts eliciting learners' expectations from the project, such as expectations related to language learning and those related to the development of intercultural competence and community-building; fears related to the project; and their overall expectations of the usefulness and difficulty of the project. The exit questionnaire posed similar questions to students and investigated their perception of positive outcomes, and fears and anxieties experienced in the course of the project, and prompted them to evaluate how difficult, entertaining, and useful the project was in retrospect. To elicit more thought-out reflections on their experiences with this type of language learning, learners were also asked to offer recommendations to students and instructors who may be involved in a similar project in the future. The 10-point Likert scale was chosen due to its established utility in the context of research on attitudes, perceptions, and beliefs about language learning experiences (Barcelos, 2003). Both entry and exit questionnaires were evaluated for face validity using the following two-step procedure: a list of questionnaire statements was first developed by one of the researchers independently based on the existing literature of attitudes, perceptions, and beliefs; then the statements were evaluated for capturing learners' attitudes and perceptions by a group of three researchers (one of the researchers was not directly involved in the project and had prior experience with psychometric evaluations of survey instruments). All confusing statements and double-barreled questions were reformulated, and the final version of the entry questionnaire was produced. Due to a small size of group populations, the questionnaire was not piloted, and ranking measurements were used instead to gauge any significant differences between pre- and post-project responses, and across project types. Given the scope and objectives of the present study, the benefits of a closed-response format facilitated direct comparisons between three intact group of learners (Appendix: see the concordance table with each item on the questionnaire classified into an overarching category/dependent variable).

A mixed-method equivalent status research design (QUAN/QUAL) (Tashakkori & Teddlie, 1998; Ware & Rivas, 2012) was used to triangulate numeric questionnaire data from the pre- and post-project questionnaires with a qualitative analysis of students' comments and reflections before and after the telecollaborative exchange with an attempt to obtain a more comprehensive understanding of L2 learners' attitudes and perceptions across exchange types and language/culture groups. As stated previously, the quantitative data obtained were analyzed using non-parametric statistical measures which were determined to be most appropriate given the small sample size and the fact that the majority of data obtained from the questionnaire were not normally distributed (Shapiro-Wilk's W test). The Wilcoxon Signed Ranks test was used to compare the responses on the entry and exit questionnaires completed by the same students (a full list of dependent variables can be found in the questionnaires in the Appendix). In addition, the Mann-Whitney U test was used to identify differences in the perceptions of the project between the learners engaging in the cross-cultural exchange and those engaging in the cross-institutional exchange. Since the aim of this study was to examine attitudes and perceptions of virtual intercultural communication in language learners, questionnaires were not collected from native Russian speakers participating in the second project (which resulted in a lower number of participants in Group #2). The qualitative data were coded using the grounded theory approach (categories were identified during the coding procedure) as well as a set of pre-established variables used in the quantitative analyses. Data triangulation was achieved by verifying the findings identified through statistical measures against qualitative data and vice versa.

4 Results

4.1 Quantitative Data

To answer Research Questions #1 and #2, the numeric data obtained from the pre- and post-project questionnaire were analyzed in two procedures.

First, responses provided in the entry questionnaire were compared to those provided in the exit questionnaire for each group in order to examine how, for instance, the *expected* usefulness of the project allowing students to practice the target language outside of the classroom compared to the *perceived* usefulness of the project at the end of the project for each student in each group (RQ #1). Second, all responses were analyzed for statistical differences between the two groups with the purpose of testing whether, for instance, Group #1 expected the project to be more difficult than Group #2 (RQ #2).

RQ#1: How do novice learners' perceptions of intercultural virtual exchange as a learning activity differ at the beginning and end of a two-week telecollaborative class project? (QUAN)

The Wilcoxon Signed Ranks test was used to compare positive expectations with perceived positive outcomes, and negative expectations (fears) with perceived negative outcomes for each group.

Group #1 (N = 35), shows a statistically significant difference in learner expectations as opposed to the perceived positive outcomes of the project for most criteria (Table 2). Students perceived that the project was not as helpful in breaking down language barriers as they hoped it would be (p = .001). More importantly, students' expectations of the project's utility for learning more language (p = .029), learning more about Russian culture (p = .000) and understanding Russian people (p = .000) exceeded

Table 2. Comparison of positive expectations and positive outcomes for Group #1

	pride 2 – pride 1	practice 2 – practice 1	barriers 2 – barriers 1	learn language 2 – learn language 1	learn about Russia 2 – learn about Russia 1	understand 2 – understand 1	community 2 – community 1	friends 2 – friends 1
Z^a	-1.649^b	-1.826^b	-3.459^b	-2.184^b	-3.648^b	-3.758^b	-2.323^b	-3.153^b
Asymp. Sig. (2-tailed)	.099	.068	.001	.029	.000	.000	.020	.002

[a] Wilcoxon Signed Ranks test for N > 10
[b] Based on positive ranks

post-test evaluations of gains on these criteria. In addition, students' perception of the usefulness of the project for finding new friends (p = .002) and becoming part of the Russian-learning community (p = .020) at the end of the project was significantly lower than their expectations in this regard at the beginning of the project. Statistical significance was not found for the difference between students' pre- and post-project evaluation of the project's usefulness for allowing additional language practice and providing an opportunity for students to take pride in their communicative ability.

The Wilcoxon Signed Ranks test did not show statistical significance for the difference between expected positive results and perceived positive outcomes as reported by students in Group #2 (N = 15), perhaps due to a small sample size. As stated above, the same statistical test was used in order to compare pre- and post-project fears and anxieties as reported by participants in each group; no statistical differences were found for either group.

RQ #2: To what extent do learners' attitudes, perceptions, and beliefs about intercultural virtual exchange, including such factors as learning gains, fears and doubts, satisfaction, etc., differ between cross-cultural and cross-institutional virtual exchange groups before and after the telecollaborative project? (QUAN)

The Mann-Whitney U test was used to compare positive expectations, positive outcomes, fears, negative outcomes, and overall project evaluation between Group #1 and Group #2 (N = 50). Mean values for each criterion are provided in parentheses as an additional reference point: M1 – mean for Group #1, and M2 – mean for Group #2. The comparison of positive expectations between the two groups showed no statistically significant differences. However, a comparison of positive outcomes did yield statistically significant results for three criteria: learning the language, learning more about Russia, and understanding Russian people better (Table 3). In particular, the Mann-Whitney U test indicated that the exchange project was more helpful for Group #2 in the category "Learn Russian language," both for vocabulary items or grammatical structures (p = .045, M1 = 6.9, M2 = 8.3). Perhaps unsurprisingly, Group #2 gave higher evaluations to the outcomes related to learning more about Russia (p = .03, M1 = 4.8, M2 = 6.9) and to understanding Russian people (p = .022, M1 = 4.3, M2 = 6.4) than Group #1. No statistically significant differences were found for the following criteria: helpfulness of the project to review material covered in the classroom; to break down language barriers; to become integrated in the Russian-speaking community; and to make new friends.

Table 3. Comparison of positive outcomes between Group #1 and Group #2

	pride 2	practice 2	barriers 2	learn language 2	learn Russian 2	understand 2	community 2	friends 2
Mann-Whitney U	213.000	238.000	177.500	169.500	161.000	155.500	222.500	184.500
Z	−1.060	−.533	−1.817	−2.005	−2.169	−2.283	−.855	−1.662
Asymp. Sig. (2-tailed)	.289	.594	.069	.045	.030	.022	.393	.097

With the exception of one criterion, no statistical significance was found for differences in pre-project fears between the two groups (Table 4). It is worth noting that the one criterion that did show a significant difference was the fear of interacting with a "cultural stranger." The Mann-Whitney U test indicates that this fear was weaker in Group #2 (M = 2.8) than for Group #1 (M = 4.9). This finding is examined further in the Discussion section.

Table 4. Comparison of pre-project fears between Group #1 and Group #2

	insufficient 1	fear-barrier 1	time 1	useless 1	stranger 1
Mann-Whitney U	165.500	165.000	171.500	146.500	118.000
Z	−.670	−.682	−.499	−1.222	−2.016
Asymp. Sig. (2-tailed)	.503	.495	.618	.222	.044

A comparison of students' evaluations of negative outcomes of the project shows two statistically significant differences (Table 5). The Mann-Whitney U test indicates that students from Group #1 were less likely to perceive their language knowledge as insufficient for virtual communication (p = .003) within the framework of this project (M = 4.3) than their peers from Group #2 (M = 6.9). Moreover, Group #1 (M = 3.4) was also significantly less aware of a language barrier (p = .022) than Group #2 (M = 5.3). Statistical significance was not found for other negative impressions (namely, for the time-consuming nature of the project, responsiveness of the partner, lacking instrumental motivation, communication with a stranger, or negative attitudes towards social networks as a medium for exchange).

Table 5. Comparison of post-project fears (negative outcomes) between Group #1 and Group #2

	stranger 2	insufficient 2	time 2	network 2	partner 2	motivation 2	fear-barrier 2
Mann-Whitney U	183.500	123.500	262.000	219.500	176.500	199.000	155.500
Z	−1.703	−2.958	−.011	−.932	−1.849	−1.353	−2.282
Asymp. Sig. (2-tailed)	.089	.003	.991	.352	.064	.176	.022

Finally, the Mann-Whitney test was used to compare students' overall perceptions of the project. Students were asked to rate the difficulty of the project, to evaluate how entertained they were by the project, and how useful they thought it was for their overall learning. While mean values are higher for all three criteria for Group #2, only differences in difficulty and usefulness were found to be statistically significant (Table 6). The Mann-Whitney U test indicates that the level of difficulty was evaluated to be significantly higher (p = .035) by Group #2 (M = 6.6) than by Group #1 (M = 5.5). At the same time, the level of usefulness of this project for learning was significantly higher (p = .01) for Group #2 (M = 7.9) as opposed to Group #1 (M = 6.1).

Table 6. Comparison of overall impressions of the project between Group #1 and Group #2 at the end of the exchange

	difficulty 2	fun 2	use 2
Mann-Whitney U	164.500	178.500	142.500
Z	−2.108	−1.799	−2.567
Asymp. Sig. (2-tailed)	.035	.072	.010

4.2 Qualitative Data

In the analysis of qualitative data, Russian learners' open-ended responses and comments in the pre- and post-project questionnaires were coded using the criteria outlined in the questionnaire: (1) positive expectations about learning; (2) positive outcomes from the intercultural experience; (3) negative outcomes from the intercultural experience; (4) attitudes and perceptions of intercultural virtual exchange as a learning activity; and (5) learner anxiety. In addition to targeted coding, an open coding procedure was completed by the authors to identify other categories in the qualitative data that were not established *a priori*. Overall, 250 responses were included in the qualitative dataset. To ensure internal validity, students' comments were first coded by each author independently, and then, two lists of coding categories were compared, and all discrepancies were reformulated, particularly for learner anxiety, where four distinct types of anxiety associated with telecollaborative activities were identified: (1) anxieties associated with target language use; (2) anxieties fueled by the use of technology and a foreign public social network; (3) fears caused by task difficulty and complexity; (4) anxieties associated with meeting with a "cultural stranger." The findings below are grouped by RQ.

RQ #1: How do novice learners' perceptions of intercultural virtual exchange as a learning activity differ at the beginning and end of a two-week telecollaborative class project? (QUAL)

At the beginning of the virtual exchange project the language gains were formulated by learners only in terms of speaking ability and speaking fluency even though this intercultural exchange was planned by the instructors primarily as an asynchronous telecollaborative writing activity with only one component involving a synchronous oral interview. Student comments did not show any qualitative differences in relation to the kinds of expectations they had for the intercultural communication between beginning-level Russian learners in two institutions in the same country or between Russian learners and native speakers. Students in both groups anticipated an opportunity to engage in the target language during the intercultural exchange, even though the individuals in Group #1 knew that their partners would be also beginning-level learners, not Russian speakers from Russia. The use of the Russia-based social networking platform as a medium was perceived by these learners as a source of cultural information to the same extent as native speaking partners in Group #2.

RQ #2: To what extent do learners' attitudes, perceptions, and beliefs about intercultural virtual exchange, including such factors as learning gains, fears and doubts, satisfaction, etc., differ between cross-cultural and cross-institutional virtual exchange groups before and after the telecollaborative project? (QUAL)

Among specific language learning gains at the end of the project most participants listed acquisition of new vocabulary and significantly improved typing skills. The social component of the telecollaborative project motivated the students in both groups to attempt extended conversations with project partners and get to know their partner on a more personal level. As one student in Group #2 wrote,

> I really liked learning more about my correspondent and about Russian culture in general. I also liked testing my knowledge and taking inspiration from the answers my correspondent gave me to formulate my own questions.

By far, the most reported gain was the opportunity to recognize (more so than to use) the linguistic structures studied with the instructor in free-flowing conversations with project partners. Noticing familiar basic vocabulary and grammatical structures had an empowering effect on many learners in this exchange – "We could use the grammar seen in the course and we could see that this grammar and vocabulary are really used in Russian language!" Learners did not comment on the gains associated with intercultural learning *per se*, possibly because most tasks involved interviewing partners on the topic of choice of foreign language and language study. However, several students in Group #2 commented on the importance of meeting people from another culture. As one student wrote, I enjoyed "learning about friends living in another country, who learn our language and whose language we learn." Group #1 learners did not perceive their partners as "cultural others" possibly due the fact that regardless of primary language affiliation (French L1 or English L1), these groups of students shared the same country of origin. Although Group #1 was not aware that Group #2 from the same university was interacting with students in Russia, some students from that group expressed preference for having a native-speaking tandem partner who learns French or English as an opportunity to learn about Russian culture in future exchanges. This comment suggests an underlying learner belief that virtual language exchange should involve target language speakers as a source of cultural information and authentic language. As a piece of advice to the instructor, one student suggested that novice learners should be given a choice of telecollaborative partner – a native speaker or another Russian learner from a different culture – based on their preference and level of comfort with beginning language skills.

RQ #3: What specific attitudes and perceptions do beginning Russian learners have towards cross-institutional and cross-cultural telecollaborative language exchange as a learning activity? (QUAL)

In the pre-project questionnaire all learners made favorable comments about their expectations for the intercultural project. Among the most anticipated positive outcomes of the intercultural exchange activity was the opportunity to practice Russian skills outside of class and in a more authentic context ("real discussion used in a more real context"). The choice of virtual exchange as an intercultural communication task was welcomed by at least half of the participants in all three groups. Many students expressed excitement about a chance to try out newly acquired language skills, and the idea of practicing Russian skills with "cultural strangers" seemed to be very appealing to most of the learners despite a significant lack of grammar and vocabulary in the target language.

The post-project questionnaire naturally contained more comments about learner-perceived gains and learning outcomes. Of the 67 comments coded as describing positive outcomes, approximately 50% described the telecollaborative project as a fundamentally different type of language learning through virtual communication with a cultural other – or, as one student metaphorically described it, "learning while improvising." For many learners, the telecollaborative activity was a test of their emerging language skills, an opportunity to prove to themselves that they were able to apply the skills and knowledge they learned in class, in what one learner called "a non-simulated environment" or a way to compare the level of Russian ability between two universities (Group #1). The social aspect of virtual language exchange was by far the most appreciated outcome of the project. Almost every participant noted the excitement they experienced when meeting a new person, a language learner or a native Russian speaker:

> The simple act of exchanging in Russian is beautiful. (Group #1 participant)
>
> I loved being able to talk for two weeks with people from another country. It allowed me to learn a lot about Russian culture and also to improve my understanding of the language. The majority of students were very friendly, which made the project even more enjoyable. (Group #2 participant)
>
> I liked being able to practice [my language skills] with a native Russian, it helped me to see how people express themselves normally. (Group #2 participant)

Interestingly, the use of "normally" in the last example hints at this novice learner's belief that language practice in the classroom is probably "not-normal" or not natural. This sentiment was expressed by several learners from both Group #1 and Group #2. The sense of enjoyment from meeting peers, however, was overshadowed by certain negative perceptions of the telecollaborative project. More learners noted in the post-project questionnaire that communicating in the target language via a social network was complicated by various logistical difficulties, including irresponsible partners (both groups), a delayed response from partner due to a time lag (Group #2), and lack of familiarity with the social networking platform (both groups). One student summarized this latter sentiment as follows: "Using an unknown social network may require some learning, getting used to it." This attitude echoed learners' dissatisfaction with a short length of the exchange resulting in a minimal use of the target language. At the end of the project many students were still overwhelmed by the amount of language they had to process daily to be able to maintain an online conversation with their project partner. No differences were observed across Group #1 and Group #2. However, naturally Group #2 learners became more aware of their linguistic limitations because their Russian speaking partners "would not adapt" to their language level. As one participant in Group #2 shared, "We may not have enough vocabulary to have a sustained conversation, but we could do it in French." This finding was confirmed with the statistical analysis of the questionnaire data in the category of difficulty associated with the target language use.

RQ #4: What fears and doubts do novice language learners have when they are asked to participate in intercultural communication in the target language? (QUAL)

With regards to fears and apprehensions, most learners in both projects initially reported the anxiety associated with the lack of language proficiency and the fear of not making themselves understood. The question about a partner's L2 identity resulted in several contradictory statements, where one student wrote that interacting with other Russian learners at the beginning level of language learning was beneficial – e.g., "I believe, [it is] highly preferable to interact with real-life interlocutors with whom we share the already rich experience of a common learning of the Russian language." This enthusiasm, however, was not shared by other learners in Group #1. Another student, for example, believed that practicing the target language with other learners was not a useful language learning activity – "I'm not sure it's the best idea to learn Russian from other students simply because they have not mastered it yet and we could mislead each other." Among other types of fears, learners reported anxieties associated with the use of public social technology – e.g., "a horror of social networks and transmission of personal information via an overseas site" or "the presence of illegitimate content" – and the nature of intercultural communicative tasks that were perceived by several learners as requiring "a lot more participation than an individual assignment" (Group #1).

Analysis of the post-project questionnaire revealed 105 mentions of anxieties caused by the nature of intercultural project activities, including 31%

(33 mentions) of the anxieties associated with the task itself, 61% (64 mentions) of foreign language anxieties, and 8% (8 mentions) of the anxieties associated with the use of the social networking platform. While it is not surprising that most learners were concerned about their lack of language ability, Group #1, however, commented more on their insufficient language skills for communication with other novice learners (also confirmed statistically). This fear of not being able to make oneself understood discouraged learners from engaging fully in the telecollaborative exchange. Several students in Group #1 also noted that they would have preferred to interact with native speakers because they would not have had a choice but to communicate only in L2 – "Here we always have English as a back-up" (Group #1 participant). This finding suggests that language learners perceive virtual telecollaborative exchange mainly as an opportunity to meet a target language speaker, rather than a way to use their L2 as a lingua franca with other L2 language speakers. At the same time, the learners in Group #2 were surprised that their native speaking partner did not make an effort to adapt to their beginning language ability when completing collaborative tasks, which made the project more challenging for this group. Among other reported anxieties, many learners noted various difficulties with navigating the Russian social website, formulating questions and responses in the target language, and typing messages using the Russian keyboard – "Typing everything in Russian was quite time-consuming and difficult" (Group #2 participant). It is important to mention that Russian language uses the Cyrillic alphabet, a writing system developed in the 9th–10th century CE for Slavic-speaking peoples of the Eastern Orthodox faith. The Cyrillic letters are not shown on the English keyboard that is most familiar to all North American students, including francophone Canadians. Learning to type Russian words and phrases on a computer typically takes time and presents a serious learning challenge not only for beginning, but also for intermediate and sometimes advanced Russian L2 learners.

5 Discussion

It has been argued that the significance of language learning tasks (the basic blocks of language instruction) as perceived by language learners themselves and shaped by their attitudes and beliefs determine their interest, motivation, and enthusiasm when practicing skills (Dörnyei, 2003). Attitudes, perceptions, and beliefs as internal forces of individual learning produce what Dörnyei (2003: 4) coins as "the motivational tapestry underlying second language acquisition (SLA)." Williams & Burden (1999: 98) maintained that "learners' perceptions and interpretations have been found to have the greatest influence on achievement," while motivation influences goal-setting, values associated with the learning process itself, learning outcomes, positive and negative consequences, expectancy of success, and perceived coping potential. It also informs new attitudes (e.g., attitudes towards the target language and its speakers) and shapes new beliefs and values in language learners (Dörnyei, 2003). In focusing on these affective domains of learning, this study has examined novice learners' attitudes and beliefs towards an intercultural virtual exchange that inform perceptions of successes and failures, including such factors as fears and anxieties, intercultural partners, perceived gains and challenges, and expected and perceived linguistic ability.

Looking at the overall picture, the findings suggest that novice learners tend to have high hopes for intercultural collaborative exchange. Analysis of the pre- and post-project questionnaires and learners' reflective comments, for example, revealed that even at the beginning level, learners become excited about the opportunity to try out their emerging language skills in authentic communicative contexts. However, as communication with "cultural strangers" progresses, learners' attitudes change, and they no longer perceive telecollaborative tasks as helpful in breaking language barriers or useful for learning and social networking with other L2 learners and native speakers. This finding is consistent with the previous research on beginning learners, making even more salient Horwitz's claim (1988) that novice L2 speakers often have unrealistic expectations about L2 learning that materialize in the form of attitudes and preconceived notions about learning tasks and teaching methods (see also Kern, 1995). Researchers, however, should not assume that learners' perceptions will remain the same as they begin to experience various types of L2 language use, including contacts with native speakers.

Learners' perceived learning gains and failures may not necessarily be accurate when compared to their actual performance as L2 beginning language users. Klimanova & Bondarenko (2018) found that low-level L2 writers can communicate with virtual partners by engaging in a creative use of familiar linguistic resources and even attempt telecollaborative tasks at the next level of L2 proficiency. They manage to control the functional aspect of written production by tapping into their expertise as digital communicators in the L1 and, despite a number of apparent linguistic obstacles, actively engage in competent written conversations within a telecollaborative writing-conducive virtual environment. These findings suggest that instructional intervention in the form of clarification, realistic goal-setting, class discussions, and awareness raising may be critical in helping beginning learners develop a more accurate understanding of the gains they should anticipate from participating in virtual communication with "cultural others." This awareness of realistic benefits and potential challenges may help shape their telecollaborative experiences in a way that is more positive, satisfactory, and motivating.

Positive expectations (pre-project responses) for the project did not differ significantly across all groups for any of the criteria tested. Learners expected that communicating with non-native speakers (NNSs) would be as useful for practicing Russian and learning more about the language and the Russian culture, as did those who were about to engage in virtual exchange with target language speakers. The act of interacting with target language speakers via a Russia-based social network was construed by the novice learners in this study as an intriguing cultural experience. Students in Group #1, however, were more aware of their linguistic limitations than Group #2 students before the project started. They felt less prepared to interact with other unfamiliar L2 learners, and expressed more concerns about not having enough language skills to complete assigned telecollaborative tasks.

The differences between groups seem to point at factors other than individual beliefs that influence learners' attitudes and perceptions. For example, partners' identities and their language affiliations in combination with task type and choice of communicative tools (Schenker & Poorman, 2017) may have had an impact on beginning learners' perceptions of learning gains. This may explain why the difference between pre- and post-project evaluations of positive outcomes did not reveal statistically significant differences in the anticipated and perceived positive outcomes for Group #2 where beginning learners successfully collaborated with students in Russia, despite various difficulties associated with this format of intercultural virtual exchange. It is possible to suggest that these difficulties were not as disillusioning for Group #2 as they were for Group #1. Previous research shows that L2 learners' perceptions of NS virtual conversation partners are generally positive, resulting in increased motivations to study the target language in novice learners (Schenker, 2018) and, regardless of the language level, leading to reported improvement in writing skills and development of more positive attitudes towards writing, the foreign language and its culture (Mahfouz, 2010), especially with a longer duration of NS-NNS written exchanges and learners' regular access to a computer (i.e., task-related factors).

Use of unfamiliar native speakers has received a great deal of attention in the previous research on online chats, particularly due to the possibility of active negotiation of meaning, a precursor of language acquisition (Long, 1996), that can take place during such online encounters (Pellettieri,

2000; O'Dowd, 2007; Schenker, 2015). Online conversations were found to promote learner noticing of errors and attention to form, while structural and lexical difficulties act as triggers for negotiation and error correction (Tudini, 2003). These additional opportunities for noticing provide learners with more developmental support, particularly since learners must first attend to, or notice, the input (or the language in front of them). Schmidt's noticing hypothesis (2001), for example, stresses the importance of noticing, and specifically the noticing of the formal features in the L2, as well as noticing gaps between a learner's interlanguage (what they already know) and the target language. Researchers have suggested that online interactions may increase learners' opportunities to notice target items in the input, potentially also leading to increased instances of intake (e.g., meta-analytic research by Ziegler, 2016).

The present study confirms previous findings but from the learner perspective and with regard to the type of interlocutor participating in the interaction. For example, Group #2 participants (partnered with students in Russia) were found to be more aware of their linguistic limitations. They reported noticing and recognizing more familiar structures while interacting with Russian partners than Group #1 participants, and found the intercultural exchange to be a useful activity to evaluate their linguistic competence. Since the tasks themselves and the contextual factors were the same in the two groups, it appears that project configurations and partner identities may be responsible for this variation. For Group #1, on the other hand, perceived positive outcomes were significantly lower than positive expectations for the project. For these students, the difficulties associated with the project may have tarnished their perceptions of the project's actual positive outcomes due to either NNS partners or a combination of NNS partner and assigned task. One possible explanation can be the differences in the language curriculum and different textbooks used in these classes. However, it seems more plausible to suggest that the NNS partner identity may have increased learners' anxieties. The fear of being compared to a peer who can be a better learner or a stronger Russian speaker triggered a feeling of insecurity and self-conscience, and impacted the learner's overall confidence in their language skills when thinking about the possibility of exposing one's linguistic limitations to another student from the same city (cf. the feared self and the ought-to-self in Dörnyei, 2009).

Furthermore, the authenticity of intercultural communication appears to have been equally threatening to both groups. Although the learners' reported fears of potential language barriers did not show great variability between two exchange types, a significant difference was found for the fear of interacting with a stranger. This fear was weaker in Group #2 (communicating with native speakers) than in Group #1 (communicating with fellow language learners). This finding is especially intriguing in that it brings our attention to the fact that learners find it less intimidating to engage in virtual communication with people who they can be sure will not judge them or they will never meet in real life. More research is needed to understand the affective complexity of partner dynamics in virtual exchanges, involving L2 learners who do not share the same cultural background and language affiliations as well as between unfamiliar L2 learners who only share the target language, but not L1 affiliations.

In addition to the aforementioned findings, there were also significant differences in perceived post-project outcomes between the two groups that require interpretation. As stated previously, in terms of positive outcomes, Group #2 seemed to have found the project to be more helpful for testing their linguistic competence and for learning more Russian language than Group #1. Moreover, Group #2 gave higher ratings to the outcomes related to learning about Russia and understanding Russian people better. These findings suggest that while Group #1 did initially perceive NNS speakers to be equally capable of sharing insights about Russian language and culture (given their responses on the entry questionnaire), at the end of the project they thought that other Russian learners were not members of the Russian community and thus did not have as much cultural insight to share. These findings are also evidenced by learners' open-ended comments about NNS partners as not being competent enough to share the knowledge of language and culture with other Russian learners. Nonetheless, no statistically significant differences between the ratings of two groups were found for the following positive outcomes: helpfulness of the project to review material covered in the classroom; to break down language barriers; to become integrated in the Russian-speaking community; and to make new friends. Thus, depending on the teaching goals of the project administrator, a cross-cultural exchange with native speakers may not be strictly the only possible configuration that would ensure better learning outcomes. In fact, previous research shows that nonnative speaker–nonnative speaker dyads may use more interactional features (see Ziegler, 2016 for more details) and provide more modified output opportunities (Sato & Lyster, 2007) when compared to native speaker–nonnative speaker dyads. However, studies have also demonstrated that native speaker interlocutors may provide more feedback (Mackey, Oliver, & Leeman, 2003), suggesting that there are differences in learners' production and development depending on interlocutor type. This consideration highlights the need for an empirical comparison across type of interlocutor, both from the perspective of learning gains as well as from the learner's perspective on the role of interlocutor in a virtual exchange.

6 Conclusion

Overall, the comparison of students' attitudes and perceptions of the two project formats shows that a cross-institutional exchange between language learners may be as beneficial for beginning learners as a cross-cultural exchange. While communication with native speakers may be a long-term target, a virtual exchange project with unfamiliar language learners (NNS) can be a stepping-stone towards that goal. This experience can teach students how to approach such projects and will help them address some of their fears as they prepare to communicate with native speaking partners in the future. As instructors and project developers, we tend to think that the effort put into cross-cultural projects for beginning learners may not be worth a minimal difference in self-reported learning gains. However, students' overall perceptions of the project show the opposite: even though Group #2 rated the project as more difficult than Group #1, it also rated it to be more useful for learning than Group #1. Still, the two groups evaluated the project to be equally entertaining. Given the dynamic nature of learners' attitudes about intercultural virtual exchange, inquiries in this research area should remain a constant in the overall landscape of studies on intercultural communication. Instructors should be informed about the impact on L2 learners of various learner and contextual factors, such as partner identities, duration of the intercultural exchange and characteristics of tasks, and learner satisfaction with intercultural communicative activities. The most practical and far-reaching impact of future research in this area will mostly take place in the classrooms where teachers will desire to understand their students' perspectives on intercultural exchange and will reconcile their expectations for such projects with those of their students.

As for most studies, in this study as well there are some limitations that restrict the generalizability and interpretability of its results. The principal limitation lies in its instrumentation, and small sample size. Effective questionnaire item writing is one of the most arduous aspects of instrument design (Brown, 2001). Although the items in the study questionnaire were carefully worded and proper procedures were undertaken to revise and validate the instrument to ensure reliability and intelligibility, some of the items may have been too specific and vague, and thus may not provide an accurate representation of beginning learners' perspectives. Besides, some of the items may not have been as clear to study participants as they were to the researchers. Open-ended responses, for example, did not always reflect the nature of the questions asked, and some students chose not to provide extended answers to some questions, thus limiting the qualitative dataset only to a partial representation of study participants. Since the questionnaire was designed specifically to suit the purposes of the study, several piloting procedures may help increase its face validity for future research. Besides, the pre- and post-project questionnaires were presented to francophone students in French and some of the nuances and meanings of the original statements may have been lost in translation.

Similarly, a small sample size may have an impact on statistical calculations. Similar studies in commonly-taught languages with larger sample sizes may indicate statistical significance for the criteria that showed no significance in this study of Russian classes. Clearly, the results of the present study can be taken as representative only of the participating population of beginning Russian learners, and, to a much lesser degree, of the larger populations of beginning learners in other languages. The use of closed-response data where the participants were forced to respond only to the set of statements permits complex statistical analyses restricting the researcher to examine only learners' questionnaire entries. Interviews with study participants can enrich future studies, providing a more personal and comprehensive account of students' experiences with intercultural virtual exchange. Within the framework adopted in this study, however, time and human constraints did not permit extended qualitative inquiry.

Finally, the short duration of the telecollaborative project and its timing towards the end of the semester may have influenced learners' perceptions of project activities. Several students indicated that the project did not constitute a significant portion of the final grade, and, hence, did not take priority among many other end-of-semester learning tasks and home assignments in their Russian classes. A larger number of participating students and a different timing of intercultural virtual exchange during the semester may warrant tentative generalizations outlined in this chapter to other educational settings and L2 classes.

The results of the present study point to critical issues in need of future research. More studies should explore various factors that influence students' ideas of effective and ineffective intercultural virtual exchange and explore how L2 learners formulate these ideas. For example, learners' previous experiences with this type of intercultural activity may have an impact on their current perspectives, particularly in relation to intercultural exchange partners, types of tasks, expectations and fears, among many others. In addition to students' perceptions, future research should explore the beliefs and attitudes of their instructors and examine ways of developing realistic expectations for language learning in a classroom setting. This area has begun to gain momentum among practitioners and researchers, and with more research attention to how learners' perceptions are formulated, students may be taught to see more benefits in this type of language learning activity. Finally, much more research should be done to explore and compare the gains and drawbacks of various types of virtual exchange, and, more specifically, the role of interlocutors, native or non-native speakers, and their impact on the way students perceive these tasks as beneficial or not beneficial for their learning. What should novice learners know about potential learning gains from participating in intercultural virtual exchanges? How can their unfavorable beliefs and attitudes be altered via an effective instructional intervention? How can instructors address novice learners' fears and anxieties via targeted classroom activities? The recommendations for future research would benefit from complex qualitative inquiry involving individual and group interviews and from studies that evaluate the impact of preparatory activities and in-class break-out sessions on learners' perceptions of learning outcomes resulting from various types and configurations of virtual exchanges.

References

Angelova, M., & Zhao, Y. (2016). Using an online collaborative project between American and Chinese students to develop ESL teaching skills, cross-cultural awareness and language skills. *Computer Assisted Language Learning*, 29, 167–185. https://doi.org/10.1080/09588221.2014.907320

Barcelos, A. M. F. (2003). Researching beliefs about SLA: A critical review. In P. Kalaja & A. M. F. Barcelos (eds.), *Beliefs about SLA: New Research Approaches* (pp. 7–33). Amsterdam: Kluwer Academic. https://doi.org/10.1007/978-1-4020-4751-0_1

Bartley, D. E. (1970). The importance of the attitude factor in language dropout: A preliminary investigation of group and sex differences. *Foreign Language Annals*, 3, 383–393. https://doi.org/10.1111/j.1944-9720.1970.tb01292.x

Belz, J. A. (2003). Linguistic perspectives on the development of intercultural competence in telecollaboration. *Language Learning & Technology*, 7(2), 68–117.

Brammerts, H. (2001). Autonomes Sprachenlernenim Tandem: Entwicklungeines Konzepts. In H. Brammerts & K. Kleppin (eds.), *Selbstgesteuertes Sprachenlernenim Tandem: Ein Handbuch* (pp. 9–16). Tübingen: Stauffenburg Verlag.

Brantmeier, C. (2005). Nonlinguistic variables in advanced second language reading: Learners' self-assessment and enjoyment. *Foreign Language Annals*, 38, 494–504. https://doi.org/10.1111/j.1944-9720.2005.tb02516.x

Brown, A. V. (2009). Students' and teachers' perceptions of effective foreign language teaching: A comparison of ideals. *Modern Language Journal*, 93, 46–60. https://doi.org/10.1111/j.1540-4781.2009.00827.x

Brown, J. (2001). *Using Surveys in Language Programs (Cambridge Language Teaching Library)*. Cambridge, UK: Cambridge University Press.

Bueno-Alastuey, M. C., & Kleban, M. (2016). Matching linguistic and pedagogical objectives in a telecollaboration project: A case study. *Computer Assisted Language Learning*, 29(1), 148–166. https://doi.org/10.1080/09588221.2014.904360

Byram, M. (1997). *Teaching and Assessing Intercultural Communicative Competence*. Clevedon, UK: Multilingual Matters.

Chen, J. J., & Yang, S. C. (2016). Promoting cross-cultural understanding and language use in research-oriented Internet-mediated intercultural exchange. *Computer Assisted Language Learning*, 29(2), 262–288. https://doi.org/10.1080/09588221.2014.937441

Chen, W. C., Shih, D., & Liu, G. Z. (2015). Task design and its induced learning effects in a cross-institutional blog-mediated telecollaboration. *Computer Assisted Language Learning*, 28(4), 285–305. https://doi.org/10.1080/09588221.2013.818557

Çiftçi, E., & Savaş, P. (2018). The role of telecollaboration in language and intercultural learning: A synthesis of studies published between 2010 and 2015. *ReCALL*, 30(3), 278–298. https://doi.org/10.1017/S0958344017000313

Condruz-Bacescu, M. (2016). E-twinning – the community for schools in Europe. New technology and redesigning learning spaces. *Proceedings of the 15th International Scientific Conference "eLearning and Software for Education"*, Volume 2, 353–359. Retrieved from https://proceedings.elseconference.eu. https://doi.org/10.12753/2066-026X-19-139.

Cziko, G. A. (2004). Electronic tandem language learning (eTandem): A third approach to second language learning for the 21st century. *CALICO Journal*, 22(1), 25–39. https://doi.org/10.1558/cj.v22i1.25-39

Dominga Miguela, A. (2007). Models of telecollaboration: E-Twinning. In R. O'Dowd (ed.), *Online Intercultural Exchange: An Introduction for Foreign Language Teachers* (pp. 85–104). Clevedon, UK: Multilingual Matters. https://doi.org/10.21832/9781847690104-007

Dörnyei, Z. (2003). Attitudes, orientations, and motivations in language learning: Advances in theory, research, and applications. *Language Learning*, 53(S1), 3–32. https://doi.org/10.1111/1467-9922.53222

Dörnyei, Z. (2009). The L2 motivational self-system. In Z. Dörnyei & D. E. Ushioda (eds.), *Motivation, Language Identity and the L2 Self* (pp. 9–42). Retrieved from https://ebookcentral.proquest.com. https://doi.org/10.21832/9781847691293

Dunne, G. B. (2014). Reflecting on the Japan-Chile task-based telecollaboration project for beginner-level learners. *TESL Canada Journal/Revue TESL du Canada*, 75(31/8), 175–186. https://doi.org/10.18806/tesl.v31i0.1193

Gardner, R. C. (2004). *Attitude/Motivation Test Battery: International AMTB Research Project*. Retrieved from http://publish.uwo.ca/~gardner/docs/englishamtb.pdf.

Guth, S., & Helm, F. (2010). *Telecollaboration 2.0: Language, Literacies and Intercultural Learning in the 21st Century*. Bern: Peter Lang GmbH, Internationaler Verlag der Wissenschaften. https://doi.org/10.3726/978-3-0351-0013-6

Hauck, M. (2007). Critical Success Factors in a TRIDEM Exchange. *ReCALL*, 19(2), 202–223. https://doi.org/10.1017/S0958344007000729

Hauck, M. (2010). Telecollaboration: At the interface between multimodal and intercultural communicative competence. In S. Guth & F. Helm (eds.), *Telecollaboration 2.0* (pp. 219–248). Bern, Switzerland: Peter Lang.

Hauck, M., & Lewis, T. (2007). The Tridem project. In R. O'Dowd (ed.), *Online Intercultural Exchange: An Introduction for Foreign Language Teachers* (pp. 250–258). Clevedon, UK: Multilingual Matters. https://doi.org/10.21832/9781847690104-015

Herring, S. C. (2007). A faceted classification scheme for computer-mediated discourse, Language@Internet 2007. Retrieved from: http://www.languageatinter-net.de/articles/2007/761.

Horwitz, E. K. (1988). The beliefs about language learning of beginning university foreign language students. *Modern Language Journal*, 72, 283–294. https://doi.org/10.1111/j.1540-4781.1988.tb04190.x

Horwitz, E. K. (2010). Foreign and second language anxiety. *Language Teaching*, 43, 154–167. https://doi.org/10.1017/S026144480999036X

Horwitz, E. K., Horwitz, M. B., & Cope, J. (1986). Foreign language classroom anxiety. *Modern Language Journal*, 70, 125–132. https://doi.org/10.1111/j.1540-4781.1986.tb05256.x

Jager, S., Nissen E., Helm, F., Baroni, A., & Rousset, I. (2019, March). *Virtual Exchange as Innovative Practice across Europe Awareness and Use in Higher Education EVOLVE Project Baseline Study*. Retrieved from https://evolve-erasmus.eu/wp-content/uploads/2019/03/Baseline-study-report-Final_Published_Incl_Survey.pdf.

Kelly, N. (2018). Student perceptions and attitudes towards the use of Facebook to support the acquisition of Japanese as a Second Language. *Language Learning in Higher Education*, 8(2), 217–237. https://doi.org/10.1515/cercles-2018-0014

Kern, R. (1995). Students and teachers' beliefs about language learning. *Foreign Language Annals*, 28, 71–92. https://doi.org/10.1111/j.1944-9720.1995.tb00770.x

Klimanova, L., & Bondarenko, M. (2018). Problematizing the notion of the beginning L2 Writer: The case of text-based telecollaboration. In J. Demperio, M. Deraîche, R. Dewart & B. Zuercher (eds.), *L'Enseignement-Apprentissage de l'Écrit / Current Trends in the Teaching and Learning of Written Proficiency* (pp. 64–89). Éditeur: Université du Québec à Montréal: UQAM Press.

Kramsch, C. (2014). Teaching foreign languages in an era of globalization. Introduction. *Modern Language Journal*, 98(1), 296–311. https://doi.org/10.1111/j.1540-4781.2014.12057.x

Kramsch, C. S., A'Ness, F., & Lam, W. (2000). Authenticity and authorship in the computer-mediated acquisition of L2 literacy. *Language Learning & Technology*, 4(2), 78–104.

Levine, G. S. (2003). Student and instructor beliefs and attitudes about target language use, first language use, and anxiety: Report of a questionnaire study. *Modern Language Journal*, 343–364. https://doi.org/10.1111/1540-4781.00194

Lin, C.-H., Warschauer, M., & Blake, R. (2016). Language learning through social networks: Perceptions and reality. *Language Learning & Technology*,

20(1), 124–147. Retrieved from http://llt.msu.edu/issues/february2016/linwarschauerblake.pdf. https://doi.org/10.1037/t64110-000

Long, M. H. (1996). The role of the linguistic environment in second language acquisition. In W. C. Ritchie & T. K. Bhatia (eds.), *Handbook of Second Language Acquisition* (pp. 413–468). New York: Academic Press. https://doi.org/10.1016/B978-012589042-7/50015-3

Mackey, A., Oliver, R., & Leeman, J. (2003). Interactional input and the incorporation of feedback: An exploration of NS-NNS and NNS-NNS adult and child dyads. *Language Learning*, 53, 35–66. https://doi.org/10.1111/1467-9922.00210

Mahfouz, S. M. (2010). A study of Jordanian university students' perceptions of using email exchanges with native English keypals for improving their writing competency. *CALICO Journal*, 27(2), 393–408. https://doi.org/10.11139/cj.27.2.393-408

Mills, N., Pajares, F., & Herron, C. (2007). Self-efficacy of college intermediate French students: Relation to achievement and motivation. *Language Learning*, 57, 417–442. https://doi.org/10.1111/j.1467-9922.2007.00421.x

O'Dowd, R. (ed.). (2007). *Online Intercultural Exchange: An Introduction for Foreign Language Teachers*. Clevedon, UK: Multilingual Matters. https://doi.org/10.21832/9781847690104

O'Dowd, R. (2011). Online foreign language interaction: Moving from the periphery to the core of foreign language education? *Language Teaching*, 44(3), 368–380. https://doi.org/10.1017/S0261444810000194

O'Rourke, B. (2007). Models of telecollaboration: E-Tandem. In R. O'Dowd (ed.), *Online Intercultural Exchange: An Introduction for Foreign Language Teachers* (pp. 42–61). Clevedon, UK: Multilingual Matters. https://doi.org/10.21832/9781847690104-005

Pellettieri, J. (2000). Negotiation in cyberspace: The role of chatting in the development of grammatical competence in the virtual foreign language classroom. In M. Warschauer & R. Kern (eds.), *Network-based Language Teaching: Concepts and Practice* (pp. 59–86). Cambridge, UK: Cambridge University Press. https://doi.org/10.1017/CBO9781139524735.006

Sato, M., & Lyster, R. (2007). Modified output of Japanese EFL learners: Variable effects of interlocutor vs. feedback types. In A. Mackey (ed.), *Conversational Interaction in Second Language Acquisition: A Collection of Empirical Studies* (pp. 123–142). Oxford, UK: Oxford University Press.

Schenker, T. (2015). Telecollaboration for novice language learners: Negotiation of meaning in text chats between nonnative and native speakers. In E. Dixon & M. Thomas (eds.), *Researching Language Learner Interactions Online: From Social Media to MOOCs* (pp. 237–259). San Marcos: CALICO.

Schenker, T. (2018). Synchronous telecollaboration for novice language learners: Effects on speaking skills and language learning interests. *ALSIC: Apprentissage des Langues et Systèmes d'Information et de Communication*, 20(2). https://doi.org/10.4000/alsic.3068

Schenker, T., & Poorman, F. (2017). Students' perceptions of telecollaborative communication tools. In C. Ludwig & K. van de Poel (eds.), *Collaborative Language Learning & New Media: Insights into an Evolving Field* (pp. 55–71). Frankfurt a.M.: Peter Lang.

Schmidt, R. (2001). Attention. In P. Robinson (ed.), *Cognition and Second Language Instruction* (pp. 3–32). Cambridge, UK: Cambridge University Press. https://doi.org/10.1017/CBO9781139524780.003

Stepp-Greany, J. (2002). Student perceptions of language learning in a technological environment: Implications for the new millennium. *Language Learning & Technology*, 6(1), 165–180.

Tashakkori, A., & Teddlie, C. (1998). *Mixed Methodology: Combining Qualitative and Quantitative Approaches* (Applied Social Research Methods Series; v. 46). Thousand Oaks, California: Sage.

Thorne, S. L. (2010). The intercultural turn and language learning in the crucible of new media. In S. Guth and F. Helm (eds.), *Telecollaboration 2.0: Language and Intercultural Learning in the 21st Century* (pp. 139–165). Berne: Peter Lang.

Tudini, V. (2003). Using native speakers in chat. *Language Learning & Technology*, 7(3), 141–159.

Vogt, K. (2006). Can you measure attitudinal factors in intercultural communication? Tracing the development of attitudes in e-mail projects. *ReCALL*, 18(2): 153–173. https://doi.org/10.1017/S095834400600022X

Ware, P., & Rivas. B. (2012). Researching classroom interaction of online language learning projects: Mixed methods approaches. In M. Dooly & R. O'Dowd (eds.), *Researching Online Foreign Language Interaction and Exchange Theories, Methods and Challenges* (1st, New ed., Telecollaboration in Education) (pp. 107–131). Bern: Peter Lang AG, Internationaler Verlag der Wissenschaften.

Wesely, P. (2012). Learner attitudes, perceptions, and beliefs in language learning. *Foreign Language Annals*, 45(S1), S98–S117. https://doi.org/10.1111/j.1944-9720.2012.01181.x

Williams, M., & Burden, R. L. (1999). Students developing conceptions of themselves as language learners. *Modern Language Journal*, 83, 193–201. https://doi.org/10.1111/0026-7902.00015

Yan, J. X., & Horwitz, E. K. (2008). Learners' perceptions of how anxiety interacts with personal and instructional factors to influence their achievement in English: A qualitative analysis of EFL learners in China. *Language Learning*, 58, 151–183. https://doi.org/10.1111/j.1467-9922.2007.00437.x

Yang, S. (2018). Language learners' perceptions of having two interactional contexts in eTandem. *Language Learning & Technology*, 22(1), 42–51.

Yashima, T. (2009). International posture and the ideal L2 self in the Japanese EFL context. In Z. Dörnyei & E. Ushioda (eds.), *Motivation, Language Identity and the L2 Self* (pp. 144–163). Clevedon, UK: Multilingual Matters. https://doi.org/10.21832/9781847691293-008

Ziegler, N. (2016). Synchronous computer-mediated communication and interaction: A meta-analysis. *Studies in Second Language Acquisition*, 38, 553–586. https://doi.org/10.1017/S027226311500025X

Appendix

Pre- and Post-exchange Questionnaire

ENTRY QUESTIONNAIRE	Categories	EXIT QUESTIONNAIRE
EXPECTATIONS (Likert scale, 1–10)		**GAINS (Likert scale, 1–10)**
1. The project will give me an occasion to be proud of myself and my knowledge of Russian language and culture	*pride*	1. The project gave me an occasion to be proud of myself and my knowledge of Russian language and culture
2. The project will allow me to practice Russian language outside of the classroom	*practice*	2. The project allowed me to practice Russian language outside of the classroom
3. The project will help me overcome language barriers	*barrier*	3. The project helped me overcome language barriers
4. The project will help me learn new words and grammar that we might not see in the classroom	*learn language*	4. The project helped me learn new words and grammar that we did not see in the classroom
5. The project will help me learn something new about Russia, Russian culture and the local Russian community	*learn about Russia*	5. The project helped me learn something new about Russia, Russian culture and the local Russian community
6. The project will help me to understand Russian people better	*understand*	6. The project helped me understand Russian people better
7. The project will help me connect to the Russian language learning community and/or to the Russian world	*community*	7. The project helped me connect to the Russian language learning community and/or to the Russian world
8. The project will help me make new friends	*friends*	8. The project helped me make new friends
9. List any expectations that have not been mentioned	*other expectations*	9. List any positive results that have not been mentioned
FEARS AND DOUBTS (Likert scale, 1–10)		**NEGATIVE IMPRESSIONS (Likert scale, 1–10)**
1. I don't like to communicate with strangers, especially on private topics	*stranger*	1. I didn't like communicating with a stranger, especially on private topics
2. I think my knowledge of Russian is not sufficient to communicate	*insufficient*	2. My knowledge of Russian was not sufficient to communicate
3. I think the project will take too much of my time	*time*	3. The project took too much of my time

4. I don't like social networks	network	4. The project forced me to use a social network and I am not comfortable with them
	partner	5. I was disappointed with my partner's attitude; he/she was not reliable and/or patient enough
	motivation	6. I was not motivated enough (in terms of the weight of the project in my final grade)
	fear-barrier	7. I had a language barrier
5. Do you have any fears, doubts or negative expectations that have not been mentioned?	other negative	8. Do you have any other negative impressions that have not been mentioned?
OVERALL IMPRESSIONS (Likert scale, 1–10)		**OVERALL IMPRESSIONS (Likert scale, 1–10)**
1. How difficult do you expect the project to be?	difficulty	1. How difficult was this project?
	difficult task	2. What was the most difficult or challenging task that you had to complete?
2. How entertaining do you think the project will be?	fun	3. How entertaining was this project?
	fun task	4. Which part of the project did you enjoy most?
	use	5. Please evaluate how useful this project was for you.
	use-details	6. What was most useful for you?
		RECOMMENDATIONS (open answer)
	advice-teacher	1. What advice would you give to your teacher if they were to carry out this project again? How can we make the project more efficient and more fun for students? How can we increase students' motivation?
	advice-student	2. What advice would you give to the students who participate in this project? What should they do or not do? What should they be warned about? What is the best strategy for the participant of this kind of project?

About the Authors

Liudmila Klimanova, PhD (Second Language Acquisition and Technology) is Assistant Professor of Russian and SLA at the University of Arizona (Tucson, AZ). Her research is situated at the intersection of technology-mediated foreign language pedagogy, social identity, and multimodal discourse studies. She has published on the topics of telecollaboration, digital identity, virtual experience, and CALL.

Valentina Vinokurova, MA (Russian Literature; Russian Linguistics) is currently a PhD student in Second Language Acquisition and Teaching at the University of Arizona (Tucson, AZ). She is interested in linguistic and instructional dimensions of L2 learning.

3 Exploring Attitude in Bilingual Virtual Exchanges: A Linguistic Perspective

Margarita Vinagre and Ana Oskoz

1 Introduction

A plethora of studies over the last thirty years have confirmed that virtual exchange (VE), an innovative activity in which students who are located in different countries collaborate in task and project work, can foster the development of knowledge and competences, especially foreign language (Bueno-Alastuey & Kleban, 2016) and intercultural skills (Kohn & Hoffstaedter, 2015; Vinagre, 2016a). Previous research has also indicated that VE can encourage the development of multiliteracies (Hauck, 2010; Guth & Helm, 2012), pedagogical knowledge (Dooly & Sadler, 2013), and teachers' telecollaborative skills (O'Dowd, 2015; Vinagre, 2017). Given its great potential, this innovative pedagogy has recently become the objective of the European Commission's Erasmus + Virtual Exchange project. This initiative aims to engage young students in VE in order to help them develop a better understanding of each other by promoting language learning and intercultural dialogue, whilst increasing awareness of the multilingual and multicultural model of society that we are immersed in. VE also offers educators an opportunity to help students develop key competences which are essential for employability (Vinagre, 2016b), in both formal and non-formal educational settings, by transcending the traditional learning classroom through the integration of technologies. Given its transnational nature, VE can also encourage internationalization on a large scale since it can offer students with economic difficulties or disabilities the possibility of experiencing intercultural exchange from their home institutions.

The principles underlying VE are of a socio-constructivist nature and they emphasize the importance of social interaction for the construction of shared knowledge. This construction process requires active participation, interaction, and reflection. In this context, quality interactions become the basic requirement for collaborative learning (Graham & Misanchuk, 2004). Lack of successful collaboration can happen for many reasons, including differences in quality and quantity of work, clash of personalities, power struggles, and poor communication (Johnstone, 2002; Vinagre, 2015). Moreover, for collaboration to be successful, interaction between members should be trustworthy and open (Wheelan & Kesselring, 2005). In this context, the importance of exploring how participants in VE convey personal attitudes in their virtual interaction has been highlighted in recent studies (Oskoz & Gimeno, 2019; Ryshina-Pankova, 2018; Vinagre & Corral, 2018; Vinagre & Corral, 2019). These studies have also approached the analysis of attitudes from a linguistic perspective, thus adding a new perspective to the content-based analysis that has become the norm in VE interaction (Belz, 2003).

2   Analyzing Attitude in Interaction

There has been a wide variety of attempts to analyze the linguistic mechanisms that speakers use to convey their personal attitudes and assessments in social interaction (Cabrejas-Peñuelas & Díez-Prados, 2014; Hunston & Thompson 2000; Martin 2003; Martin & White, 2005; White, 2002). These proposals differ in the methodologies they have used for their analysis, with these varying approaches including consideration of affect (Ochs & Schieffelin, 1989), evaluation (Thompson & Hunston, 2000), stance (Biber & Finegan, 1989), and appraisal (Martin, 2003). Despite these differences, they all focus on the interpretation of the speaker's assessment, the linguistic realizations of stance, and the function of evaluation in building and maintaining relations between speakers and listeners.

The appraisal framework, which examines "the semantic resources (used by interlocutors) to negotiate emotions, judgements, and valuations, alongside resources for amplifying and engaging with these evaluations" (Martin, 2000: 144), has increasingly been applied to VE discourse (Belz, 2003; Oskoz, Gimeno, & Sevilla, 2018; Oskoz & Gimeno, 2019; Ryshina-Pankova, 2018; Vinagre & Corral, 2018, 2019). Based on the theory of systemic-functional linguistics (Eggins & Slade, 1997), the appraisal framework makes it possible to systematically connect the discourse-semantic aspects of VE interaction with their realizations through particular linguistic resources. In this model, the language of evaluation or appraisal is organized as three interacting components: attitude, engagement, and graduation. The attitude component (see Table 1) is further subdivided into affect (What emotional reaction do participants exhibit?), judgment (How special, capable, or dependable is someone?), and appreciation (How valuable is someone or something?). Affect reflects people's positive or negative emotions or feelings (un/happiness, in/security, dis/satisfaction, dis/inclination). Judgment refers to the linguistic resources employed to assess people's behavior ethically (morally and legally). Appreciation evaluates aesthetically semiotic and natural phenomena and is concerned with impact and quality (reaction), balance and complexity (composition), and valuation (social value). The subcategories of affect, judgment, and appreciation can have positive and negative values. The two other components of appraisal, namely engagement and graduation, were not used in this study because the focus was on the extent to which learners attached intersubjective values to participants and processes rather than on the intensity of their statements (graduation) or on the position learners took with regard to particular statements (engagement).

Table 1. Martin & White's (2005) attitudinal component

Appraisal: Attitude		
Affect	**Judgment**	**Appreciation**
– Happiness	– Social esteem	– Reaction
• cheer	• positive normality	• positive impact
• affection	• negative normality	• negative impact
– Unhappiness	• positive capacity	• positive quality
• misery	• negative capacity	• negative quality
• antipathy	• positive tenacity	– Composition
– Security	• negative tenacity	• positive balance
• confidence	– Social sanction	• negative balance
• trust	• positive veracity	• positive complexity
– Insecurity	• negative veracity	• negative complexity
• disquiet	• positive propriety	– Valuation
• surprise	• negative propriety	• positive valuation
– Satisfaction		• negative valuation
• interest		
• pleasure/admiration		
– Dissatisfaction		
• ennui		
• displeasure		
– Inclination		
• desire		
– Disinclination		
• fear		

As regards the use of evaluative language in VEs, several studies have looked into the differences or similarities in terms of attitude between groups (Belz, 2003; Oskoz & Gimeno, 2019; Vinagre & Corral, 2018, 2019). Vinagre & Corral (2018) found that learners, regardless of the country of origin, used more affect markers than judgment and appreciation markers. This is in line with previous research confirming second language learners' tendency to use positive affective language in order to create a close and friendly atmosphere in virtual environments to facilitate effective collaboration and learning (Morand & Ocker, 2003). Despite these similarities, research has also found culture-specific linguistic patterns that seem to affect the use of appreciation and judgment markers. For example, Belz (2003) showed that American learners tended to use more positive appreciation markers than their German counterparts. Vinagre & Corral (2018) and Oskoz & Gimeno (2019) found that students from Spain tended to use more judgment markers than their American partners. These three studies suggest that there might be cultural differences behind these behaviors. In Spanish culture, being critical (i.e., making value judgments about specific behaviors, ideas, and opinions) is considered a positive trait (Vinagre & Corral, 2018). German learners are more direct, explicit, and likely to provide *ad hoc* formulations (Belz, 2003) whereas American learners tend to be more indirect and use linguistic routines to express their ideas whilst avoiding being critical and opinionated (Oskoz & Gimeno, 2019).

Despite potential overarching cultural differences in linguistic behavior, Belz's (2003) analysis of Germans' and Americans' attitudinal tokens in VE revealed that participants did not just exhibit their own culturally-specific linguistic patterns; they also accommodated, to some degree, to the norms of interaction in the foreign language. Belz (2003) suggests that this type of lingua-pragmatic hybridity is a desired outcome of foreign language learning and that an inadequate knowledge of (or failure to acknowledge) culture-specific patterns of interaction in a partner's language may hinder communication. More recently studies suggest that, in VE, specific patterns emerge regarding the use of appraisal. Participants tend to notice and imitate their partners' use of attitudinal resources, a strategy whose aim is to converge with the other in order to avoid conflict (Vinagre & Corral, 2018). In their study, these authors found that Spanish and American students used a similar number of affect and appreciation tokens in their interaction. Similarly, these students predominantly used affect tokens and, regardless of category type, the vast majority of tokens had a positive polarity (positive values). This last finding is also corroborated by Vinagre & Corral (2019) who suggest that the use of more positive markers than negative markers is the result of the students' desire to create a positive atmosphere in telecollaborative environments (Liaw & English, 2017; Morand & Ocker, 2003). Belz's and Vinagre & Corral's studies suggest that in virtual interaction, linguistic hybridity reflects "a natural and emerging state of multicompetence, that is, the state of mind with two (or more) languages, in the learner" (Belz, 2003: 92). Moreover, in VE, the fact that the partners have to collaborate through an electronic medium also contributes to the occurrence of acts of hybridity that show that the students acknowledge their peers' culture-specific linguistic patterns and pragmatic discursive strategies, and adapt and integrate them into their own discourse (Vinagre & Corral, 2018).

Given the current proliferation of studies using the attitudinal component of appraisal for the analysis of virtual interaction, and in order to discover whether the appraisal patterns found in previous studies can be substantiated by further research, the aim of this chapter is to compare the findings from two unrelated bilingual VEs organized between university students in Madrid and New York (Study 1) and university students in Valencia and Maryland (Study 2). The main research questions guiding this study are as follows:

RQ1: What are the similarities or differences in the use of attitude by participants in two unrelated VEs?

RQ2: What are the similarities or differences between the use of attitude by the Spanish participants and American participants in two unrelated VEs?

3 Method

3.1 Participants

In the first study (see Table 2), a group of students from a university in Spain and another from a university in the USA engaged in a telecollaborative exchange for two and a half months. The Spanish students were 49 fourth-year undergraduate students aged between 21 and 22, who were enrolled on a course titled *Information and Communication Technologies*. As regards gender, 10 students were male and 39 were female. Instructors and students met twice a week and tasks were carried out mostly online, working in small groups inside and outside the classroom. The level of experience with the use of the technology was very similar among participants and they had no previous experience of online collaborative learning, although some were familiar with the use of some ICT tools (i.e., blogs, Skype) and most of them used social networks (i.e., Facebook, WhatsApp, Twitter). The American students were also undergraduates aged between

21 and 22, from all concentrations, who were taking an *Intermediate I* or *II Spanish* course (depending on the semester of implementation). This group was composed of 14 males and 35 females. As regards their competence in the foreign language, the Spanish students' level of English ranged between a B2 and C2 whilst the American students' level was a B2, according to the *European Framework of Reference for Languages*.

For the second study, two groups of learners, one from a technical university in Spain and the other from a mid-sized Atlantic coast university in the USA, engaged in a telecollaborative encounter over one and a half months. There were 12 Spanish students, all of whom were majoring in aerospace engineering and who were enrolled in an optional 3rd-year 6-credit higher intermediate English-language class, and 12 North American students enrolled in a 3rd-year 3-credit Spanish history and culture class as a requirement for their major or minor in Spanish. Similar to the previous group, the participants did not have previous experience of online collaborative learning, although several of them were familiar with the use of some ICT tools and most of them used social networks. There were 12 female students and 12 male students and they were between 17 and 24 years old. According to the *Common European Framework of Reference for Languages*, the US-based students' level of Spanish proficiency ranged between B2 and C1, while the Spanish students' level of English ranged between B2 and C2.

Table 2. Rationale followed in Studies 1 and 2

	Study 1		Study 2	
	Madrid	New York	Valencia	Maryland
Student number	49 students	49 students	12 students	12 students
Course	Information and Communication Technologies	Intermediate Spanish I or II	High-intermediate English-language	España y sus culturas
Language level	B2–C2 (English)	B2 (Spanish)	B2–C2 (English)	B2–C1 (Spanish)
ICT Tool	Email and Skype		Google+ community	
VE model	E-Tandem		E-Tandem	
Process	In pairs, students discussed eight cultural topics ranging from daily life to health systems and political elections		In groups of four, students discussed two cultural topics: immigration and nationalism	

3.2 Tools

In Study 1, following an e-Tandem approach, the students worked in pairs and used email to discuss a series of topics relating to each other's cultures. Given that there was also a focus on form in the project, the asynchronous nature of email facilitated error correction and provision of feedback. For the final task, the students took some photographs of their respective cities and uploaded them onto Cityscapes, a platform especially designed for this project by Columbia University. Students also used Skype or Zoom for synchronous discussions of the topics and Movie Maker for a final self-reflection video.

Study 2 also followed an e-Tandem approach. In this case, the instructors/researchers created a private community using Google+ and the students were invited to join. As it was a closed community, this safeguarded the learners' privacy and, in some cases, overcame their unwillingness to share their profile with the outside world. Despite Google products being very popular both in the US and Spain, not all of the participants had Google accounts prior to the project, so those who did not had to register for one. The asynchronous nature of the postings was also a feature sought by the instructors to allow students time to think through and plan their responses (Guth & Thomas, 2010). For the final task, students completed a podcast based on one of the topics discussed that was uploaded to the Google+ platform. Students also used Skype for synchronous discussions of the topics.

3.3 Procedure

In Study 1, after sending an introductory message, the students worked in pairs and discussed (in bilingual email messages written half in English and half in Spanish) a series of culture-related topics (stereotypical beliefs, history and politics of their countries, colloquial expressions, literature and music, and other topics of their choice). The cultural discussions were initiated by the teachers in class, since the selected topics for discussion were included in the syllabus of the American students' courses. After the initial in-class conversation, students continued the discussion online with their foreign counterparts. They were required to send a minimum of two emails per week providing information and sharing experiences about their own culture but also showing an interest in and requesting information about the foreign culture. Students corrected each other's errors and provided feedback with examples and explanations in order to help their partners improve their foreign language skills. In order to carry out the final task, an exploration of the linguistic landscape of their respective cities, the dyads met via

Skype or Zoom to discuss what they had discovered in the foreign language. Finally, students reflected on what they had learned throughout the entire exchange in a self-reflection video.

In Study 2, after preliminary introductions, the students participated in three discussions within the Google+ community, each of which took place over a period of two weeks. The first discussion focused on the YouTube video *The Danger of a Single Story* by Chimamanda Adichie (2009, July). The second and third discussions (analyzed in this study) focused on immigration and nationalism and patriotism. To give all the learners the opportunity to interact in their target language, the discussion on immigration took place entirely in Spanish, whilst the discussion on nationalism took place entirely in English. Students were divided into groups of four, with each group comprising two participants from the US and two participants from Spain.

The cultural discussions were always initiated in class under the guidance of the instructors, who also provided links and articles to boost the conversation. Both groups used the same links and articles as a starting point. After the initial in-class conversation, learners continued the online discussion in their respective groups for two weeks. The two discussions analyzed in this study (immigration and nationalism) addressed topics that were very significant at the time of the study and were having huge repercussions in the news in both countries. Discussions continued throughout the two weeks in student-led teams. All of the group members were required to provide personal opinions and share personal experiences, integrate ideas from their classmates' contributions into their own comments, search for additional information, and ask questions that would help maintain the conversation. All of the learners were required to post a minimum of four comments on each topic.

3.4 Data Collection and Analysis

After the exchange finished, and once consent was given by students to collect and analyze their data for research purposes, a subset of learners' contributions was subjected to quantitative and qualitative analyses. In the first study, the content, generated by 20 dyads selected at random, comprised a corpus of 211 messages and 59,908 words. In the second study, the researchers gathered the content from three groups (12 students). These groups, which were selected because they had completed all the interactions, comprised a corpus of 85 posts and 23,425 words.

Using the appraisal model (Martin & White, 2005), the researchers qualitatively analyzed and manually tagged both corpora using the T-unit (that is, a "main clause with all subordinate clauses attached to it") (Hunt, 1965: 20) as the element of analysis. The T-unit was selected because "these units are the shortest grammatically allowable sentences into which the theme could be segmented" (Hunt, 1965: 21). Within each T-unit, the researchers looked for lexico-grammatical items (adverbs, adjectives, verbs, and nominalizations), that is, a single word, a part of a word, or a chain of words that form the basic elements of a language lexicon. Then, the T-units were coded as either expressing positive or negative emotions or values. In those cases where there was not an inherently positive or negative polarity, decisions about token type (affect, judgment, and appreciation) were made based on the context of the conversation. In the next step, the researchers decided whether each T-unit represented affect, judgment, or appreciation, since sometimes the same lexico-grammatical item could represent more than one attitudinal marker depending on the context (e.g., a sad song [appreciation] versus a sad man [affect]).

In order to guarantee the consistency of this analysis, in both studies only one of the two researchers involved analyzed all tokens. However, to ensure internal reliability, the second researchers analyzed 25% and 20% of all tokens, respectively. In those cases in which there were discrepancies, the researchers discussed them until consensus was reached. Internal reliability coefficient (Study 1) and Cohen's κ (Study 2) were run to determine if there was agreement between the two independent raters regarding segmentation and tagging of the T-units. After discussions to clarify those T-units or tokens that could represent more than one attitudinal marker, strong agreement was achieved between the two raters in each study with an inter-rater reliability coefficient of 83.3% (Study 1) and $\kappa = 1.000$, $p < .0005$ (Study 2).

Quantitative analyses were additionally performed to calculate relative frequencies. Attitude tokens were calculated against non-attitude tokens and then the different subcategories of attitude (affect, judgment, and appreciation) were calculated against the totals of appraisal tokens found in the interaction per group. We also calculated the frequencies per 100 words of text to draw comparisons between both groups in both studies. Finally, we used the chi-square test to investigate whether the results of affect, judgment and appreciation tokens used by the participants in each group signaled actual differences between the studies or occurred randomly. Since the chi-square test is extremely sensitive to sample size, after consulting an expert, the total number of tokens was divided by 10 in order to ensure reliability of results.

4 Results and Discussion

The purpose of this study is to examine the validity of appraisal as an effective framework to assess learners' attitudinal interactions in virtual exchange (VE). To do so, we present and compare the findings from two bilingual VEs organized between university students in two similar contexts (undergraduate students in Spain and the US) but with differences in the studies (i.e., tasks and topics, number of students, and time on tasks).

The first research question (RQ1) aimed at examining the similarities and differences in the use of attitude by participants in these two unrelated VE interactions. Results from the quantitative analyses can be found in Tables 3 and 4 below:

Table 3. Total tokens of attitudinal appraisals by participants in Study 1

ATTITUDE	SPANISH STUDENTS			AMERICAN STUDENTS		
	Total	Words between appraisals (Total 32,257 words)	Rate per 100 words (Total 32,257 words)	Total	Words between appraisals (Total 27,651 words)	Rate per 100 words (Total 27,651 words)
Affect	1,102 (52.30%)	29.27	3.41	1,034 (56.68%)	26.74	3.73
- Positive	910 (39.30%)	35.44	2.82	842 (46.15%)	32.83	3.04
- Negative	192 (13%)	168.00	0.59	192 (10.53%)	144.01	0.69
Judgment	512 (24.29%)	63.00	1.58	364 (19.20%)	75.96	1.31
- Positive	377 (17.88%)	85.56	1.16	294 (15.50%)	94.05	1.06
- Negative	135 (6.41%)	238.94	0.41	70 (3.7%)	395.01	0.25
Appreciation	493 (23.41%)	65.43	1.52	426 (23.35%)	64.90	1.54
- Positive	311 (14.76%)	103.72	0.96	267 (14.63%)	103.56	0.96
- Negative	182 (8.65%)	177.23	0.56	159 (8.72%)	173.90	0.57
Total	2,107	15.30	6.53	1,824	15.32	6.59
- Positive	1,598 (75.84%)	20.18	4.95	1,403 (76.91%)	19.70	5.07
- Negative	509 (24.16%)	63.37	1.57	421 (23.09%)	65.67	1.52

Table 4. Total tokens of attitudinal appraisals by participants in Study 2

ATTITUDE	SPANISH STUDENTS			AMERICAN STUDENTS		
	Total	Words between appraisals (Total 7,580 words)	Rate per 100 words (Total 7,580 words)	Total	Words between appraisals (Total 15,845 words)	Rate per 100 words (Total 15,845 words)
Affect	88 (13.04%)	86.14	1.16	213 (16.19%)	74.39	1.34
- Positive	47 (6.96%)	161.28	0.62	142 (10.79%)	111.58	0.90
- Negative	41 (6.07%)	184.88	0.54	71 (5.40%)	223.17	0.45
Judgment	343 (50.81%)	22.10	4.53	537 (40.81%)	29.51	3.39
- Positive	219 (32.44%)	34.61	2.89	398 (30.24%)	39.81	2.51
- Negative	124 (18.37%)	61.13	1.64	139 (10.56%)	113.99	0.88
Appreciation	244 (36.15%)	31.07	3.22	566 (43.01%)	27.99	3.57
- Positive	110 (16.30%)	68.91	1.45	282 (21.43%)	56.19	1.78
- Negative	134 (19.85%)	56.57	1.77	284 (21.58%)	55.79	1.79
Total	675	139.30	8.91	1,316	131.89	8.31
- Positive	376 (55.70%)	264.80	4.96	822 (62.46%)	207.58	5.19
- Negative	299 (44.30%)	302.57	3.94	494 (37.54%)	392.95	3.12

As seen in Table 3, participants in the Madrid-New York exchange (Study 1) presented more instances of affect, followed by instances of judgment and appreciation. Participants in the Maryland-Valencia exchange (Study 2), however, presented more instances of judgment, followed by appreciation and affect (see Table 4). Results per subcomponent also show that affect percentages and relative frequencies were significantly higher in Study 1 than in Study 2 (3.41 and 3.73 versus 1.16 and 1.34). These noticeable differences in the number of affect tokens maybe the result of several factors including social presence, time spent on tasks, nature of tasks, and topics of discussion. In this respect, previous studies have illustrated that affective value, or social presence, tends to increase as students engage in discussions during the semester and relationships are formed (Arnold,

Ducate, Lomicka, & Lord, 2005). We believe this to be one of the main contributing factors to the results of our study since, whilst students in Study 1 collaborated for two and a half months (which gave time for students to develop close and friendly relationships), participants in Study 2 interacted in Google+ for one and a half months. Another relevant factor (time spent on tasks) relates to continued collaboration. Thus, while participants in Study 1 took part in eight tasks that involved sending a minimum of two emails per task and a final task that required discussing the linguistic landscapes of their respective cities with the partner via Skype, participants in Study 2 participated in two tasks a minimum of four times each. It seems likely that the length of the exchange and the amount of time that each pair and group spent on the tasks influenced the presence of affect markers. In addition, learners in Study 2 focused on topics such as immigration and nationalism/patriotism, whereas learners in Study 1, despite discussing the health and political systems of their respective countries, also engaged in topics of a more personal nature, such as getting to know each other, university life, or music preferences. It is possible that these latter topics might have encouraged students in Study 1 to express more emotional states that their counterparts in Study 2. As Arnold et al. (2005) suggest, tasks that require learners to share their personal (and even vulnerable) experiences lead to higher levels of affective indicators than those tasks in which students are required to answer specific questions. Another relevant factor to consider refers to the instructions provided in the tasks, which were very different. While students in Study 1 were required to provide factual information about the different topics together with their personal opinions, in Study 2 emphasis was placed on students looking for additional information and providing evidence to support their opinions as objectively as possible. As Oskoz & Gimeno (forthcoming) pointed out, the perceived formality of the tasks in Study 2 might have also deterred students from exhibiting high numbers of affective markers, favoring judgment and appreciation markers to convey their meanings.

In addition to these differences in the presence of affect markers, there are also differences in how these markers were used in both studies (see Table 5). Within the affect subcomponent, students in Study 1 used mostly tokens of satisfaction-interest (15.94% for Spanish students and 20.61% for American students, relative frequencies 1.04 and 1.35 respectively), and happiness-affection (13.00% for Spanish students and 13.26% for American students, relative frequencies 0.84 and 0.88 respectively) in their interaction, with very few instances of negative affect. Students in Study 2 used mostly inclination-desire (2.52% for Spanish students and 3.88% for American students, relative frequencies 0.32 in both groups) and unhappiness-misery

(2.37% for Spanish students and 2.36% for American students, relative frequencies 0.21 and 0.21 respectively). These findings reflect the types of emotional resources that students in both studies used in their interaction to elicit reactions from their partners and they are consistent with the factors previously mentioned (nature of task, time on task, and topic). Although all students favored the use of mostly positive appraisals (i.e., satisfaction, happiness, inclination) which supports students' desire to create a positive atmosphere (Liaw & English, 2017; Morand & Ocker, 2003), in both studies there is a noticeable presence of unhappiness-misery. The presence of this negative affective marker as the second most frequent appraisal type in Study 2, and with high results in Study 1, was mostly associated to the discussion of the 2016 US presidential elections. This discussion resulted in students reacting with disbelief, sadness, anger, and dismay at the results. Following Vinagre & Corral (2018), it is possible that, by commiserating with each other, students were seeking to build trust and empathy in order to facilitate interaction and encourage collaboration. Results from the chi-square test proved to be statistically significant ($\chi^2 = 31.6124$, $df = 13$, $p = .00001$, $p < .05$), which indicates that the patterns exhibited by participants in both studies regarding the use of affect represent a departure from chance.

Appreciation, despite being the second most common category in both studies, had a significantly higher presence in Study 2 (36.15% for Spanish students and 43.01% for American students, with relative frequencies of 3.22 and 3.55 respectively); while in Study 1, despite showing higher numbers of appraisals, percentages and relative values were lower (23.41% for Spanish students and 23.35% for American students, with relative frequencies of 1.52 and 1.54 respectively). Interestingly though, as seen in Table 6, reaction ("it is exciting") was the subcategory most frequently used in both studies (10.25% for Spanish students and 9.26% for American students, with relative frequencies of 0.66 and 0.61 respectively in Study 1; 30.82% for Spanish students and 35.33% for American students, with relative frequencies of 2.75 and 2.94 respectively in Study 2). This suggests that participants in both studies chose to evaluate the product/process in terms of the impact it made or its quality. As Thompson (2008: 172) suggests, these categories fundamentally reflect the values of a culture, what is "normal" for members of that culture, and "the parameters within which they 'place' their experiences." Rather than focusing on human behavior, students seem to have been more interested in discovering the practices, policies, and norms of both countries regarding the cultural topics under discussion. As suggested by Belz (2003) and Vinagre & Corral (2018), the use of similar attitudinal tokens by participants in VE, regardless of their culture, seems to

Table 5. Comparison of Affect markers per study

	STUDY 1							STUDY 2					
	SPANISH STUDENTS			AMERICAN STUDENTS				SPANISH STUDENTS			AMERICAN STUDENTS		
Affect	Total tokens	Percent-age	Rate per 100 words (32,257)	Total tokens	Percent-age	Rate per 100 words (27,651)		Total tokens	Percent-age	Rate per 100 words (7,580)	Total tokens	Percent-age	Rate per 100 words (15,845)
Affect	1,102	52.30%	3.41	1,034	56.68%	3.73		88	13.04%	1.16	213	16.19%	1.34
Happiness	361	17.13%	1.11	274	15.02%	0.99		9	1.33%	0.12	29	2.20%	0.18
cheer	87	4.12%	0.26	32	1.75%	0.11		1	0.15%	0.01	10	0.76%	0.06
affection	274	13.00%	0.84	242	13.26%	0.88		8	1.19%	1.11	19	1.44%	0.12
Unhappiness	98	4.65%	0.30	107	5.86%	0.38		17	2.52%	0.22	34	2.58%	0.21
misery	85	4.03%	0.26	89	4.87%	0.32		16	2.37%	0.21	31	2.36%	0.20
antipathy	13	0.61%	0.04	18	0.98%	0.06		1	0.15%	0.01	3	0.23%	0.02
Security	140	6.64%	0.43	112	6.14%	0.40		5	0.74%	0.07	28	2.13%	0.18
confidence	88	4.17%	0.27	74	4.05%	0.26		2	0.30%	0.03	13	0.99%	0.08
trust	52	2.46%	0.16	38	2.08%	0.13		3	0.44%	0.04	15	1.14%	0.09
Insecurity	74	3.51%	0.22	62	3.39%	0.22		16	2.37%	0.21	21	1.60%	0.13
disquiet	71	3.36%	0.22	46	2.52%	0.16		6	0.89%	0.08	6	0.46%	0.04
surprise	3	0.14%	0.00	16	0.87%	0.05		10	1.48%	0.13	15	1.14%	0.09
Satisfaction	372	17.65%	1.15	430	23.57%	1.55		17	2.52%	0.22	34	2.58%	0.21
interest	336	15.94%	1.04	376	20.61%	1.35		7	1.04%	0.09	20	1.52%	0.13
pleasure/admiration	36	1.70%	0.11	54	2.96%	0.19		10	1.48%	0.13	14	1.06%	0.09
Dissatisfaction	20	0.94%	0.06	23	1.26%	0.08		4	0.59%	0.05	8	0.61%	0.05
ennui	5	0.23%	0.01	5	0.27%	0.01		0	0.00%	0.00	0	0.00%	0.00
displeasure	15	0.71%	0.04	18	0.98%	0.06		4	0.59%	0.05	8	0.61%	0.05
Inclination	37	1.75%	0.11	26	1.42%	0.09		16	2.37%	0.21	51	3.88%	0.32
desire	37	1.75%	0.11	26	1.42%	0.09		16	2.37%	0.32	51	3.88%	0.32
Disinclination	0	0.00%	0.00	0	0.00%	0.00		4	0.59%	0.05	8	0.61%	0.05
fear	0	0.00%	0.00	0	0.00%	0.00		4	0.59%	0.05	8	0.61%	0.05

Table 6. Comparison of Appreciation markers per study

	STUDY 1								STUDY 2							
	SPANISH STUDENTS			AMERICAN STUDENTS				SPANISH STUDENTS				AMERICAN STUDENTS			
	Total tokens	Percent-age	Rate per 100 words (32,257)	Total tokens	Percent-age	Rate per 100 words (27,651)			Total tokens	Percent-age	Rate per 100 words (7,580)		Total tokens	Percent-age	Rate per 100 words (15,845)
Appreciation	493	23.39%	1.52	426	23.35%	1.54			244	36.15%	3.22		566	43.01%	3.57
Reaction	216	10.25%	0.66	169	9.26%	0.61			208	30.82%	2.75		465	35.33%	2.94
+ impact	69	3.27%	0.21	63	3.45%	0.22			12	1.78%	0.16		56	4.26%	0.35
– impact	17	0.80%	0.05	4	0.21%	0.01			34	5.04%	0.45		96	7.29%	0.61
+ quality	91	4.31%	0.28	71	3.89%	0.32			81	12.00%	1.07		171	12.99%	1.08
– quality	39	1.85%	0.12	31	1.69%	0.11			81	12.00%	1.07		142	10.79%	0.90
Composition	130	6.16%%	0.40	109	5.97%	0.39			20	2.97%	0.69		66	5.02%	0.87
+ balance	46	2.18%	0.14	29	1.58%	0.10			2	0.30%	0.03		1	0.08%	0.01
– balance	46	2.18%	0.14	40	2.19%	0.14			1	0.15%	0.01		7	0.53%	0.04
+ complexity	13	0.61%	0.04	5	0.27%	0.01			11	1.63%	0.15		41	3.12%	0.26
–complexity	25	1.18%	0.07	35	1.91%	0.12			6	0.89%	0.08		17	1.29%	0.11
Valuation	147	6.97%	0.45	148	8.11%	0.53			16	2.37%	0.21		35	2.66%	0.22
+ valuation	92	4.36%	0.28	99	5.42%	0.35			2	0.30%	0.03		12	0.91%	0.08
– valuation	55	2.61%	0.17	49	2.68%	0.17			14	2.07%	0.18		23	1.75%	0.15

Table 7. Comparison of Judgment markers per study

	STUDY 1								STUDY 2							
	SPANISH STUDENTS			AMERICAN STUDENTS			SPANISH STUDENTS			AMERICAN STUDENTS		
	Total tokens	Percent-age	Rate per 100 words (32,257)	Total tokens	Percent-age	Rate per 100 words (27,651)	Total tokens	Percent-age	Rate per 100 words (7,580)	Total tokens	Percent-age	Rate per 100 words (15,845)
Judgment	512	24.29%	1.58	364	19.95%	1.31	343	50.81%	4.53	537	40.81%	3.39
Social esteem	298	14.14%	0.92	194	10.63%	0.70	187	27.71%	2.47	265	20.14%	1.67
+ normality	87	4.12%	0.26	63	3.45%	0.22	104	15.41%	1.37	137	10.41%	0.86
− normality	52	2.46%	0.16	38	2.08%	0.13	35	5.19%	0.46	43	3.27%	0.27
+ capacity	83	4.03%	0.26	41	2.24%	0.14	18	2.67%	0.24	56	4.26%	0.35
− capacity	69	3.27%	0.21	44	2.41%	0.15	25	3.70%	0.33	25	1.90%	0.16
+ tenacity	7	0.33%	0.02	8	0.43%	0.02	3	0.44%	0.04	4	0.30%	0.03
− tenacity	0	0.00%	0.00	0	0.00%	0.00	2	0.30%	0.03	0	0.00%	0.00
Social sanction	214	10.15%	0.66	170	9.32%	0.61	156	23.10%	2.06	272	20.67%	1.72
+ veracity	68	3.22%	0.27	67	3.67%	0.24	84	12.44%	1.11	186	14.13%	1.17
− veracity	3	0.14%	0.00	1	0.05%	0.00	3	0.44%	0.04	6	0.46%	0.04
+ propriety	132	6.26%	0.40	95	5.20%	0.34	10	1.48%	0.13	15	1.14%	0.09
− propriety	11	0.52%	0.03	7	0.38%	0.02	59	8.74%	0.78	65	4.94%	0.41

be a discursive strategy with the aim of showing solidarity and convergence with the partner in order to facilitate collaboration. Results from the chi-square test also proved highly significant (χ^2=31.3103, df=9, p=.00001).

In terms of judgment (see Table 7), participants' discourse patterns were also very similar in both studies. This category was the most common in Study 2 (50.81% for Spanish students and 40.81% for American students, with relative frequencies of 4.53 and 3.39 respectively) and the least common in Study 1 (24.29% for Spanish students and 19.95% for American students, with relative frequencies of 1.58 and 1.31 respectively) with chi-square results proving significant (χ^2 = 30.3586, df = 9, p = .00001). Most participants showed a preference for social esteem (personal judgments of admiration or criticism) over social sanction (moral judgments of praise or condemnation). Thus, in Study 1, totals for social esteem were 14.14% for Spanish students and 10.63% for American students, with relative frequencies of 0.92 and 0.70, whereas totals for social sanction were 10.15% for Spanish students and 9.32% for American students, with relative frequencies of 0.66 and 0.61. In Study 2, although the Spanish participants also preferred social esteem appraisals (27.71%, relative frequency 2.47) rather than social sanction (23.10%, relative frequency 2.06), the American students favored social sanction slightly more (20.67%, relative frequency 1.72) over social esteem (20.14%, relative frequency 1.67). The explanation for this difference is likely to be found in the nature of the topics for discussion (i.e., the 2016 US presidential elections). Students from the United States felt strongly about this topic and they approached the topic from a legal or moral perspective, since judgments of social sanction raise issues about the legality and morality of the person under scrutiny (Martin & White, 2005).

Within social esteem, the subcategory with the highest number of tokens in both studies was positive normality: "how unusual someone is" (in Study 1 this was 4.12% for Spanish students and 3.45% for American students, with relative frequencies 0.26 and 0.22; in Study 2, 15.41% for Spanish students and 10.41% for American students, with relative frequencies 1.37 and 0.86). The second highest subcategory in both groups belonged to social sanction, although it was different in both studies. Thus, while participants in Study 1 preferred positive propriety: "how ethical someone or something is" (6.26% for Spanish students and 5.20% for American students, with relative frequencies of 0.40 and 0.34 respectively), participants in Study 2 favored positive veracity: "how truthful someone or something is" (12.44% for Spanish students and 14.13% for American students, with relative frequencies of 1.11 and 1.17 respectively). Even though we could consider that these two subcategories are very closely related, the fact that students in each study used the same type of judgment tokens reinforces the idea of the use of similar discursive strategies to create solidarity (Belz, 2003; Vinagre & Corral, 2018).

With regard to RQ2, which aimed to investigate whether there were any similarities or differences in the way the Spanish students in both studies and the American students in both studies deployed appraisal, results from the chi-square test for affect proved statistically significant despite the differences in totals. Thus, for the use of affect among Spanish students in both studies, results from the chi-square statistic were $\chi^2 = 11.1674$, $df = 13$, $p = .000832$. Similarly, chi-square test results for the American students in both studies also proved statistically significant ($\chi^2 = 19.344$, $df = 13$, $p = .000011$). These results indicate a high degree of association in both cases.

A more detailed look into the subcategories within affect (see Table 8), reveals that similar attitudinal patterns can be observed between the Spanish and American students who participated in the studies. For instance, when looking at the commonalities between the students from Spain, participants in both studies used mostly positive markers, favoring satisfaction appraisals in their interaction (17.65% in Study 1 and 2.52% in Study 2, relative frequencies of 1.15 and 0.22). As regards those subcategories that they used the least, they also coincide in the lack of appraisals of disinclination (0% in Study 1 and 0.59% in Study 2, relative frequencies of 0 and 0.05) and dissatisfaction (0.23% in Study 1 and 0.59% in Study 2, relative frequencies of 0.01 and 0.05). However, there were also striking differences between the two groups, such as the presence of high totals of happiness (17.13%, relative frequency of 1.1) and security tokens (6.64%, relative frequency of 0.43) in Study 1 versus high totals of unhappiness (2.52%, relative frequency of 0.22) and insecurity tokens (2.37%, relative frequency of 0.21) in Study 2. As regards the contributions from students in the United States in both groups, the results showed that satisfaction was also the subcategory that participants in both studies shared the most (23.57% in Study 1 and 2.58% in Study 2, relative frequencies of 1.51 and 0.21). Participants in both studies also presented a lack of disinclination (0% in Study 1 and 0.61% in Study 2, relative frequencies of 0 and 0.05) and dissatisfaction appraisals (0.27% in Study 1 and 0.61% in Study 2, relative frequencies of 0.01 and 0.05). When looking at the differences in the use of affect, the most significant is again the presence of high totals of happiness (15.02%, relative frequency of 0.99) and security tokens (6.14%, relative frequency of 0.40) in Study 1, versus high totals of inclination (3.88%, relative frequency of 0.32) and unhappiness (2.58%, relative frequency of 0.21) in Study 2.

The clear similarities in the use of affect by the Spanish participants and American participants in each of the studies reinforces the idea that participants from the same culture share common traits in their discourse (Belz, 2003). Yet, it is noteworthy that participants in each of the studies, regardless of their culture, also used the same type of affect tokens, indicating the presence of lingua-pragmatic hybridity (Belz, 2003), which is considered crucial for successful intercultural interaction in VEs. As suggested by Vinagre & Corral (2018: 33), it is likely that the online environment contributed to the occurrence of acts of hybridity demonstrating that the participants "acknowledge their peers' linguistic patterns and pragmatic discursive strategies and adapt and integrate them into their own discourse." The differences in the use of polarity (i.e., the use of positive and negative values) between participants in Study 1 (main affect subcategories were positive) and those in Study 2 (main affect subcategories were negative) may be linked to the different nature of the tasks and topics discussed in each of the studies (as already suggested in RQ1).

Regarding appreciation, results from the chi-square statistic (χ^2 = 9.2864, df = 9, p = .0002309) are significant at $p < .05$, indicating a high degree of association between the two Spain-based groups. When examining the discourse patterns of the Spanish students (see Table 9), the most common category was reaction (10.25% in Study 1 and 30.82% in Study 2, relative frequencies of 0.66 and 2.75 respectively). Within reaction, positive quality ("it is innovative") was also the preferred strategy by Spanish students in both studies (4.31% in Study 1 and 12.00% in Study 2, relative frequencies of 0.28 and 1.07 respectively). Other relevant subcategories were positive valuation (4.36%, relative frequency of 0.28) and positive impact (3.27%, relative frequency of 0.21) by participants in Study 1, whilst participants in Study 2 favored negative quality (12.00%, relative frequency of 1.07) and negative impact (5.04%, relative frequency of 0.45). Similar to the affect results above, polarity totals by Spanish students in both studies showed that while in Study 1 the presence of positive appreciation appraisals outnumbered the negative (311, 63% positive appreciation tokens versus 182, 37% negative appreciation tokens), in Study 2 it was the reverse (134, 55% negative appreciation tokens versus 110, 45% positive appreciation tokens).

When looking into the presence of appreciation appraisals by the American groups, the chi-square test results also proved statistically significant (χ^2 = 18.602, df = 9, p = .000016), which indicates a high degree of association between the two groups. Similar to students from Spain, the most common category was reaction (9.26% in Study 1 and 35.33% in Study 2, relative frequencies of 0.61 and 2.94 respectively). Within reaction, positive quality was also the preferred strategy by American students in both studies (3.89% in Study 1 and 12.99% in Study 2, relative frequencies of 0.32 and 1.08 respectively). Similar to their Spanish counterparts,

Exploring Attitude in Bilingual Virtual Exchanges 83

Table 8. Comparison of Affect markers per group

	SPANISH STUDENTS (Study 1)			SPANISH STUDENTS (Study 2)			AMERICAN STUDENTS (Study 1)			AMERICAN STUDENTS (Study 2)		
	Total tokens	Percent-age	Rate per 100 words (32,257)	Total tokens	Percent-age	Rate per 100 words (7,580)	Total tokens	Percent-age	Rate per 100 words (27,651)	Total tokens	Percent-age	Rate per 100 words (15,845)
Affect	1,102	52.30%	3.41	88	13.04%	1.16	1,034	56.68%	3.73	213	16.19%	1.34
Happiness	361	17.13%	1.11	9	1.33%	0.12	274	15.02%	0.99	29	2.20%	0.18
cheer	87	4.12%	0.26	1	0.15%	0.01	32	1.75%	0.11	10	0.76%	0.06
affection	274	13.00%	0.84	8	1.19%	1.11	242	13.26%	0.88	19	1.44%	0.12
Unhappiness	98	4.65%	0.30	17	2.52%	0.22	107	5.86%	0.38	34	2.58%	0.21
misery	85	4.03%	0.26	16	2.37%	0.21	89	4.87%	0.32	31	2.36%	0.20
antipathy	13	0.61%	0.04	1	0.15%	0.01	18	0.98%	0.06	3	0.23%	0.02
Security	140	6.64%	0.43	5	0.74%	0.07	112	6.14%	0.40	28	2.13%	0.18
confidence	88	4.17%	0.27	2	0.30%	0.03	74	4.05%	0.26	13	0.99%	0.08
trust	52	2.46%	0.16	3	0.44%	0.04	38	2.08%	0.13	15	1.14%	0.09
Insecurity	74	3.51%	0.22	16	2.37%	0.21	62	3.39%	0.22	21	1.60%	0.13
disquiet	71	3.36%	0.22	6	0.89%	0.08	46	2.52%	0.16	6	0.46%	0.04
surprise	3	0.14%	0.00	10	1.48%	0.13	16	0.87%	0.05	15	1.14%	0.09
Satisfaction	372	17.65%	1.15	17	2.52%	0.22	430	23.57%	1.55	34	2.58%	0.21
interest	336	15.94%	1.04	7	1.04%	0.09	376	20.61%	1.35	20	1.52%	0.13
pleasure/admiration	36	1.70%	0.11	10	1.48%	0.13	54	2.96%	0.19	14	1.06%	0.09
Dissatisfaction	20	0.94%	0.06	4	0.59%	0.05	23	1.26%	0.08	8	0.61%	0.05
ennui	5	0.23%	0.01	0	0.00%	0.00	5	0.27%	0.01	0	0.00%	0.00
displeasure	15	0.71%	0.04	4	0.59%	0.05	18	0.98%	0.06	8	0.61%	0.05
Inclination	37	1.75%	0.11	16	2.37%	0.21	26	1.42%	0.09	51	3.88%	0.32
desire	37	1.75%	0.11	16	2.37%	0.32	26	1.42%	0.09	51	3.88%	0.32
Disinclination	0	0.00%	0.00	4	0.59%	0.05	0	0.00%	0.00	8	0.61%	0.05
fear	0	0.00%	0.00	4	0.59%	0.05	0	0.00%	0.00	8	0.61%	0.05

Table 9. Comparison of Appreciation markers per group

	SPANISH STUDENTS (Study 1)			SPANISH STUDENTS (Study 2)			AMERICAN STUDENTS (Study 1)			AMERICAN STUDENTS (Study 2)		
	Total tokens	Percent-age	Rate per 100 words (32,257)	Total tokens	Percent-age	Rate per 100 words (7,580)	Total tokens	Percent-age	Rate per 100 words (27,651)	Total tokens	Percent-age	Rate per 100 words (15,845)
Appreciation	493	23.39%	1.52	244	36.15%	3.22	426	23.35%	1.54	566	43.01%	3.57
Reaction	216	10.25%	0.66	208	30.82%	2.75	169	9.26%	0.61	465	35.33%	2.94
+ impact	69	3.27%	0.21	12	1.78%	0.16	63	3.45%	0.22	56	4.26%	0.35
– impact	17	0.80%	0.05	34	5.04%	0.45	4	0.21%	0.01	96	7.29%	0.61
+ quality	91	4.31%	0.28	81	12.00%	1.07	71	3.89%	0.32	171	12.99%	1.08
– quality	39	1.85%	0.12	81	12.00%	1.07	31	1.69%	0.11	142	10.79%	0.90
Composition	130	6.16%	0.40	20	2.97%	0.69	109	5.97%	0.39	66	5.02%	0.87
+ balance	46	2.18%	0.14	2	0.30%	0.03	29	1.58%	0.10	1	0.08%	0.01
– balance	46	2.18%	0.14	1	0.15%	0.01	40	2.19%	0.14	7	0.53%	0.04
+ complexity	13	0.61%	0.04	11	1.63%	0.15	5	0.27%	0.01	41	3.12%	0.26
– complexity	25	1.18%	0.07	6	0.89%	0.08	35	1.91%	0.12	17	1.29%	0.11
Valuation	147	6.97%	0.45	16	2.37%	0.21	148	8.11%	0.53	35	2.66%	0.22
+ valuation	92	4.36%	0.28	2	0.30%	0.03	99	5.42%	0.35	12	0.91%	0.08
– valuation	55	2.61%	0.17	14	2.07%	0.18	49	2.68%	0.17	23	1.75%	0.15

Exploring Attitude in Bilingual Virtual Exchanges   85

Table 10. Comparison of Judgment markers by group

	SPANISH STUDENTS (Study 1)			SPANISH STUDENTS (Study 2)			AMERICAN STUDENTS (Study 1)			AMERICAN STUDENTS (Study 2)		
	Total tokens	Percent-age	Rate per 100 words (32,257)	Total tokens	Percent-age	Rate per 100 words (7,580)	Total tokens	Percent-age	Rate per 100 words (27,651)	Total tokens	Percent-age	Rate per 100 words (15,845)
Judgment	512	24.29%	1.58	343	50.81%	4.53	364	19.95%	1.31	537	40.81%	3.39
Social esteem	298	14.14%	0.92	187	27.71%	2.47	194	10.63%	0.70	265	20.14%	1.67
+ normality	87	4.12%	0.26	104	15.41%	1.37	63	3.45%	0.22	137	10.41%	0.86
− normality	52	2.46%	0.16	35	5.19%	0.46	38	2.08%	0.13	43	3.27%	0.27
+ capacity	83	4.03%	0.26	18	2.67%	0.24	41	2.24%	0.14	56	4.26%	0.35
− capacity	69	3.27%	0.21	25	3.70%	0.33	44	2.41%	0.15	25	1.90%	0.16
+ tenacity	7	0.33%	0.02	3	0.44%	0.04	8	0.43%	0.02	4	0.30%	0.03
− tenacity	0	0.00%	0.00	2	0.30%	0.03	0	0.00%	0.00	0	0.00%	0.00
Social sanction												
+ veracity	214	10.15%	0.66	156	23.10%	2.06	170	9.32%	0.61	272	20.67%	1.72
− veracity	68	3.22%	0.27	84	12.44%	1.11	67	3.67%	0.24	186	14.13%	1.17
+ propriety	3	0.14%	0.00	3	0.44%	0.04	1	0.05%	0.00	6	0.46%	0.04
− propriety	132	6.26%	0.40	10	1.48%	0.13	95	5.20%	0.34	15	1.14%	0.09
	11	0.52%	0.03	59	8.74%	0.78	7	0.38%	0.02	65	4.94%	0.41

other relevant subcategories were positive valuation (5.42%, relative frequency of 0.35) and positive impact (3.45%, relative frequency of 0.22) by participants in Study 1, whilst participants in Study 2 favored negative quality (10.79%, relative frequency of 0.90) and negative impact (7.29%, relative frequency of 0.61).

As regards total results for polarity, similar findings to those from the Spanish group were also found here. In Study 1, the presence of positive appraisals outnumbered the negative (267, 62.6% positive appreciation tokens versus 159, 37.4% negative appreciation tokens), whereas in Study 2 negative appreciation was more abundant (285, 50.4% negative appreciation tokens versus 281, 49.6% positive appreciation tokens).

These results, similar to those from the affect component, corroborate findings from previous studies that point to the presence of specific patterns and cultural discourse practices among students from the same country (Belz, 2003; Vinagre & Corral, 2018). The remarkable similarities in the use of subcategory types by participants in each of the studies (quality, valuation, and impact) also suggest a desire to notice and imitate the other in order to adapt and converge in communication. In addition, the consistency in the expression of positive attitudes by participants in Study 1 versus negative attitudes by participants in Study 2 also indicates that, in addition to cultural differences, there is a need to examine the effect that the nature of task and topic for discussion have on virtual interaction. As suggested by Oskoz & Gimeno (forthcoming), the perceived seriousness of a topic might lead students to focus on different implications of cultural practices and policies. These aspects, no doubt, have a direct effect on the presence of positive and negative markers in participants' discourse.

Results from the judgment component also showed similarities between the Spanish students in the two studies. Results from the chi-square statistic for judgment markers was significant at < .05 ($\chi^2 = 24.8524$, $df = 9$, $p < .00001$) which indicates a high degree of association for this variable between these two groups. When looking into the similarities in discourse patterns (see Table 10), Spain-based participants employed more instances of social esteem than social sanction (14.14%, relative frequency of 0.92 versus 10.15%, relative frequency of 0.66 in Study 1; and 27.51%, relative frequency of 1.37 versus 23.10%, relative frequency of 1.37 in Study 2). Within social esteem, students in both studies favored the use of positive normality (4.12%, relative frequency of 0.26 in Study 1 versus 15.41%, relative frequency of 1.37 in Study 2). As regards the differences, whilst Spain-based students in Study 1 showed more positive propriety appraisals (6.26%, relative frequency of 0.40), the Spain-based students in Study 2 used positive veracity more often (12.44%, relative frequency of 1.11).

As regards the American students in both studies, the chi-square test results also proved significant ($\chi^2 = 21.002$, $df = 9$, p < .00001). The main observable difference between these two groups is that while US-based students in Study 1 favored social esteem over social sanction, like the Spanish groups (10.63%, relative frequency of 0.70 versus 9.32%, relative frequency of 0.61), the US-based students in Study 2 preferred social sanction over social esteem (20.67%, relative frequency of 1.71 versus 20.14%, relative frequency of 1.67). As already mentioned, it is likely that the nature of some of the issues discussed (i.e. US elections) may have triggered these students' reaction to judge them according to some set of rules or regulations, more or less explicitly codified by their culture. These rules may be legal or moral and therefore, judgments of social sanction raise questions about the legality and morality of the issues being evaluated.

Finally, the fact that in both studies, Spain-based participants presented higher instances of judgment (24.29%, relative frequency of 1.58 in Study 1 and 50.81%, relative frequency of 4.53 in Study 2) versus US-based students (19.95%, relative frequency of 1.31 in Study 1 and 40.81%, relative frequency of 3.39 in Study 2) provides further support to the idea that being critical is considered a positive personality trait in Spanish culture, while in American culture being "critical" and "opinionated" are considered negative traits and therefore should be avoided (Vinagre & Corral, 2018).

5   Conclusion

The results of this study are threefold. First, the application of the appraisal model (Martin & White, 2005) to analyze how the participants used attitudinal resources in two unrelated telecollaborative studies confirms that there are observable cultural discourse differences between participants from different countries. Second, when interacting virtually, participants from different countries also adopt and integrate each other's pragma-linguistic discourse patterns. These findings corroborate results from previous studies (Belz, 2003; Vinagre & Corral, 2018) and suggest that virtual exchanges can provide a fruitful arena where students engage in effective intercultural dialogue. Third, the impact of task type and nature of topic for discussion on learners' discourse patterns cannot be undervalued.

Despite these encouraging results, there are several limitations to this study. First, the different sample size in terms of participants and number of interactions may have affected the results. In the future, it would be of interest to compare the interactions from the same number of participants in separate exchanges but who interact similarly over the same period of time. Second, the differences in the range of tasks to be carried out by participants in the two studies have no doubt influenced the results. The fact that in Study 1 participants talked about a wide range of topics, while in Study 2 the students were limited to two heated topics, has likely resulted in the differences in polarity (positive versus negative) that can be observed in the three attitudinal components (affect, judgment, and appreciation). In future studies, providing students from two different exchanges with the same topics would offer us a more accurate depiction of how participants use appraisals in their encounters. Third, neither of these studies collected information on the students' intercultural and linguistic backgrounds or on their initial opinions about the topics discussed. This information would provide further insights into how learners approach the different discussions and how their discourse patterns reflect their opinions and reactions.

From a pedagogical perspective, the results of this study illustrate how online interactions in VEs are ideal venues for participants to learn from each other's pragma-linguistic practices. When designing a task, the instructor needs to be aware that task design and topic selection are not neutral and therefore may have implications on learners' discourse patterns. Overall, by engaging in meaningful discussions in which they share their emotional responses to the evaluation of behaviors, objects, and products, learners are a step closer to becoming effective intercultural communicators.

References

Adichie, C. (2009). *Chimamanda Adichie: The Danger of a Single Story* [video file]. Retrieved from
https://www.ted.com/talks/chimamanda_adichie_the_danger_of_a_single_story?language=en

Arnold, N., Ducate, L., Lomicka, L., & Lord, G. (2005). Using computer-mediated communication to establish social and supportive environments in teacher education. *CALICO Journal*, 22, 537–566.
https://doi.org/10.1558/cj.v22i3.537-566

Belz, J. A. (2003). Linguistic perspectives on the development of intercultural competence in telecollaboration. *Language Learning & Technology*, 7(2), 68–99.

Biber, D., & Finegan, E. (1989). Styles of stance in English: Lexical and grammatical marking of evidentiality and affect. *Text*, 9(1), 93–124.
https://doi.org/10.1515/text.1.1989.9.1.93

Bueno-Alastuey, C., & Kleban, M. (2016). Matching linguistic and pedagogical objectives in a telecollaboration project: A case study. *Computer Assisted Language Learning*, 29(1), 148–166.
https://doi.org/10.1080/09588221.2014.904360

Cabrejas-Peñuelas, A. B., & Díez-Prados, M. (2014). Positive self-evaluation versus negative other-evaluation in the political genre of pre-election debates. *Discourse & Society*, 25(2), 159–185. https://doi.org/10.1177/0957926513515601

Dooly, M., & Sadler, R. (2013). Filling in the gaps: Linking theory and practice through telecollaboration in teacher education. *ReCALL*, 25(1), 4–29. https://doi.org/10.1017/S0958344012000237

Eggins, S., & Slade, D. (1997). *Analysing Casual Conversation*. London: Cassell.

Graham C., & Misanchuk M. (2004). Computer-mediated learning groups: Benefits and challenges to using groupwork in online learning environments. In T. Roberts (ed.), *Online Collaborative Learning: Theory and Practice* (pp. 181–202). Hershey-USA: IGI Global. https://doi.org/10.4018/978-1-59140-174-2.ch008

Guth, S., & Helm, F. (2012). Teaching culture through CALL. In A. Arnold & L. Ducate (eds.), *Present and Future Promises of CALL: From Theory and Research to New Directions in Language Teaching* (pp. 211–256). San Marcos, TX: CALICO.

Guth, S., & Thomas, M. (2010). Telecollaboration with Web 2.0 tools. In S. Guth and F. Helm (eds.), *Telecollaboration 2.0: Language, Literacy and Intercultural Learning in the 21st Century* (pp. 39–68). Bern: Peter Lang.

Hauck, M. (2010). The enactment of task design in Tellecollaboration 2.0. In M. Thomas & H. Reinders (eds.), *Task-based Language Learning and Tteaching with Technology* (pp. 197–217). London: Continuum.

Hunston, S., & Thompson, G. (eds.) (2000). *Evaluation in Text: Authorial Stance and the Construction of Discourse* (pp. 1–27). Oxford: Oxford University Press.

Hunt, K. W. (1965). *Grammatical Structures Written at Three Grade Levels*. Champaign, IL: National Council of Teachers of English.

Johnstone, B. (2002) *Discourse Analysis*. Blackwell Publishers: Malden, MA.

Kohn, K., & Hoffstaedter, P. (2015). Flipping intercultural communication practice: opportunities and challenges for the foreign language classroom. In J. Colpaert, A. Aerts, M. Oberhofer, & M. Gutiérez-Colón Plana (eds.), *Task Design & CALL: Proceedings of the CALL 2015 Conference* (pp. 1–6). Belgium: Universiteit Antwerpen.

Liaw, M.-L., & English, K. (2017). Identity and addresivity in the Beyond these Walls program. *System*, 64, 74–86. https://doi.org/10.1016/j.system.2016.12.005

Martin, J. (2000, 2003). Beyond exchange: Appraisal systems in English. In S. Hunston & G. Thompson (eds.), *Evaluation in Text* (pp. 142–175). Oxford: Oxford University Press.

Martin, J. R., & White, P. R. (2005). *The Language of Evaluation: Appraisal in English*. New York, NY: Palgrave. https://doi.org/10.1057/9780230511910

Morand, D. A., & Ocker, R. J. (2003). Politeness theory and computer-mediated communication: A sociolinguistic approach to analyzing relational messages. Paper presented at the Proceedings of the 36th Hawaii International Conference on System Sciences, Hawaii. https://doi.org/10.1109/HICSS.2003.1173660

Ochs, E., & Schieffelin, B. (1989). Language has a heart. *Text*, 9(1), 7–25. https://doi.org/10.1515/text.1.1989.9.1.7

O'Dowd, R. (2015). Supporting in-service language educators in learning to tele-collaborate. *Language Learning & Technology*, 19(1), 63–82.

Oskoz, A., & Gimeno-Sanz, A. (2019). Engagement and attitude in telecollaboration: Topic and cultural background effects. *Language Learning & Technology*, 23(3), 136–160. http://hdl.handle.net/10125/44700.

Oskoz, A., & Gimeno-Sanz, A. (forthcoming). Exploring L2 learners' engagement and attitude in an intercultural encounter. *Language Learning & Technology*, 24(1).

Oskoz, A., Gimeno-Sanz, A., & Sevilla Pavón, A. (2018). Exploring learner written discourse in a university telecollaboration project. In B. Mousten, S. Vandepitte, E. Arnó, & B. Maylath, (eds.), *Multilingual Writing and Pedagogical Cooperation in Virtual Learning Environments* (pp. 200–220). Hershey, PA: IGI Global.

Ryshina-Pankova, M. (2018). Discourse moves and intercultural communicative competence in telecollaborative chats. *Language Learning & Technology*, 22(1), 218–239.

Thompson, G. (2008). Appraising glances: Evaluating Martin's model of appraisal. *WORD*, 59(2), 169–187. https://doi.org/10.1080/00437956.2008.11432585

Thompson, G., & Hunston, S. (2000). Evaluation: An introduction. In S. Hunston & G. Thompson (eds.), *Evaluation in Text: Authorial Stance and the Construction of Discourse* (pp. 1–27). Oxford: Oxford University Press.

Vinagre, M. (2015). Training teachers for virtual collaboration: A case study. *British Journal of Educational Technology*, 47(4), 787–802. https://doi.org/10.1111/bjet.12363

Vinagre, M. (2016a). Promoting intercultural competence in culture and language studies: Outcomes of an international collaborative project. In E. Martín-Monje, I. Elorza, & B. García Riaza (eds.), *Technological Advances in Specialized Linguistic Domains: Practical Applications and Mobility* (pp. 23–35). London: Routledge.

Vinagre, M. (2016b). Developing key competences for life-long learning through virtual collaboration: Teaching ICT in English as a medium of instruction. In C. Wang & L. Winstead (eds.), *Handbook of Research on Foreign Language Education in the Digital Age* (pp. 170–187). Hershey: IGI Global. https://doi.org/10.4018/978-1-5225-0177-0.ch008

Vinagre, M. (2017). Developing teachers' telecollaborative competences in online experiential learning. *System*, 64 (Special Issue on Telecollaboration), 34–45. https://doi.org/10.1016/j.system.2016.12.002

Vinagre, M., & Corral, A. (2018). Evaluative language for rapport building in virtual collaboration: An analysis of appraisal in computer-mediated interaction. *Journal of Language and Intercultural Communication*, 18(3), 335–350. https://doi.org/10.1080/14708477.2017.1378227

Vinagre, M., & Corral, A. (2019). Tracing the development of intercultural competence in telecollaborative interaction: An analysis of evaluative language in eTandem exchanges. In C. Tardieu & C. Horgues (eds.), *Redefining Tandem Language and Culture Learning in Higher Education*. London: Routledge.

Wheelan, S., & Kesselring, J. (2005). Link between faculty group development and elementary student performance on standardized tests. *The Journal of Educational Research*, 98(6), 323–330.

White, P. (2002). Appraisal: The language of attitudinal evaluation and intersubjective stance. In J. Verschueren, J. O. Östman, J. Blommaert, & C. Bulcaen (eds.), *Handbook of Pragmatics* (pp. 1–23). Amsterdam: John Benjamins.

About the Authors

Margarita Vinagre is Associate Professor at Autónoma University of Madrid where she teaches Educational Technologies and English Language and Linguistics. Her main research interests are the integration of technologies in the foreign language classroom, computer-mediated communication, and the implementation of intercultural exchanges for the development of linguistic and generic competences. She has published widely on these topics and is currently the coordinator of the VELCOME project on the integration of virtual exchange for key competence development in higher education, with twenty participating researchers from five countries.

Ana Oskoz is Professor of Spanish and Applied Linguistics at the University of Maryland, Baltimore County (UMBC). Her research interests include different aspects of online learning and telecollaboration, with a special focus on the development of second language digital literacies and intercultural communicative competence. Her publications have appeared in professional journals including *Foreign Language Annals*, *ReCALL*, and *Language Learning & Technology*. She is co-editor of *CALICO Journal*.

4 Linguistic and Non-Linguistic Choices and Attitudes in an East-West Telecollaboration

Carolin Fuchs, Tsz Yan Lo, and Sneha Thapa

1 Introduction

In the last two decades, telecollaboration has facilitated the virtual link between students in international classroom settings through the use of digital tools (e.g., O'Dowd, 2018). It has been well documented that this can result in communication failure (e.g., O'Dowd & Ritter, 2006; Ware, 2005), or in compelling, surprising, or problematic situations (e.g., Liaw & Bunn-Le Master, 2010; see also Çiftçi and Savaş's 2018 meta-analysis of studies published between 2010 and 2015).

The term "telecollaboration" implies participants' online interaction with peers across different contexts using digital tools. From a sociocultural perspective, social interaction and "participation in culturally organized activity" lie at the center of all learning (Lantolf & Thorne, 2006: 214). One important aspect of such interaction is participant attitude. Attitude, from the perspective of interculturality, is part of social competence and has been defined as the "curiosity and openness, readiness to suspend disbelief about other cultures and belief about one's own," and it is reflected in one's willingness to seek out "to engage with otherness in a relationship of equality" (Byram, 1997: 50). While social psychologists have established that the attitude-and-behavior relationship is complex, dynamic, and not causal (Ajzen & Fishbein, 2005), linguistic or non-linguistic choices made during digitally mediated team negotiations can be indicative of participants' learned predisposition to behave favorably or unfavorably towards their telecollaborative partners. In this study, the goal was to identify such choices to see if they facilitated or hindered negotiations during different task stages by four focus teams in a Hong Kong–Germany telecollaboration.

In order to take a closer look at team interactions, this study[1] further draws on what Breen & Littlejohn (2000) have coined interactive negotiation,[2] which looks at the overt and social interactions whereby participants have used, modified, or restructured their language to indicate their understanding or failure to understand something. Closely linked is the concept of procedural negotiation, whereby participants engage in discussions with others with the ultimate goal of making key decisions: "who will work with whom, in what ways, with what resources and for how long, upon what subject matter or problems, and for what purposes" (Breen & Littlejohn, 2000: 8). This requires collaborative decision-making and constant balancing of different agendas and particular goals, personal purposes and preferences for learning (see also Johnson, Johnson, & Smith, 1991). In this telecollaboration, each task required telecollaborative teams to fully collaborate and support one another to achieve their mutual goals, which meant they needed to be willing to navigate and engage with each other's linguistic, cultural, technological, and socio-institutional systems.

2   Literature Review

Prior research in telecollaboration and online interaction has addressed attitude-related factors such as agreement and cooperation, communication strategies and style, and non-linguistic factors such as emoticons and Facebook "likes." While there is ample research conducted in Western languages regarding online communication (e.g., Belz, 2003; Darhower, 2008; Sadler & Dooly, 2016; see also the volume edited by Jager, Kurek, & O'Rourke, 2016), fewer telecollaborations deal with Asia-European contexts. Overall, it has been established that participants' attitudes towards one another are important factors in the negotiation process that requires participants to collaboratively make key decisions in order to achieve their mutual task goals. Communication style and agreement are thus crucial elements in this process. Group interaction styles have been categorized into

1   This study is part of a larger project (Fuchs, 2018, 2019) and was funded by a 2016 Start-Up Grant from the City University of Hong Kong. An earlier version of this chapter was presented at the American Association for Applied Linguistics 2019 Conference in Atlanta.
2   Breen & Littlejohn (2000) distinguish three different but interrelated types of negotiation: personal (on individual level, where one analyzes and synthesizes); interactive (on group level, where people share, check, and clarify meaning); procedural (on group level, where people with different interests or perspectives make key decisions).

"constructive" (e.g., suggesting a solution), "aggressive" (e.g., confrontational behavior), and "passive" (e.g., conforming behavior) communication, and analyzed across different synchronous and asynchronous media (González-Navarro, Orengo, Zornoza, Ripoll, & Peiró, 2010: 1475). While an in-depth discussion of Chinese and German intercultural communication is beyond the scope of this chapter, some main tendencies have been pointed out. Lewis (2005: 70) explains that Chinese speakers have a "reactive" communication style, in which people are "courteous, amiable and compromising"; Germany, on the other hand, has a "linear-active culture," where people prefer "straightforward and direct discussions," a discourse style which may be perceived as rude due to a lack of appreciation. Given the cultural distance between Asian and Western communication styles, it is quite likely that this will affect interaction, and the attitudes speakers show towards their interlocutors. In her discourse analysis of German–Chinese face-to-face conversations, Günthner (1993) established that though avoiding direct disagreement might be adequate for small-talk situations, speakers express disagreement often in a very direct and unmitigated form when engaged in argumentative sequences and confrontational discussions.

With regard to telecollaboration, Helm & Guth (2012) have argued that agreement tends to be preferred and that participants tend to be superficial to avoid conflict. In a case study on foreign language education in secondary schools, Hoffstaedter & Kohn (2016: 291) found that dyad strategies were predominantly supportive and consensual; participants' online lingua franca conversations were "marked by a high degree of cooperative autonomy with an emphasis on creating common ground, negotiating a shared line of argumentation, ensuring a supportive and consensual atmosphere, and solving communication problems on the fly." Participants also expressed praise towards telecollaborative partners in what has been termed "complimenting behavior" (Sanchez, 2015: 187). While complimenting can mean that participants either genuinely appreciate or validate their partners' suggestions, it can also mean that they try to keep a positive face even if their attitude towards one another is not positive. What is of interest is to learn what linguistic and non-linguistic resources L2 learners employ that result in different constructive, aggressive, or passive ways that enhance or hinder joint project negotiations.

A number of L2 studies have analyzed communication strategies (e.g., L1 use, mutual responsiveness, use of emoticons) in synchronous and asynchronous computer-mediated communication (e.g., Magnan, 2008). For instance, the use of the L1 in the second language learning process has been found to serve critical socio-cognitive functions to perform L2 tasks (Antón & Dicamilla, 2002). Darhower (2008), who analyzed linguistic affordances (e.g., providing translation or L1 use) in telecollaborative chat exchanges between advanced learners of Spanish and English, concluded that while it is important for language learners to practice co-constructing meaning with their interlocutors in their L2, learners also employed bilingual linguistic resources by drawing on linguistic affordances available to them whenever they found it relevant. On the other hand, code-switching to the L1 has been found to decrease in synchronous, task-based chat with increasing levels of proficiency by second-semester German students (Kost, 2008).

In telecollaborative US–German groups of students, Ware (2005) found that those who were more successful at co-constructing their online relationship in mutually compatible ways displayed the following strategies: responding to and elaborating on questions, following up on other-initiated topics, and converging on a conversational tone. However, factors such as differing norms and expectations, social and institutional factors, and student motivation and investment can impact telecollaboration negatively (Basharina, 2007). Belz (2003) also found that the functional social relationship can be affected by participants' unawareness of culture-specific interaction and argued that this was due to participants' lacking knowledge of culture-specific interaction patterns (directness, critique, mitigation).

Non-linguistic factors such as emoticons in computer-mediated communication also play a role due to their increasing popularity in social media discourse and their affective orientation ("affect display," Vandergriff, 2014: 11). Drawing on speech act theory, Dresner & Herring (2010) postulate that emoticons as indicators of illocutionary force can be regarded as an expansion of text in the same way that punctuation such as question marks and exclamation marks can change a question into a statement. Yet, the authors also stress the importance of contextual factors given that, despite a shared function of commonly-used Western-style emoticons in English, the forms and meanings of emoticons (smiling faces, winking faces) vary considerably in actual use. Derks, Bos, & von Grumbkow (2007) found that emoticons are more often used in informal, playful communication than in formal or task-focused contexts. Xu, Xu, & Yi's (2007) research on the use of emoticons in Instant Messenger indicated that people used emoticons to make themselves approachable to unfamiliar people. In her comparative analysis between native and non-native speaker use of emoticons, Vandergriff (2014) argued that non-native English speakers use emoticons more frequently than their English-speaking native counterparts, possibly to compensate for any linguistic shortcomings. Emoticon overuse, however, can diminish their impact, as Walther & D'Addario observed in an early investigation of emoticons in email communication (2001).

When given a choice of communication features, a corpus study comparing responses to compliments in Spanish in non-institutionalized face-to-face interaction versus social networking (Facebook) found that emoticon use was infrequent (3%) – as opposed to the more frequently used "liking" function on Facebook (Maiz-Arévalo, 2013). In fact, the Facebook "liking" function was found to be used for bonding or gratification purposes in open forums (Ozane, Cueva Navas, Mattila, & Van Hoof, 2017). As West (2015: 144) suggested, the "like" button's success in terms of frequency of use and proliferation in Internet culture is owing to its basic function in conversation as a "quick and inexplicit backchanneling device" that fills the gap in case a post is met with silence. Whereas the previous studies focused on non-institutional settings, it is of interest to learn whether L2 learners make use of this non-linguistic feature in a formal, task-focused setting. Furthermore, given that it has been established that attitude-related factors play a role in the decision-making process in telecollaboration, and choices such as language use and communication styles as well as non-linguistic factors such as emoticons and Facebook "likes" are important, this study examines the following research questions:

1. What linguistic choices did members make that facilitated or hindered their task negotiations?
2. What non-linguistic choices did members make that facilitated or hindered their task negotiations?

The next section will provide a detailed description of project stages, focus teams, and the data collection and analysis procedure.

3   Methodology

In this classroom-based case study,[3] Author 1 (principal investigator) co-designed the project with her colleague in Germany and taught the course in Hong Kong. She was the researcher-instructor. Author 2 was the project's teaching assistant and primary research assistant, who was part of the project from the planning stages onward, and Author 3 was the secondary research assistant, who came on board toward the end of the project. Both Authors 2 and 3 were participant-observers in the study. Triangulating different *"slices of data"* (Glaser & Strauss, 1967: 65, emphasis in original)

---

3   The focus team data presented here are from a previously unanalyzed subset of a larger set of data (see Fuchs, 2018, 2019).

from Facebook interactions and post-questionnaires[4] served the purpose to understand categories such as "accommodating propositions," or "pragmatic presupposition" from different viewpoints. The triangulation of data is in line with the emic and holistic principles of an ethnographic approach (van Lier, 1988). In order to provide "information-rich cases" and to go beyond typical and representative cases (Antoniadou & Dooly, 2017: 252), focus teams were chosen specifically based on their inter-group and intra-group compositions including cultural and linguistic backgrounds, and task performance, as specified in Table 1 below.

3.1 Task Stages

Since one goal was to model for Hong Kong (hereinafter HK) and German (hereinafter DE) participants how social media can afford online engagement and collaborative writing in the language classroom, the telecollaborative teams used social media tools to communicate and participated in three sequential project stages (see O'Dowd & Ware, 2009). Task content was based on chapters on linguistic and educational topics from the HK textbook.[5] HK members were graded for all tasks.

Stage 1: Introductions and themed discussions

The purpose of Stage 1 was for participants to get to know each other, their contexts, express goals and expectations for the project through (a) individual introductions and (b) team videos, as well as comment on their peers' posts using the comment function on Facebook. Next, each team engaged in procedural negotiation for a team name and a team philosophy, which they subsequently posted on their Facebook group site. Afterwards, students posted responses to theme-based Facebook discussions led by instructor prompts.

Stage 2: Comparing and contrasting educational contexts in a literature review

From Stage 2 onwards, telecollaborative teams engaged in procedural negotiation to consolidate the division of labor and timeline. First, members jointly negotiated a topic of interest for further research based on the themed discussions in the previous stage (see Table 1 below for topic choices). In

4   The post-questionnaire elicited information on participants' motivation regarding the telecollaboration and their satisfaction with final outcomes.
5   Mooney, A., & Evans, B. (2015). *Language, Society and Power: An Introduction* (4th ed.). London: Routledge.

this stage, students compared and contrasted their socio-institutional and educational systems (HK, China, Germany). Next, they developed research questions about their topic, and conducted research before collaboratively writing a Literature Review on Google Docs.

Stage 3: Publishing recommendations on a jointly designed team website

In Stage 3, which also encompassed procedural negotiation, teams posted a synthesis of their findings from the Literature Review and generated recommendations, which they then posted on their team website on Wix.[6]

3.2 Participants and Focus Teams

Participants in the eight-week telecollaboration included 58 English majors in a master-level sociolinguistics core course at a HK public research institution, who telecollaborated with 15 EFL student-teachers in an elective course in language teaching and new media at a DE public education institution. In HK, students self-selected their 11 HK teams; a few weeks after, when the German course started, the DE instructor paired his students with the HK teams. While it was desirable to have pairs of students on the German side for mutual support, numbers had to match the 11 HK teams. This meant that some DE members were chosen by the instructor to work solo. In the present study, out of the original set of 11 HK–DE teams, four focus teams were selected after the telecollaboration for subsequent data analysis. Table 1 shows the composition of these four focus teams (1, 2, 8, 11), their topics, linguistic and cultural backgrounds, and task performance. Names are pseudonyms,[7] and all data are verbatim. Interaction during team formation took place primarily on the instructor-created Facebook[8] site for the project. For intra-team negotiations, teams could choose any social media tool (e.g., WhatsApp, WeChat, Facebook Messenger).

---

6 Wix is a tool for website design.
7 Pseudonyms were assigned by Authors 2 and 3.
8 The HK instructor created a closed FB group site, and students logged in with their private accounts. Facebook was used based on Author 1's positive experience with the tool for discussion in a 2016 telecollaboration between HK and the US. Originally, for the present study, the instructors planned to use Google Apps because of the multi-functionality of Blogger, Google Sites, Google Docs, and Google Hangouts; however, this was not possible due to the lack of access in Mainland China for those students who were going back after graduation. Google Docs was used because documents can be easily downloaded.

Table 1. HK focus teams

Team names/Topics	Linguistic/Cultural background	Task performance
1 *Sevensome Travelistas* Chan-Chong, Honey, Kerry, Mary, Caitlin *Petra, Lotte* "EMI vs. CLIL in secondary education"	1 Cantonese/HK 4 Mandarin/Mainland 2 DE	High scores in all task stages
2 *4x2* Judy, Annie, Venus, Carla, Carmen, Elsa *Ada, Sofia* "Critical reading/writing skills"	6 Mandarin/Mainland 2 DE	High score in Stage 2, significantly lower score in Stage 3
8 *Magic 10* Madison, Cecile, Felicia, Tina, Madeleine, Connie, Edith, Sumaya *Max, Adelbert* "Gender stereotypes in textbooks"	4 Cantonese/HK 4 Mandarin/Mainland 2 DE	High scores in all task stages
11 *The Carpenters* April, Yu, Rikki, Kala *Erika* "Different teaching approaches"	4 Cantonese/HK 1 DE	High score in Stage 2, significantly lower score in Stage 3

In Team 1, four students were from Mainland China and one was from HK. In Team 2, all students were all from Mainland China, while in Team 11, all were from HK. Team 8, the largest team, had an equal mix of students from HK and Mainland China. All the teams had two German partners with the exception of Team 11, which had one. With regard to task performance, the four teams were representative of high-achieving (Teams 1, 8) and low-achieving (Teams 2, 11) teams.

3.3 Data Collection and Analysis

This case study triangulates data from social media and post-questionnaires. The data were a subset from a broader ethnographic analysis of participants and are qualitative and exploratory in nature. Descriptive quantitative data from Likert Scale items in the questionnaires were generated by Qualtrics. Qualitative data from Facebook and the post-questionnaires were coded by Authors 2 and 3 using MAXQDA. Codes taken verbatim from the subjects, or *in vivo* codes (Strauss & Corbin, 1998), from Facebook interactions were annotated thematically in MS Word and grouped into categories (e.g., L1 use, emoticon use, constructive communication style).

4 Results

With regard to Research Question 1 (What linguistic choices did members make that facilitated or hindered their task negotiations?), we examined L1 use and other linguistic sources (e.g., adjectives, adverbs, phrases, exclamation marks) to express agreement or validation.

In terms of the use of the L1, in Stage 1, during the themed Facebook discussions, two instances of L1 use were identified, one by HK2[9] and one by HK8. After having read the textbook chapter on Language and Ethnicity, participants were asked to provide examples from their first language.

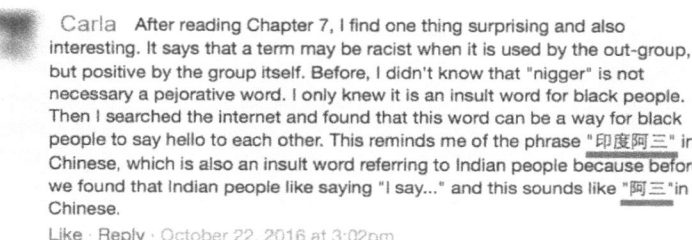

Figure 1. Team 2, Facebook Prompt 1 (emphasis added)

As seen in Figure 1, Carla (HK2) showed critical cultural awareness when drawing parallels between a derogatory term in English for African-Americans and a derogatory term in Chinese for Indians. Yet, when she used the phrase "印度阿三" (which means literally, "India number three," a pejorative term in Chinese) in her native language, she did not provide a translation in the lingua franca. While most of Carla's HK classmates were able to understand Mandarin, the instructor, her German colleague and his students were not.

Similarly, in the fourth Facebook prompt (Global Englishes), Felicia (HK8) provided a link to a Chinese article about US President Trump, which was published by a Mainland website (Figure 2).

---

9   Abbreviations are used for purposes of brevity: for instance, HK2 stands for "Hong Kong Team 2."

Figure 2. Team 8, Facebook Prompt 4

Unlike Carla, who explained the use of the four Chinese characters in English, Felicia did not provide any further explanations or an English translation for the article that she posted. In contrast, DE8 partners Adelbert and Max posted German examples with English translations in the commenting functions, which demonstrates perspective-taking. For example, in his Facebook Prompt 4 response, Adelbert posted a link to an article from *Der Spiegel Online*[10] about Russian President Putin, US President Trump, and Chinese President Xi along with an English translation. Likewise, his colleague Max provided a translation of an interview from the same news magazine on a similar political topic. Neither of them presupposed that their peers overseas would be able to understand the German original.

During Stage 3, when the teams had to finalize their websites, all four teams relied heavily on text messaging and sending pictures or videos. In Team 2, instances of L1 use resulted in a rather aggressive communication style. HK members used Mandarin for discussion in their intra-team chats without providing English translations or explanations (cf. Carla's explanation of her use of Chinese in Figure 1); DE partners Ada and Sofia raised this issue directly as shown below in Figure 3.

Here, one of the DE2 members (first turn) expressed the DE team's confusion and possible frustration by diverging from a conversational tone ("Girls we really don't get your plans."). Next, she recommended that their team discusses in English "all the time." Although one of the HK members replied immediately after the other DE member commented (second turn), the HK member was unresponsive to her DE partner's request but shifted the topic to the organization of the Wix website they had been working

10 An internationally renowned German news magazine.

102 *Understanding Attitude in Intercultural Virtual Communication*

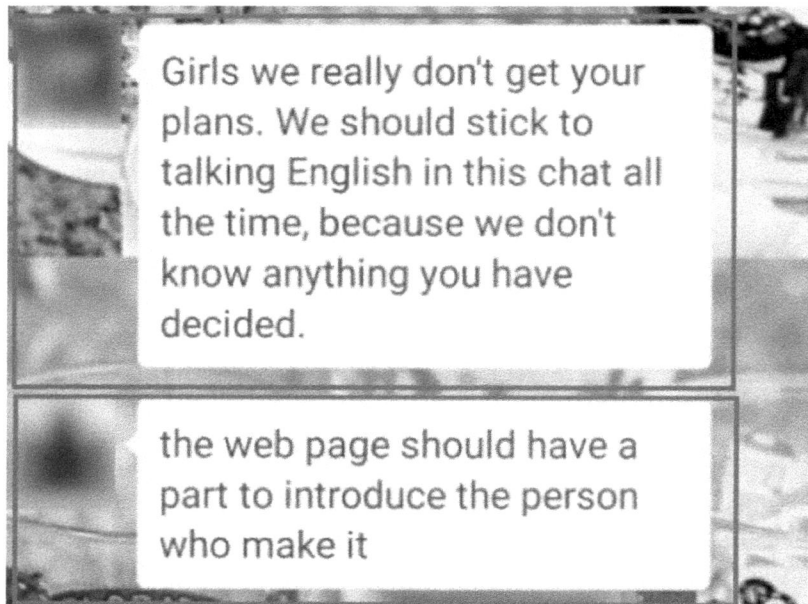

Figure 3. Team 2, WeChat (12/8/16, emphasis added)

on. DE2 members Ada and Sofia further stated in their post-questionnaire responses that they felt excluded because their HK partners texted in Chinese to discuss something that concerned only them: "[HK members] discussed their ideas in their group but not exactly with us. In our group chat, they wrote in Chinese most of the time. So the communication within their group was good, but not with us" (Sofia). Likewise, Ada (DE2) rated her motivation for the telecollaboration "unmotivated." Regarding the last stage of the project she said: "I didn't have the feeling that we were working in a group at all." She felt there was a "[l]ack of team spirit – [as there were] two separate teams (Chinese + Germans)." Sofia (DE2) concurred that the final product "was not a group outcome." This implies that their intra-team relationship was adversely affected. HK members for their part during this final stage of the project, gave their DE partners the option of working on either the "home page" or the "about us page" but not the main content pages of their joint Wix website.

In addition to the L1, participants also used a variety of other sources to express agreement and validation to elaborate on and extend their topic discussions. Team 1, for instance, appeared more successful than Teams 2 or 11 in that their constructive communication style of making concrete suggestions enabled them to move their task procedures forward.

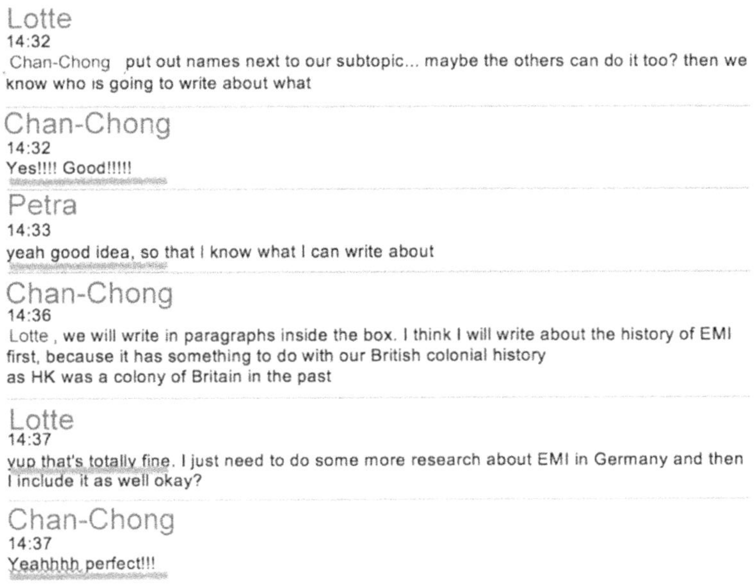

Lotte
14:32
Chan-Chong put out names next to our subtopic... maybe the others can do it too? then we know who is going to write about what

Chan-Chong
14:32
Yes!!!! Good!!!!!

Petra
14:33
yeah good idea, so that I know what I can write about

Chan-Chong
14:36
Lotte , we will write in paragraphs inside the box. I think I will write about the history of EMI first, because it has something to do with our British colonial history as HK was a colony of Britain in the past

Lotte
14:37
yup that's totally fine. I just need to do some more research about EMI in Germany and then I include it as well okay?

Chan-Chong
14:37
Yeahhhh perfect!!!

Figure 4. Team 1, Facebook Messenger (11/3/16, emphasis added)

Figure 4 shows an excerpt from Team 1's discussion of the Literature Review in Stage 2. This excerpt is representative of how this team used positive feedback to show agreement or positive judgment toward each other's propositions. Specifically, Chan-Chong acknowledged Lotte's ideas by exclaiming: "Yes!!!! Good!!!!!" and "Yeahhhh perfect!!!" Chan-Chong's complimenting behavior appears genuine, as expressed in her use of the adjective "perfect" followed by several exclamation marks. When Chan-Chong proposed another idea, Lotte responded: "yup that's totally fine." While Lotte's statement also expresses agreement, it does not come across in the same complimenting way because she uses the term "fine" (albeit accentuated by the adverb "totally") and ends with a period, not with an exclamation mark. Moreover, Team 1 displays a constructive communication style in that they combined agreement with specific suggestions for next steps to take. For example, Lotte took the lead in writing down names next to subtopics for easier recognition and suggested others did the same. Next, Chan-Chong specified what the HK team would tackle next ("write about the history of EMI"), which then prompted Lotte's proposal to do more research on EMI in Germany. When further discussing their ideas for their EMI versus CLIL topic, Lotte and Petra (DE1) made sure to clarify what they did not understand, e.g., "Okay what do you mean by drawbacks then? Sorry I'm confused" or "okay, I thought we need 5 parts because we are 7. Am I wrong?" Team 1 demonstrated responsiveness to each other's questions. Later in the project, Chan-Chong accommodated Lotte's wish to leave a photo on their website unchanged, which demonstrated responsiveness to other-initiated items.

Despite the constructive nature of Team 1's communication styles, based on statements by their DE partners, it became clear that in most teams, decisions were primarily made by the HK partners, which consequently limited discussion. According to Lotte's (DE1) post-questionnaire response, "HK team speaker responsible for the communication, already discussed and agreed on a lot of things without including us. only included on our request make our contributions." Lotte found it problematic that HK students were making "decisions on 'one side' and simply informing the others." This shows that HK students were not inclusive of their partners' opinions in that there was no validation, and that the collaborative nature of the project tasks was thus at odds with the division of labor in the team.

In Team 8, DE members also tended to accommodate HK members' suggestions but in a more passive and conforming way. For example, Madison (HK8) provided the following topic suggestion: "How about the topic about gender? This might be good for 'Magic 10' because hopefully we could have different perspectives from Boys and girls as well as east and west" (Facebook, November 2, 2016 at 7:19am). In his response, Max (DE8) expressed his interest and underscored the relevance of the topic by rephrasing her statement ("adding the differences of cultures"); yet, he did not further develop the idea or suggest how to proceed, thus not following up on his partner's topic suggestion. Similarly, in Team 11's topic negotiation for the Literature Review, Erika (DE11) agreed with her partners' suggestions as shown in Figure 5.

When April proposed an idea about the topic, HK partner Yu immediately commented the idea was "quite interesting." Their DE partner Erika agreed: "would be absolutely fine with me, as well :)". In the same exchange, when distributing the work for each person in Stage 2, Kala (HK11) suggested how much Erika (their sole German partner) should write: "You may write less for each. For some of them I am sure they are same as Hong Kong then basically there's not much to write too haha." Erika concedes: "you're probably right :) :)". In these examples, telecollaborative partners did not respond to or elaborate on questions, nor did they follow up on partner-initiated topics – except for agreeing with the proposition rather passively.

Choices and Attitudes in an East-West Telecollaboration 105

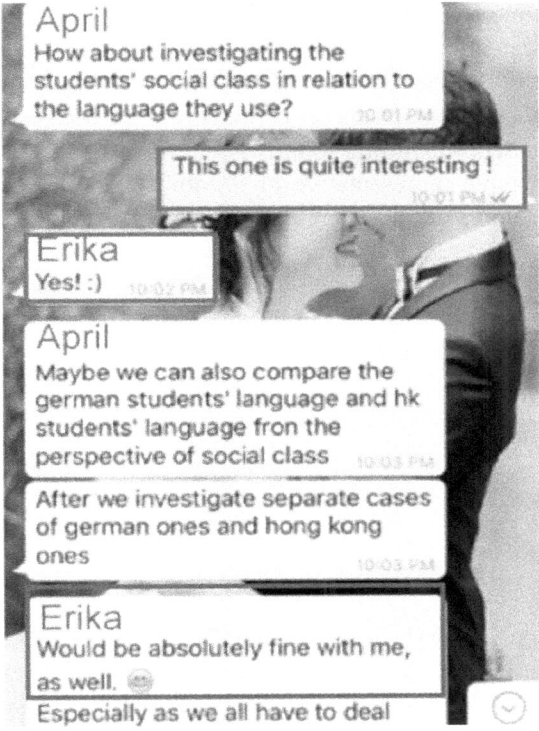

Figure 5. Team 11, WhatsApp (n.d., emphasis added)

In contrast, a more "aggressive" communication style was observed by HK8 at the end of Stage 2 (Figure 6).

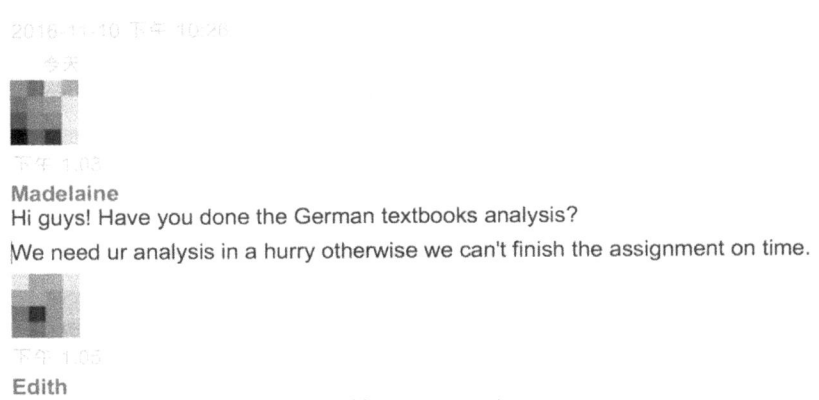

Figure 6. Team 8, Facebook Messenger

Here, HK8 members reminded their DE partners to submit their work when the due date for the Literature Review was approaching. Madeleine's urgent message ("We need ur analysis in a hurry") is underlined by Edith shortly after when she confronts her partners with the potential consequence of the HK members submitting solo.

Another example representative of the imbalance in decision-making comes from Team 11 during Stage 3. Overall, HK11 members took the initiative to share different references related to the topic with one another. Erika (DE11) typically conformed to her HK partner's suggestions without providing additional input. Once an issue was solved, she became passive and did not participate much in the discussion process any more. She was barely seen participating in the latter stage of the discussion except for asking for clarification (Figure 7).

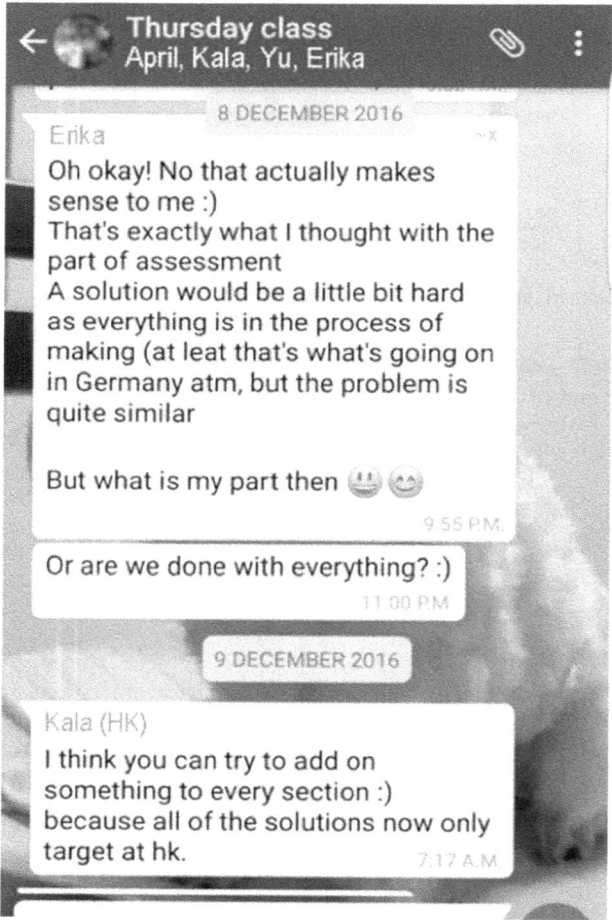

Figure 7. Team 11, WhatsApp (12/8/16)

Choices and Attitudes in an East-West Telecollaboration 107

The exchange in Figure 7 took place at the end of the HK project deadline and illustrates that Erika and her four HK partners seemed unclear about their work division and timeline. A day after Erika inquired about her part, Kala mitigated the face-threatening potential of her request – "I think you can try to add on something to every section" – by adding a smiley emoticon. This also added a more conversational tone to her request.

As Erika DE11 pointed out in her post-questionnaire, it was: "difficult to set up skype dates or dates to work together on the google doc with a large number of partners […]." The team's struggle to divide their work was most problematic during the final stages and could be attributed to the asymmetry in team member numbers (in addition to the time difference).

In terms of Research Question 2 (What non-linguistic choices did members make that facilitated or hindered their task negotiations?), teams used the Facebook "like" function and emoticons. Overall, the "like" function was used frequently. During the Team Videos discussions, there were a total of nine comments and 21 "likes," with HK1 being responsible for the bulk of the comments. Only a few members (e.g., DE8) commented on the actual content of the team videos or their project expectations. Mostly, the discussion was limited to one or no exchanges between members. For the Team Philosophy discussion, HK1 was the only team with multiple comments, while the other teams did not post comments or "likes."

In terms of emoticons, as can be seen in the chat, they were used regularly by all four focus teams. Teams used smiley emoticons primarily at the end of statements. For instance, Figure 8 shows that smiley emoticons were used for being polite, conversational, or courteous – "Ladys first :)" – or for negotiating work processes and procedures – "If you'd like to chat via Wechat just tell us :)".

11/4, 9:06pm

Max

[…]

1. skype/video chat - is there a date and time where most or all of you could online chat with us? Because we are so many I think once a week should be quite funny as well :)

2. nothing to add. but I think its alright to chat via facebook right?

3. Color code for google docs. Ladys first :) you're allowed to choose a color first and afterwards the boys :)

4. we heard from our classmates that some of them chat via Wechat. Its not familiar to us but looks like whatsapp, right? If you'd like to chat via Wechat just tell us :)

5. keep up the good work.

Cheers magic10

Figure 8. Team 8, Facebook Messenger

Figure 8 is also representative of the most frequent use of emoticons, i.e., at the end of a statement. Other examples of emoticon use in this study include making a request – "Please kindly check :)", Madison, 11/19, 1:49pm; asking for help – "If anyone can help, thanks :)", Sumaya, 11/21, 9:24am; or expressing gratitude to others – "thank you for the collaboration :)", Max, 11/21, 9:41pm.

5 Discussion

The purpose of this study was to explore what team members' linguistic and non-linguistic choices revealed about their attitudes towards their telecollaborative engagement. The first research question explored linguistic choices that members made that facilitated or hindered their team negotiation processes in task stages. The results of the study suggest that a constructive communication style that involved being sensitive toward each other by asking and clarifying questions facilitated interaction and moved the task forward, while L1 use did not.

In terms of L1 use, we observed that the use of and interaction in L1 Mandarin (HK) was one of the linguistic choices that hindered communication. Carla (HK2) and Felicia (HK8) set an exclusive precondition for their linguistic interaction with their German partners presupposing all members to understand Mandarin (Potts, 2016). Not explaining their Mandarin examples thus excluded the non-Mandarin speakers. Furthermore, the tendency among some HK members of the groups to converse in their L1, despite their fluency in English, during the actual negotiation processes – without restructuring or modifying their language – may have compromised a more cooperative or effective working relationship with DE partners (cf. Breen & Littlejohn, 2000). German students, however, had no way of deriving meaning because they did not know their partners' native language. While the use of the native language is in line with Darhower's (2008) findings that students use their L1 as a bilingual affordance when deemed appropriate, given that in this lingua franca exchange the German participants had no knowledge at all of their partners' L1, code-switching had the negative consequence of partners feeling excluded and may have thus impacted their attitude negatively.

If the use of the L1 hindered the interaction among students, members across teams tended to accommodate each other's suggestions, albeit often without engaging in more in-depth conversation. Agreeing with and accommodating partners aided the decision-making process and could mean that they shared the line of argumentation (Hoffstaedter & Kohn, 2016); another interpretation could be that this passiveness was a way to avoid disagreement. This would then support Helm's & Guth's (2012) findings about participants' tendency to agree with their telecollaborative partners and keep exchanges superficial to stay away from major conflicts. Another factor that supports the latter interpretation was the absence of inquisitive questions about each other or about their socio-institutional context. Here, however, it is unclear whether this was due to the participants' attitude towards working with one another, or to unfavorable external circumstances (e.g., timeline and asymmetrical team member numbers).

Learners' specific use of praise, compliments, and validation (or lack thereof) was a consequence of their telecollaborative interactions. For instance, the frequent interactions of Team 1 and how they elicited each other's opinions by reinforcing compliments with exclamation marks, and clarifying misunderstandings, led them to a constructive communication style. Members on both sides appeared enthusiastic, which they expressed through frequent praise, compliments, and validation when working on the tasks (Hoffstaedter & Kohn, 2016; Sanchez, 2015). One reason could be the concept of "face" in Asian cultures; "interpersonal communication in Chinese is a 'relationship game'" (Chang, 2008: 310), and maintaining positive face is of high importance. It also supports Lewis's (2005) suggestion that Chinese speakers are courteous, amiable, and compromising. Yet, the two low-scoring teams (8 and 11), on the other hand, displayed more hindering communication issues such as L1 use or "aggressive" or "passive" communication styles (González-Navarro, et al., 2010). It is possible that in Teams 8 and 11, HK students felt under time pressure to complete the task, and therefore were more direct and less courteous (Günther, 1993). This may have put telecollaborative partners on the spot and thus resulted in resentment and negative attitudes.

HK members also came up with their team topic and developed their content rather quickly by themselves – up to the point where DE students felt excluded. This was not productive for jointly making key decisions. While this shows that teams did not appear to maintain a "relationship of equality" (Byram, 1997: 91), it is unclear if this was due to participants' attitudes toward each other, or was the culmination of a number of socio-institutional constraints (Basharina, 2007) that prevented a more in-depth discussion about each other's contexts and experiences and may have compromised a more balanced approach with DE members. It is also possible that HK members felt more pressed for time due to grading pressure and coordination difficulty with a large number of team members. The fact that they outnumbered their DE partners by far may have also resulted in their feeling more responsible for project results.

The second question explored the non-linguistic choices team members made that facilitated or hindered their team negotiation processes. Emoticon use aided team negotiations, whereas "liking" on Facebook (which came at the expense of more elaborate discussion in the comment section) did not facilitate the process. While "liking" each other's posts on Facebook served as acknowledgement, the "likes" were accompanied by little or no interaction in the comment section. Learners might have used the "like" function as a way to bond with their groupmates and create a positive environment. They did not use the "dislike" (thumbs-down) function in response to their partners' posts, which indicates that they were either in full agreement with everything, or that they tried to keep a positive rapport and create a friendly environment. Whereas the "like" button can demonstrate a positive attitude and aid in establishing rapport quickly when using it for bonding or gratification purposes (Ozane et al., 2017; Xu et al., 2007), in the present study, "liking" seemed less conducive to team negotiation processes. In fact, it may have come at the expense of a more in-depth discussion in the Facebook comment function, especially in the beginning stage of the project where participants review each other's experiences and expectations, which sets the tone for subsequent interactions. Unlike emoticons, which offer a variety of different options, a "like" has only two response options (like/dislike as expressed in the thumbs-up and thumbs-down icons on Facebook), and may thus not be further discussed in the comment function – especially if it is followed by more "likes." While it does not come as a surprise that students would choose the immediate agreement function of a thumbs-up to show validation, it seemed odd that not more students would use the Facebook text comment function when it was a task requirement (e.g., Stage 1). The fact that there was little text-based response to each other's introductions could be interpreted as a lack of interest in better getting to know their partners and their socio-institutional and educational environments. This may seem surprising given that the two contexts were different culturally and linguistically from one another. Yet, it could have been precisely this distance that the language student teachers in this study may have perceived as not relevant for their future English teaching career. Or, the lack of responses could have simply been due to a lack of time given the labor-intensive nature of the collaborative tasks.

Teams used smiley emoticons frequently throughout their conversations. This served the purpose of positioning themselves positively in the communication with their telecollaborative partners (Derks et al., 2007; Xu et al., 2007). Similar to the "like" button on Facebook, the use of smiley emoticons can be reflective of a positive attitude. Emoticon use was observed especially at the end of participants' posts and when making propositions as an expansion of text (Dresner & Herring, 2010) in that a smiley, for instance, can reinforce a positive statement or mitigate a negative one. The conversational tone a smiley creates can have a positive impact on their group dynamics (see Ware, 2005). The fact that students used them so frequently, though, may have resulted in a decreased impact (Walther & D'Addario, 2001) in that students may not have paid attention anymore to the meaning of emoticons when they occurred at the end of most statements. If the smiley becomes a default, statements without smileys could then be interpreted as a negative attitude towards either their teammates or the task, or both.

As teams moved closer to their first submission deadline (the Literature Review), emoticon use became more infrequent and communication styles more direct and less mitigated, which supports findings by Derks et al. (2007) that in task-oriented contexts, subjects used the fewest emoticons. Participants may have not engaged with each other more because they did not deem "off topic" exchanges relevant for task completion. It is likely that the formality of the Literature Review task, together with the approaching deadline, might have had students' focusing on the task accomplishment rather than on the development of friendships. In contrast, focusing on an exploration of telecollaborative partners' identities, however, can have a positive impact on students' views of and attitudes towards one another (Liaw & English, 2016).

6 Conclusion

The results of this study indicate that a constructive communication style was reflective of students' positive attitudes. In contexts where external circumstances (such as the tight timeline and asymmetrical team member numbers) may be overwhelming, how learners communicate with one another deserves explicit attention. Future research could thus focus on eliciting information about participants' communication style preferences in order to raise awareness and avoid any problems that may arise. Another issue that deserves attention is the use of L1 in lingua franca exchanges where students' L1s are different such as Mandarin and German and where L1 use may lead to negative attitudes and frustration. It is therefore critical to discuss with participants the need to use the lingua franca as well as potential consequences this may have for team negotiation and decision-making. It could also be of interest to examine in more detail the positive or negative impact of students' use of emoticons or "likes" in their negotiation processes. To this end, students could annotate some of their transcripts retroactively commenting on their specific instances of use (agreement, validation, mitigation, etc.).

Furthermore, the immediacy of non-linguistic choices available may impact how quickly participants accommodate each other's propositions and thus prevent more in-depth discussion, as was seen in most focus teams. Nonetheless, in an asymmetrical telecollaboration such as the present one, having these resources available may help participants keep in touch more easily. This deserves a systematic analysis – especially from the perspective of different usages in the East–West contexts.

The limitations of this study are as follows. First, the main focus of analysis was on the Hong Kong context because the authors were located there. Second, only a limited number of focus team participants filled out all post-questionnaire questions – in addition to the small overall pool of participants of the four focus groups. In order to get a fuller picture, all teams would need to be analyzed. Third, with regard to the analysis of the chat data, teams had been encouraged to submit their full conversations; yet, some provided selected excerpts of their private chat discussions and the authors in HK had no direct access to intra-team exchanges by DE students. In order to get a fuller picture, students could be asked to use Facebook exclusively; however, it might come at the expense of negotiation efficiency if teams cannot choose the tool that is the most convenient for them. Fourth, participants' perspectives were limited to questionnaire responses, when focus-team interviews could have provided further insight into participants' attitudes and motivation.

From a pedagogical perspective, this telecollaboration provided participants in Hong Kong the opportunity to explore similarities and differences between their own and the Chinese and German socio-institutional and educational systems. It was hoped that the process of analyzing and publishing their results on a joint website would encourage students to demonstrate openness towards each other's perspectives. Despite not having fully achieved our purpose, we believe that collecting regular participant reflections on initial beliefs and expectations – and how they might change throughout the project – can shed some light on students' attitudes towards their partners and this mode of learning, especially against the backdrop of the potential of telecollaborative tasks in an exam-based learning culture.

References

Ajzen, I., & Fishbein, M. (2005). The influence of attitudes on behavior. In D. Albarracín, B. T. Johnson, & M. P. Zanna (eds.), *The Handbook of Attitudes* (pp. 173–221). Mahwah, NJ: Erlbaum.

Antón, M., & Dicamilla, F. (2002). Socio-cognitive functions of L1 collaborative interaction in the L2 classroom. *The Modern Language Journal*, 83(2), 233–247. https://doi.org/10.1111/0026-7902.00018

Antoniadou, V., & Dooly, M. (2017). Educational ethnography in blended learning environments. In E. Moore & M. Dooly (eds.), *Qualitative Approaches to Research on Plurilingual Education* (pp. 237–263). Research-publishing.net. https://doi.org/10.14705/rpnet.2017.emmd2016.630

Basharina, O. K. (2007). An activity theory perspective on student-reported contradictions in international telecollaboration. *Language Learning & Technology*, 11(2), 82–103. http://dx.doi.org/10125/44105

Belz, J. A. (2003). Linguistic perspectives on the development of intercultural competence in telecollaboration. *Language Learning & Technology*, 7(2), 68–117.

Breen, M. P., & Littlejohn, A. (2000). The significance of negotiation. In M. P. Breen & A. Littlejohn (eds.), *Classroom Decision-making: Negotiation and Process Syllabuses in Practice* (pp. 5–38). Cambridge: Cambridge University Press.

Byram, M. (1997). *Teaching and Assessing Intercultural Communicative Competence*. Clevedon: Multilingual Matters.

Chang, Y. Y. (2008). Cultural "faces" of interpersonal communication in the U.S. and China. *Intercultural Communication Studies*, XVII(1), 299–313.

Çiftçi, E. Y, & Savaş, P. (2018). The role of telecollaboration in language and intercultural learning: A synthesis of studies published between 2010 and 2015. *ReCALL*, 30(3), 278–298. https://doi.org/10.1017/S0958344017000313

Darhower, M. (2008). The role of linguistic affordances in telecollaborative chat. *CALICO Journal*, 26(1), 48–69.

Derks, D., Bos, A. E. R., & von Grumbkow, J. (2007). Emoticons and social interaction on the Internet: the importance of social context. *Computers in Human Behavior*, 23, 842–849. https://doi.org/10.1016/j.chb.2004.11.013

Dresner, E., & Herring, S. (2010). Functions of the nonverbal in CMC: Emoticons and illocutionary force. *Communication Theory*, 20, 249–268. https://doi.org/10.1111/j.1468-2885.2010.01362.x

Fuchs, C. (2018). Of tools and tasks: A Hong Kong–Germany telecollaboration. *The European Journal of Applied Linguistics and TEFL Special Issue on Educational Technology in English Language Learning and Teaching*, 7(2), 137–156.

Fuchs, C. (2019). Critical incidents and cultures-of-use in a Hong Kong-Germany telecollaboration. *Language Learning & Technology*, 23(3), 74–97. http://hdl.handle.net/10125/44697.

Glaser, B. G., & Strauss, A. L. (1967). *The Discovery of Grounded Theory: Strategies for Qualitative Research*. Chicago: Aldine Publishing Company.

González-Navarro, P., Orengo, V., Zornoza, A., Ripoll, P., & Peiró, J. M. (2010). Group interaction styles in a virtual context: The effects on group outcomes. *Computers in Human Behavior*, 26, 1472–1480. https://doi.org/10.1016/j.chb.2010.04.026

Günthner, S. (1993). *Diskurs strategien in der interkulturellen Kommunikation: Analysen deutsch-chinesischer Gespräche*. Tübingen: Niemeyer. https://doi.org/10.1515/9783110953459

Helm, F., & Guth, S. (2012). Open intercultural dialogue: Educator perspectives. *Journal of E-Learning and Knowledge Society*, 8(3), 129–139.

Hoffstaedter, P., & Kohn, K. (2016). Cooperative autonomy in online lingua franca exchanges: A case study on foreign language education in secondary schools. In S. Jager, M. Kurek, & B. O'Rourke (eds.), *New Directions in Telecollaborative Research and Practice: Selected Papers from the Second Conference on Telecollaboration in Higher Education* (pp. 291–296). Research-publishing.net. https://doi.org/10.14705/rpnet.2016.telecollab2016.520

Jager, S., Kurek, M., & O'Rourke, B. (eds.). (2016). *New Directions in Telecollaborative Research and Practice: Selected Papers from the Second Conference on Telecollaboration in Higher Education*. Dublin, Ireland: Research-Publishing.net. https://doi.org/10.14705/rpnet.2016.telecollab2016.9781908416414

Johnson, D. W., Johnson, R. T., & Smith, K. A. (1991). *Active Learning: Cooperation in the College Classroom*. Edina, MN: Interaction Book Company.

Kost, C. (2008). Use of communication strategies in a synchronous CMC environment. In S. Magnan (ed.), *Mediating Discourse Online* (pp. 153–189). Philadelphia: John Benjamins. https://doi.org/10.1075/aals.3.11kos

Lantolf, J. P., & Thorne, S. L. (2007). Sociocultural theory and second language learning. In B. van Patten & J. Williams (eds.), *Theories in Second Language Acquisition* (pp. 201–224). Mahwah, NJ: Lawrence Erlbaum.

Lewis, R. D. (2005). *Finland, Cultural Lone Wolf*. Yarmouth, ME: Intercultural Press.

Liaw, M.-L., & Bunn-Le Master, S. (2010). Understanding telecollaboration through an analysis of intercultural discourse. *Computer Assisted Language Learning*, 23(1), 21–40. https://doi.org/10.1080/09588220903467301

Liaw, M.-L., & English, K. (2016). Identity and addressivity in the "Beyond These Walls" program, *System*, 64, 74–86. https://doi.org/10.1016/j.system.2016.12.005

Magnan, S. (ed.). (2008). *Mediating Discourse Online*. Philadelphia: John Benjamins. https://doi.org/10.1075/aals.3

Maiz-Arévalo, C. (2013). Just click "Like": Computer-mediated responses to Spanish compliments. *Journal of Pragmatics*, 51, 47–67. https://doi.org/10.1016/j.pragma.2013.03.003

O'Dowd, R. (2018). From telecollaboration to virtual exchange: state-of-the-art and the role of UNI Collaboration in moving forward. *Journal of Virtual Exchange*, 1, 1–23. Research-publishing.net. https://doi.org/10.14705/rpnet.2018.jve.1

O'Dowd, R., & Ritter, M. (2006). Understanding and working with "failed communication" in telecollaborative exchanges. *CALICO Journal*, 23, 623–642. https://doi.org/10.1558/cj.v23i3.623-642

O'Dowd, R., & Ware, P. (2009). Critical issues in telecollaborative task design. *Computer Assisted Language Learning*, 22(2), 173–188. https://doi.org/10.1017/S0958344017000313

Ozane, M., Cueva Navas, A., Mattila, A. S., & Van Hoof, H. B. (2017). An investigation into Facebook "liking" behavior an exploratory study. *Social Media + Society*, 3(2), 1–12. https://doi.org/10.1177/2056305117706785

Potts, C. (2016). Presupposition and implicature. In S. Lappin & C. Fox (eds.), *The Handbook of Contemporary Semantic Theory* (pp. 1–52). New Jersey: Wiley-Blackwell.
https://web.stanford.edu/~cgpotts/manuscripts/potts-blackwellsemantics.pdf.
https://doi.org/10.1002/9781118882139.ch6

Sadler, R., & Dooly, M. (2016). Twelve years of telecollaboration: What we have learnt. *ELT Journal*, 70(4), 401–413. https://doi.org/10.1093/elt/ccw041

Sanchez, B. J. (2015). *The Dynamics of Social Interaction in Telecollaborative Tandem Exchanges.* Doctoral dissertation, University of Iowa, 2015. https://doi.org/10.17077/etd.201gog4v

Strauss, A., & Corbin, J. (1998). *Basics of Qualitative Research: Techniques and Procedures for Developing Grounded Theory* (2nd ed.). London: Sage.

van Lier, L. (1988). *The Classroom and the Language Learner.* London, New York: Longman.

Vandergriff, I. (2014). A pragmatic investigation of emoticon use in nonnative / native speaker text chat. *Language@Internet*, 11, Article 4.

Walther, J. B., & D'Addario, K. (2001). The impacts of emoticons on message interpretation in computer-mediated communication. *Social Science Computer Review*, 19, 324–347. https://doi.org/10.1177/089443930101900307

Ware, P. (2005). "Missed" communication in online communication: Tensions in a German-American telecollaboration. *Language Learning & Technology*, 9(2), 64–89.https://doi.org/10.1111/j.1540-4781.2005.00274.x

West, L. E. (2015). *Responding (or not) on Facebook: A Sociolinguistic Study of Liking, Commenting, and Other Reactions to Posts.* Doctoral dissertation, Georgetown University, ProQuest Dissertations Publishing, 2015.

Xu, L., Xu, Y., & Yi, C. (2007). Emotional expression online: The impact of task, relationship and personality perception on emoticon usage in Instant Messenger, 11th Pacific-Asia Conference on Information Systems. Retrieved February 20, 2019, from http://citeseerx.ist.psu.edu/viewdoc/download;jsessionid=4145059E B78C3FBC5D03EB34B5DCD97B?doi=10.1.1.617.7692&rep=rep1&type=pdf

About the Authors

Carolin Fuchs is Teaching Professor in the World Languages Center at Northeastern University, where she also coordinates online teaching and learning for the College of Social Sciences and Humanities. She holds a PhD in English Studies from the Justus-Liebig University Giessen and an MA in TESOL from the Middlebury Institute of International Studies at Monterey. Her research interests include different aspects of online learning and telecollaboration (e.g., learner autonomy, task design). Carolin has published in *CALICO Journal*, *CALL*, *Language Learning & Technology*, *ReCALL*, and *TESOL Quarterly*. She currently serves as one of the Editors-in-Chief of the *CALICO Journal*.

Tsz Yan (Fion) Lo currently teaches English and interview skills at Hong Kong Glory Education & Technology Limited, which is headquartered in Shenzhen, China. She holds an MA in Education from the University College London (UCL) and a BA in English from the City University of Hong Kong. Fion was a Research and Teaching Assistant in the Department of English at the City University of Hong Kong between 2016 and 2017. Her research interests include educational technology, telecollaboration, and social media language learning. She has presented at the American Association for Applied Linguistics 2019 Conference in Atlanta.

Sneha Thapa holds an MA in Applied Linguistics from University College London (UCL). She coordinates a community project for the Nepalese community in the United Kingdom, which has been funded by The National Lottery Community Fund, and she also teaches English and Math. Prior to that, Sneha worked as a Research Assistant at the City University of Hong Kong between 2016 to 2017, where she completed her BA in English Studies. She is interested in the areas of identity, ageing, and migration. She has presented at the American Association for Applied Linguistics 2019 Conference in Atlanta.

5 Understanding L2 Teachers' Attitudes via Their Uses of Multimodal Resources in Telecollaboration

Meei-Ling Liaw and Sabrina Priego

1 Introduction

Intercultural competence is an essential requirement for teachers in the globalized world. Interculturally competent teachers understand the importance of intercultural sensitivity. They realize that the validity of one's frame of cultural reference may affect communication styles and behaviors in specific local and intercultural contexts. Telecollaboration, projects connecting internationally dispersed learners in parallel classes for social interaction and intercultural exchanges, has been reported to have positive effects on developing intercultural competence and digital literacies for teachers (Sadler & Dooly, 2016). O'Dowd (2016) points out that one of the emerging directions in telecollaborative learning is multimodal communication. The multimodal approach allows participants of telecollaboration to exploit a mix of words, images, and other resources to comprehend and communicate more effectively (Farías, Obilinovic, & Orrego, 2007) and thus should be inculcated in instructed second or foreign language (L2 or FL) settings (Berglund, 2009; Hampel, 2006; Hauck & Youngs, 2008). Teacher education programs play a critical role in preparing teachers to meet the needs of their students by creating contexts and experiences for pre-service and in-service teachers to cultivate their ability to integrate multimodal resources in teaching (Hauck & Kureck, 2017). In addition, the effects of telecollaboration for teacher education cannot be adequately interpreted without a sound understanding of how multimodal communication may affect teachers' attitudes or abilities to "decenter" (Byram, 1989) from pre-existing notions of language learning and teaching. In this chapter, we report on a telecollaborative project that provided L2 teachers in different countries with opportunities to engage in professional dialogues via multimodal means. We specifically focused on the participating teachers' attitudes and the changes during the telecollaboration.

2 Literature Review

2.1 Multimodal Literacy and Language Teacher Education

One of the emerging trends and new directions in telecollaboration is multimodal communication (O'Dowd, 2016). The multimodal approach allows learners to exploit a mix of words, images, and other resources to comprehend and express themselves. In language learning, it may help learners to communicate more effectively, enhance awareness of the target language, or even motivate learning (Farías et al., 2007). However, in telecollaboration, partners' levels of multimodal communicative competence may affect how they can benefit from the interaction (Hauck & Youngs, 2008). When students are not able to manage their communicative affordances, multimodality may not have an equalizing effect on their verbal interactions (Berglund, 2009). In some cases, the multimodality afforded by technology may even have adverse effects on communication (Hampel, 2006). Researchers thus assert that multimodal intercultural communication should be inculcated in instructed L2 or FL settings (Hampel, 2006; Hauck & Youngs, 2008).

To support students' new literacy needs, teacher education courses must create contexts and experiences for pre-service and in-service teachers to cultivate their ability to integrate multimodal resources in their teaching practices (Chandler, 2017; Ryan, Scott, & Walsh, 2010; Yi & Angay-Crowder, 2016). Early, Kendrick, & Potts (2015) argued for the need to bring issues of multimodality and meaning-making squarely into the center of language teachers' concerns. In fact, researchers and educators have been calling for a teacher education curriculum reform. The term "multimodal pedagogy" has been used to refer to "curriculum, pedagogy, and assessment practices focus[ed] on mode as a defining feature of communication in learning environments" (Stein, 2008: 121). As opposed to digital technologies, multimodal pedagogy is considered a more realistic depiction of digital technologies in teaching because it foregrounds creativity and effective communication as well as modal affordances in the classroom (Archer & Newfield, 2014).

2.2 Understanding Multimodal Communication

Dooly & Hauck (2012) argue that the transition from text to screen and the recognition of various communication channels have brought about a growing presence of multimodality and have rendered an imperative need to investigate multimodal communicative competence (MCC) or intercultural communicative competence (ICC) in telecollaborative projects. Similarly, Avgousti (2018) suggests that as multimodality in Web 2.0 tools and applications affects ICC development in multiple ways, more research on telecollaboration in multimodal environments needs to be conducted.

The effects of telecollaboration for teacher education cannot be adequately interpreted without a good understanding of multimodal communication. To understand multimodal communication, multimodal discourse analysis has been proposed and applied (Jaipal, 2009; Jewitt, 2017; Jones, 2013). From the multimodal discourse perspective, all modes consist of sets of semiotic resources that people use in specific moments and places to represent events and relationships; language, whether as speech or as writing, is one means among many that are available for representation and for making meaning. An analysis of speech or writing may only reveal the partial meaning that resides in the language (Kress, 2011). Multimodal discourse analysis is "an approach to discourse which focuses on how meaning is made through the use of multiple modes of communication" (Jones, 2013: 1). Based on this perspective, an analysis of the modal resources used by teachers or students may provide insights into the relationship between the use of semiotic resources and the production of knowledge, student/teacher subjectivity, and pedagogy (Jewitt, 2017).

The relationship between modes and media is intimate and complex; the development of technologies and the social practices governing their uses in different contexts affects the functions and significance of various modes (Kress & van Leeuwen, 1996). Research has been conducted to understand the ways in which modes are configured and made available for teaching and learning via new technologies. In the field of L2/FL learning for example, Malinowski & Nelson (2010) argue that understanding multimodality is crucial in all human communication and illustrate the complex interplay between language and multisemiotic composition in the context of digital storytelling. As for teaching, studies have looked into how the dynamic nature of the interplay of modalities has helped teachers make decisions on how to select and sequence modalities to support students' learning. For instance, Jaipal (2009) employed a four-level multimodal semiotics discourse analysis framework by extending Kress's model to illuminate meaning-making possibilities during the teaching of a science concept. However, in the area of L2/FL teacher education, especially in the context of telecollaboration for professional development, no research has been conducted to understand the meaning-making processes of L2 teachers from different cultural backgrounds from the multimodal perspective.

Technology plays a powerful role in the shaping of literacy practices. Even though computer-assisted language learning (CALL) and technology-enhanced language learning (TELL)[1] are already widely acknowledged as well-established academic and education disciplines and much research has been conducted to examine the impact of technology on language learning and teaching, they may not have made the impact on language teacher education that researchers and educators have generally expected (Hubbard, 2007; Kessler, 2006). The need for teacher education programs to provide teachers with adequate competency to integrate technologies in their instruction goes beyond language education. The European Union outlines a framework to ensure that European teachers in all fields of education are better equipped with and more willing to apply technology to their everyday teaching routines (Kelly, Grenfell, Allan, Kriza, & McEvoy, 2004). In other parts of the world, including Taiwan and Quebec, guidelines for curriculum development and material design also explicitly stipulate that technologies should be brought into classrooms to facilitate teaching and learning (Quebec Education Ministry, 2001; Taiwan Ministry of Education, 2016). CALL and TELL, despite having undergone stages of evolution in accordance with changes in beliefs of how languages are learned and with advancements of information technologies, have not been adequately used by language teachers to meet the needs of their students in today's globally connected world. The gap between what teachers do for school teaching and their students' use of technologies outside of the classroom still exists; the activities in the classroom are often top-down and teacher-controlled rather than student-centered (Dooly, 2010; Dooly & O'Dowd, 2018; Dooly & Sadler, 2013). As technological developments exert growing influence on our daily lives in general and play a significant role in shaping literacy practices, teachers and teacher educators have the responsibility to understand their impact.

---

1 The distinction between CALL and TELL is that the latter places direct importance on the media of communication made possible by technology, which itself often remains unseen, rather than on the computer itself (Bush & Roberts, 1997, cited in Patel, 2015).

2.3 Computer-Mediated Communication (CMC) and Language Teacher Intercultural Competence

The spread of Internet technology has changed the nature and the role of culture in language teaching. Increasingly, language learners "stress the relationality of self and others across multiple timescales in a decentered perspective" in which learners themselves construct social reality in the ongoing discourse (Kramsch, 2013: 67). The concept of intercultural communicative competence (ICC), theorized by Michael Byram in 1997, emphasizes the importance of engaging, through a foreign language, in intercultural communication and interaction with interlocutors with different culturally influenced values, beliefs, and assumptions.

Byram & Zarate (1997) offered an ICC framework comprising five *savoirs* that constitute intercultural competence: *savoirs* (knowledge of self and other; of interaction, individual and societal); *savoir apprendre/faire* (skills to discover and/or interact); *savoir comprendre* (skills to interpret and relate); *savoir s'engager* (critical cultural awareness, political education); *savoir être* (attitudes: relativizing self, valuing others). Byram, Gribkova, & Starkey (2002) point out that, on the one hand, knowledge and skills are usually the focus of language teaching; attitudes and values, on the other hand, are implicit objectives of a lesson. Nevertheless, teachers must respond to this inadequacy and help learners to "decenter, to make the strange familiar and the familiar strange" (Byram et al., 2002: 14). Intercultural competence is a crucial skill for teachers in all learning environments, especially in language classrooms where teachers are likely to play the role of mediators between communities and cultures (Byram & Feng, 2004; Durham, 2018).

Among studies on teacher interculturality in L2 teaching, Menard-Warwick (2008) explored how two teachers, one who lived in California and the other in Chile, constructed their intercultural identities and how they used their transnational experiences to develop intercultural competence and a meta-awareness of this competence when approaching cultural topics in their classrooms. The researcher concluded that transnational and intercultural teachers bring to English language teaching valuable pedagogical resources and this, in turn, facilitated teacher attitudinal changes.

As computer-mediated communication (CMC) becomes easily accessible and commonly used in education settings, international telecollaboration now functions as a means of experiential learning and model teaching in FL teacher education. Participation in such a partnership may facilitate the development of both ICC and critical media literacy (Müller-Hartmann, 2006).

2.4 Intercultural Telecollaboration and Teachers' Ability to "De-Center"

Teacher education programs may set up telecollaborative activities for knowledge sharing and enhancing of intercultural and instructional competence for teachers across different institutions or even cultures. Such projects and studies on the effects of telecollaboration on teacher education have yielded encouraging results. The intercultural telecollaborative project conducted by Keranen & Bayyurt (2006) paired up in-service teachers in Mexico and pre-service teachers in Turkey who used English for communication. The findings showed that the telecollaborative approach encouraged the participants to further their existing understanding of other cultures via such exchanges. Haley (2012) arranged for pre-service teacher candidates in China and in the US to have electronic exchanges. The participants discussed topics related to culture and teaching in the two countries. Similar to Keranen & Bayyurt's (2006) findings, Haley also found that the participants learned much about each other and shared more similarities than differences in regard to what they learned from such a cultural exchange (for example, why they want to become teachers, what they will contribute to the teaching profession, etc.).

In addition to linking teachers for intercultural discussions, some telecollaborative projects have been implemented for enhancing teacher pedagogical competence. For example, Innovating Teacher Education through ICT-Based Interaction employed telecollaboration to shift teachers in training in Spain and in the US from knowledge consumers to collaborative knowledge producers (Dooly, 2011). The researcher found that, in addition to the participants' previous knowledge, acceptance, experience, and willingness to adapt to the available communication channels, their interactions varied according to the available communication modes as they constructed "membership" identities in the virtual interaction. Along the same line of research, Dooly & Sadler's (2013) project introduced student teachers in Spain and in the US to innovative methods for communicative-based language learning. The results of this study suggest that the collaboration enhanced teacher development and attitude change through opportunities not available in more traditional teacher education classrooms and enabled pre-service teachers to make connections between theory and practice. In a more recent study, Altstaedter & Falasca (2015) linked two groups of participants in Argentina and in the US to explore how pre-service teachers' prior beliefs and experiences shaped their teaching selves. The researchers found that the intercultural communication experience affected the participants' current beliefs and attitudes. They concluded that their findings carry practical implications for teacher education programs.

Findings of telecollaboration for teacher education have indicated positive effects on teacher professional development. O'Dowd (2015), after consulting a large group of experts and experienced practitioners by employing the Delphi technique,[2] has developed a model of telecollaborative competence for teachers containing four sections – organizational, pedagogical, digital competencies, and attitudes and beliefs. Quite importantly, the model requires that teachers have open and tolerant attitudes of partner-teachers with "alternative pedagogical beliefs and aims" (O'Dowd, 2015: 12). He further urges that teacher educators and teachers put this model into action.

As the literature review shows, research on the effects of intercultural telecollaboration for L2 language teacher professional development is relatively new. Studies looking into the processes and effects of teacher telecollaboration through the lens of multimodal communication are few. In this chapter, we report on a study that addresses the multimodal communication aspects in teacher telecollaboration as well as the participating teachers' attitudes or ability to "decenter" (Byram, 1989). Because the design of the project provided opportunities for intercultural dialoguing of pedagogical issues, there were possibilities for decentering in this communication context by departing from one's existing knowledge of language teaching and learning.

This study examines the specificities and traits of multimodal discourse that account for the participants' intercultural competence development and socially constructed knowledge related to language teaching. In particular, it has sought to answer the following research questions:

1. What types of multimodal resources do L2 teachers use in a telecollaborative project for intercultural dialoguing of pedagogical issues?
2. How does the use of multimodal resources facilitate or hinder the development of L2 teachers' ability to "decenter" (Byram, 1989) from pre-existing notions of language learning and teaching?

3 Method

3.1 Participants and Settings

A total of 14 pre- and in-service L2/FL teachers who were taking graduate-level language education courses at three universities in Canada and Taiwan

2   The Delphi technique is a three-stage iterative questionnaire-based research technique that combines the findings of the literature with the input of practitioners.

participated in the study. At the university in Canada, all the students registered in an elective graduate-level course participated in the project. The group was composed of three Canadian students, one Italian student, one German student, and one Colombian student. The project was integrated into the course syllabus and represented 25% of the final mark. The eight Taiwanese participants who volunteered to take part in the project were from two universities in central Taiwan. The researchers of the project were also the instructors of the courses. Of the 14 participants, 10 had teaching experiences ranging from 2 to over 15 years. Some of the Canadian participants, in addition to speaking French, also spoke an additional language including Spanish, Italian, and German. The Taiwanese participants all spoke Mandarin Chinese.

The telecollaborative project was designed to provide the participants with opportunities to enhance their intercultural competence and professional knowledge via social constructive meaning-making processes. The design of the activities was informed by Halliday's (1989) social-semiotic framework and Kress & van Leeuwen's (2001) understanding of multimodality, which included the affordances of modes for making meaning through the new media; the tasks in the project prompted the participants to exchange information, engage in discussion via information technology, and create multimodal products to represent their co-constructed meanings.

3.2 Implementation Procedures

First, each of the participants introduced her/himself by posting one photo and a brief description of her/himself on a Padlet[3] file created by one of the instructors-researchers. The participants were then put into three groups. The members of each group consisted of participants from all three sites. The tasks for them to collaborate on were (1) discussing "Language teaching in the 21st century," (2) creating collages to summarize/conclude discussion results, and (3) jointly reflecting on the processes of intercultural collaboration by posting their afterthoughts on Google Docs. The instructors created Google Docs as platforms for group discussions. The platforms allowed the participants to express themselves in multiple modes and to co-construct multimodal compositions to represent their ideas. Other than Google Docs, they could choose other means for discussions. The collages summarizing discussion results were created by using Padlets too. Figure 1 illustrates the project design and implementation procedures.

---

3   Padlet (https://padlet.com) is a digital canvas that allows users to share and edit text, graphs, audio, and video files among themselves.

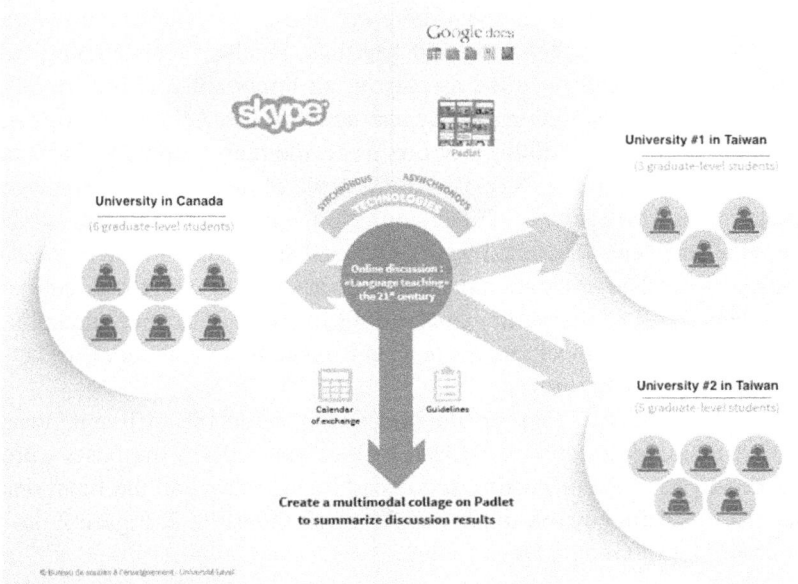

Figure 1. Project design and implementation procedures

3.3 Data Collection and Analysis

The data collected for the study included Google Docs discussions, the collages created, and joint reflections. One group also used Skype to communicate and posted their video recording of a Skype meeting on their collage. The audio recording was transcribed verbatim and coded as well.

For getting insights into how the different groups collaborated via multimodal means to communicate and to co-construct knowledge of the discussion topic, a four-level social semiotic discourse analysis was employed to analyze the collages, Google Docs discussions, and Skype meeting transcriptions. Jaipal (2009) and Jaipal Jamani (2011) extended Lemke's (1998, 2002) semiotics typology of meaning for discourse analysis and notions of multimodal communication proposed by Kress & van Leeuwen (2001) and constructed an analysis framework including presentational, organizational, orientational, and epistemological aspects. According to Lemke (1998), a language in use always creates three interdependent kinds of social and cultural meaning. They are (1) verbal presentations of events, activities, and relationships other than itself, (2) relations of parts to wholes within its own text and between itself and its contexts, and (3) social relationships among participants and points of view. The analysis framework extends Lemke's typology by considering an additional epistemological aspect of meaning to interpret how multimodal signs represent and communicate the nature of knowledge related to teaching and learning. Teachers' epistemological beliefs have long been regarded as playing an important role in virtually all aspects of decision-making about instruction (Gill, Ashton, & Algina, 2004; Sun, 2017; White, 2000). For our study, the representational aspects are the concepts/ideas/events related to the topic of discussion, "Language teaching in the 21st century." The organizational aspects focus on how the concepts/ideas/events discussed were organized and related in the intercultural discussion. The orientational aspects are associated with the affective/attitude capacities of the participants during intercultural communication. The epistemological aspects are the teachers' epistemological beliefs of language teaching and learning.

For data analysis, the group members who made the different posts were first identified to answer Research Question 1. Then the posts were sequenced by the time of posting and coded by modality and the functions of the four-level framework to answer Research Question 2. Figure 2 provides examples of Google Docs coding.

Student	posts	Sequence and Interplay of Modalities	Presentational	Organizational	Orientational	Epistemological	Other
A 6 October 2016, 20:01	Teachers in the 21st Century need the 6 C's. what do you guys think?	Written text of a question			open-minded, tentative	pedagogical knowledge can be socially constructed	Inviting input from other members
	[diagram]	A diagram of 6Cs of education for the future	presenting the 6Cs proposed by scholars	6Cs forming an integrated whole (equally important) (each component can be broken down to smaller parts/skills)	assertive, explanatory	the knowledge can be compartmentalized and organized, factual	
	The Seven Cs - 21st Century Lifelong Skills [diagram]	A diagram of 7Cs of 21st century lifelong skills	presenting the 7Cs proposed by scholars	7Cs forming an integrated whole (each component can be broken down to smaller parts/skills)	assertive, explanatory	the knowledge can be compartmentalized and organized, factual	
A 9 October 2016, 18:44	What images, videos, and/or text would you guys like to post on Padlet?	Written text of a question	n/a	n/a	Open-minded, tentative	Whole to part (deductive) pedagogical Knowledge can be socially constructed	Inviting others to post/contribute to the meaning-making
A 9 Octobe	[puzzle image]	Figure of a puzzle	Presenting learning goals for language, culture, and 21st	knowledge is consisted of smaller parts to form an integrated	assertive	knowledge can be compartmentalized and analyzed, knowledge is	taking initiative to provide input

Figure 2. Sample of data coding (Group 3)

Student	Transcript	Modalities	Presentational Meaning	Organizational Meaning	Orientational Meaning	Epistemological Meaning	Other
E	Ok so let's talk about what you guys think when we talk about 21st century language teachers what's the image that comes to your mind? I think the image that comes to my mind is a very busy teacher	verbal	Presenting the idea about images of busy teachers	n/a	positive	Social constructivist	Opening discussion Initiating idea of images of teachers
C	Oh I do agree I think it's also a very open one	verbal	Adding "openness" to "busy"	"Openness" is parallel to "busy"	Positive	Social constructivist	Agreeing to E's idea and adding a new idea
D	yeah	verbal	n/a	n/a	positive	Social constructivist	Agreeing with C
C	so they have like to be open to either like cultural suggestion from their students and from like the school their working at so they have to adapt to pretty much every environment that they can be in	verbal	Adding "cultural backgrounds of student" and "adaptive" to teaching environments	Supporting information of "openness"	positive	Social constructivist	adding new ideas to support what was proposed by E
D	yeah ok	verbal	n/a	n/a	positive	Social constructivist	Agreeing to C's points
B	and they also have to adapt to the new technologies	verbal	Adding "technology"	Supporting the idea of	positive	Social constructivist	Adding new idea for others

Figure 3. Example of Skype meeting coding

The verbatim transcription of the audio file was also analyzed by using the framework. Figure 3 gives examples of the coding of the audio recording transcription.

The reflective thoughts posted on another Google Docs discussion were analyzed qualitatively to understand, from participants' perspectives, how the technological tools, especially the multimodal affordances, were used and whether they were conducive to decentering processes, the processes of "mak[ing] the strange familiar and the familiar strange" (Byram, Gribkova, & Starkey, 2002: 14) in the ongoing multimodal discourse. Lastly, the finalized collages by the three groups were analyzed using the framework as well. The functions of each posting on the collages were identified. The analysis results of the finalized collages, the Google Docs discussions (and the audio recording in the case of Group 3), and final reflections were compared. All coding was done by the two authors. Differences in the coding were discussed until mutual agreement was reached.

4 Results and Discussion

Regarding the first question, the type of multimodal resources L2 teachers used in a telecollaborative project for intercultural dialoguing on pedagogical issues, the analysis of the data indicated that all three groups used a host of multimodal resources to express and communicate in the Google Docs discussions. Group 1 used (1) sixteen posts of written text, (2) three diagrams, (3) one link to YouTube video, (4) one link to a Doodle survey, (5) two comic strips, and (6) three photos. The posts by Group 2 included (1) twenty-five posts of text, (2) five diagrams, (3) two photos, (4) four pictures, (5) eight links to YouTube videos, (7) two links to academic articles, and (8) one screenshot. As for Group 3, in addition to Google Docs, they Skyped using only audio chat. The meeting lasted for 25 minutes and consisted of 165 turn-takings among four participants (one member was not able to join). The four participants contributed 27, 63, 47, and 28 turns respectively. Their Google Docs each contained (1) five posts of text, (2) five diagrams, (3) one table, (4) one link, and (5) two screenshots. Table 1 is an overview of the multimodal resources used by the three groups.

When looking at how L2 teachers used the multimodal resources for the discussion of pedagogical topics, we applied the four-level social semiotic discourse analysis framework to the Google Docs discussions. We first identified the main concepts related to "Language Teaching in the 21st Century" raised by the different groups and how the multimodal resources were used to interact and to co-construct pedagogical knowledge.

Table 1. Summary of multimodal resources used by the groups

Multimodal resources	Group 1	Group 2	Group 3
Written texts	16	25	5
Diagrams	3	5	5
Links to YouTube videos	1	8	
Link to Doodle survey	1		
Comic strips	2		
Photos	3	2	
Pictures		4	
Links to academic articles		2	
Screenshots		1	2
Table			1
Link to audio recording of Skype meeting			1

In terms of the ideas and concepts being discussed, Group 1 focused on delineating 21st-century teachers' roles and the importance for teachers to understand students' multicultural backgrounds. They asserted the urgency for teachers to gain technological competences as the world has become increasingly globalized due to technological advancements. Their own teaching experiences were referenced to support their viewpoints. As for Group 2, they started off with challenges and problems faced by 21st-century teachers. They then moved on to discussing the characteristics (e.g., optimistic, patient, open-minded, creative, etc.), competencies (e.g., know-how to use new teaching tools and methods, etc.), and skills (e.g., learning and innovative skills, media and technology skills, life and career skills, etc.) that teachers should have. They also pointed out how classroom settings are different from what they used to be and what skills needed to be taught in the 21st-century language classroom. Group 3 took a different approach by first looking into the skills that students would always need, which included critical thinking and problem-solving skills, collaboration across networks, agility and adaptability, etc. They then went on to discuss the characteristics of teaching in the 21st century. Similar to Group 2, they also compared and contrasted the differences between teaching in the 20th and in the 21st century.

To understand the affordances of the multimodal resources used by the participants, the functions of the modes of resources were analyzed. The analyses showed that written texts were used by all three groups. Except for Group 3, who used a face-to-face online meeting as the main means of communication, the other two groups relied on written texts for most of the discussions.[4] Diagrams were another mode used by all three groups to present their ideas. They supplemented written texts and verbal discussions to illustrate the relationships among the different concepts being presented. An examination of the diagrams posted by the different groups showed that they were all obtained from the Internet.[5] The participants seemed to have regarded the Internet as an important source of knowledge and information.

4   Group 1 had a brief Skype meeting for group members to get acquainted before switching to Google Docs discussions.
5   The diagrams were from the following sources:
    https://district.franklinlakes.k12.nj.us/apps/pages/index.jsp?uREC_ID=421073&type=d&pREC_ID=920188
    https://helloliteracy.blogspot.tw/2011/08/super-skills-of-21st-century.html
    https://www.slideshare.net/piphowell/
    st-century-skills-in-the-foreign-langauge-classroom
    http://www.bamradionetwork.com/edwords-blog/the-6-c-s-squared-version-of-education-in-the-21st-century

In addition to getting diagrams from the Internet, the participants also obtained other forms of pictorial representations (e.g., comic strips, pictures, photos) to represent their concepts. They were also supplements to written texts and verbal descriptions. In comparison to diagrams, these types of pictorial resources functioned not so much as to display complex relationships among different elements of the topics or summarizing their ideas, but rather to help them emphasize certain points of arguments. For example, Group 2 used photos and pictures to highlight the differences between classroom settings in the past and today (see Figure 4).

Hyperlinks were another multimodal resource used by Groups 1 and 2. One of the participants in Group 1 shared his experience of teaching in an immersion program for disadvantaged populations in Colombia by posting a link to a YouTube video.[6] This video presented the participant's personal passion for teaching and assertions of his belief that could not have been otherwise expressed. The links chosen by Group 3, on the other hand, were resources for members to enrich their knowledge of the topics being discussed. The eight hyperlinks to YouTube videos included a news report on great teachers and the teaching methods they used, TED talks on pedagogical changes and teaching methods, and language programs for diverse

Figure 4. The use of pictorial representations

---

https://www.pinterest.com/pin/208995238935322702/
http://depts.washington.edu/celtweb/
https://delenibrahim.wordpress.com/research/
https://chrischiversthinks.weebly.com/
blog-thinking-aloud/-investigation-or-research
http://slideplayer.com/slide/274645/
http://slideplayer.com/slide/2976446/
http://www.richardnelsononline.co.uk/blog/pcet/teacher-as-researcher
https://nishrym.wordpress.com/page/2/

6 Immersion Rooms. Secretaría de Educación del Distrito de Bogotá.

learners, etc.[7] The hyperlinks to academic articles were to "justify what [had been] discussed" (Amy,[8] Group 3).[9]

In terms of organization of communication processes, the analysis reveals that all three groups approached discussions by presenting broad concepts (i.e., changing world, changing student populations, challenges in education) to more specific ideas, including teacher competence, skills, and characteristics, as well as skills needed by students. Besides the whole-to-part approach, another commonly shared feature in their written texts was presenting concepts and viewpoints by bullet points or numbered points. The participants used them as semiotic cues to help organize information and to make it easier for their partners to understand. This may also suggest that the concepts perceived could be divided up and compartmentalized into a number of related ideas or solutions. See Figure 5 for examples.

The findings from the analysis of multimodal resources used by the participants suggest that the various modes served specific functions in the processes of communication. Written texts, the "canonical mode par excellence" (Kress, 2009: 70), as well as verbal communication were maintained as the main means for describing, explaining, and relationship-building. At the same time, images including diagrams, tables, cartoons, videos, etc. also played an indispensable role; they took on the functions of depicting relationships among concepts and providing additional information. The participants' use of these modes, along with the hyperlinks to academic articles and YouTube videos, do resonate with Bezermer & Kress's (2016) assertion that canonical representations of knowledge are giving way to increasingly diverse multimodal resources. In addition, because of the use of information technology, knowledge can be constructed anywhere and by anyone, teachers included, as the outcome of processes of design motivated by individual interest (Kress, 2009).

In terms of the second question (i.e., to what extent does the use of multimodal resources facilitate or hinder the development of L2 teachers' ability

---

7   https://www.youtube.com/watch?v=33OINi3xVbc
    https://www.youtube.com/watch?v=CmVQCjtWirU
    https://www.youtube.com/watch?v=hvS-yPug8Vk
    https://www.youtube.com/watch?v=_Df9c7-aMMI
    https://www.youtube.com/watch?v=ZlpBZPLJ0lA
    https://www.youtube.com/watch?v=7bIQ4-3XSxU
    https://www.youtube.com/watch?v=3fMC-z7K0r4
    https://www.youtube.com/watch?v=dEJ_ATgrnnY
8   For ethical reasons, all names are pseudonyms.
9   http://www.edutopia.org/discussion/15-characteristics-21st-century-teacher
    http://www.sens-public.org/article667.html?lang=fr

1. I think the 21st Century teacher needs to be innovative in teachings, knowledgeable, culturally aware, excited, be a good leader, and good with perhaps even in technology.
2. Teachers today are perhaps different in ways that children they teach could be very diverse in background, I feel being culturally aware and teaching kids to be interested in other cultures and languages is very important, as globalization progresses...
3. We may encounter cultural differences.
4. Keep up by getting continued education or interacting with other teachers in the field.

Effective Teaching in the 21st Century
- Believe in the potential learning for each student. (No student behind!)
- Create a positive learning environment to include everyone. (collaboration, feedback from peers!)/(diversity, develop understanding and respecting of individual's differences among students)
- Show students the material is both relevant and useful to their daily life; (Make it meaningful!)
  adjust or redesigned the curriculum to meet the needs of unique individual learners
- Promote self-learning and help develop critical thinking skills. (Train students to seek out answers through exploration!)

1. I picture the 21st century language teacher as a facilitator: someone who will *help* you learn the language, and not just give you rules and examples to follow. This teacher has to be flexible, resourceful, open-minded, understanding and culturally aware, but should also be able to provide a framework and guided environment for the development of students, as well as have lots of knowledge about the language taught (and maybe even the students' different first languages).

2. The biggest difference is, I think, the attitude towards students. It should be (and usually is nowadays) interaction between peers, and between the teacher and students, not just the teacher talking. No more empty repetition, now it's meaningful conversation!

3. More and more students have different first language backgrounds and cultures in the language class, which is a big challenge compared to a class with a common mother tongue and cultural background. The inclusion of technology is another challenge, especially for older teachers. I think another challenge is that teachers should constantly review their methodology to see if it's appropriate to the context of a new class, or just to keep up with the most recent developments in the field of language teaching.

4. I personally read a lot of research articles on specific topics that are relevant to my current teaching situation. This way I can challenge my own perception of certain methods, and question whether I could include certain activities in my classes to the benefit of my students. We also have regular training and teacher meetings at work, so we can share ideas (for example, last week we met to share flashcard games).

Figure 5. Examples of the common organizational feature in text postings (by the three Group 1 participants)

to "decenter" from pre-existing notions of language learning and teaching), analysis of the Google Docs discussions reveals that from their first exchanges, several participants explicitly described themselves as having attitudes of openness to incorporate new ideas and adopt different teaching methods. For example, Yvonne (Group 1) explained that she had read many research articles on specific topics that were relevant to her current teaching situation to challenge her own perception of certain methods, and to question whether she had included certain activities in her classes to the benefit of her students. Another participant of the same group (Kay, Group 1) mentioned that she adjusted her teaching techniques based on her students' feedback. Then, through the course of Google Docs discussions, it was clear that, coming from similar professional backgrounds, they shared understandings of the meanings that are associated with the language they used. They frequently responded with positive remarks such as "I agree with Kim and Elle on the whole" (Ivy, Group 1) or "That's very true" (Rita, Group 3). They further added their own perspectives on the issues discussed with the support of personal experiences. For example, Peter (Group 1) wrote, "I would like to share my teaching experience. I teach in a very rural town ... in central Taiwan ... To me, teachers in the 21st century are the ones that give students visions of the future." Another participant (Jack, Group 1) added his views on the importance of technology in teaching and posted a link to a video recording of his own teaching.

The multimodal approach allowed the participants to exploit and design a mixture of texts, images, and other resources to convey their attitudes to not only the discussion topics but also toward the collaboration. For example, Cathy (Group 2) stated, "I decided to share with you this video. It is a very interesting project called 'Building Bridges.' Maybe this video can help us better understand what it means to be a teacher in the 21st century." Following Cathy's video posting, Penny (Group 2) added her own viewpoints and posted links to three videos to support her ideas. Then Amanda (Group 2) did the same and posted three more videos.

The analysis of joint reflections confirms the open-minded attitudes of the participants. Language and cultural diversity brought different views to the same issue. Through reasoning and explanations, the diversity among group members, in turn, contributed to the productivity and effectiveness of collaboration. This is illustrated in the following examples:

> Since our group is so diverse in terms of language and culture (Germany, Canada, USA, and Taiwan), we benefited a lot from the interaction and the immense knowledge gained from the collaboration ... (Lily, Group 3)

> It is indeed a fresh experience for me to collaborate with students with diverse backgrounds and I am so glad to have this opportunity ... each of us has our own perspectives on this topic, and sometimes we can easily accept others' views because that was what we were thinking and it seems like "great minds think alike." But sometimes we could not totally agree with the other's opinions, so we came up with our own and stated the reasons and even gave examples to illustrate the exception. (Amanda, Group 2)

The participants were clearly aware that the effective communication and the opportunity to embrace different perspectives were achieved with help afforded by multimodal resources and intercultural encounters. They acknowledged the role of Google Docs discussions in helping them to "easily achieve a consensus" because "[they] had time to make up [their] mind[s] before [their] Skype session, so it was more a matter of discussing esthetics and getting to know each other than debating" (Lisa, Group 3). The pictures, diagrams, and photos helped not only with aesthetics but also nudged them into taking on perspectives different from theirs and achieving agreement. As one participant wrote (Cathy, Group 2), "Probably, one initial idea ...was partly set aside ..., but this was done with the consent of all members since our discussion allowed us to compare our ideas and the realities in which we live."

Reflection findings also show evidence of students' epistemological decentering being a result of intercultural communication. For example, Cathy (Group 2) explained how she had come to realize how her perception of the challenges teachers face nowadays was shaped by the context in which she worked:

> Before our conversation, I started thinking about what it means for me to be a teacher in the 21st century. I immediately thought about the problems teachers encounter when they have in their class immigrant students. However, when I started talking about this topic with the other members of my group I realized that my point of view was influenced by the place where I live. Not all countries are facing the problem of immigration, thus the presence of many immigrant students in schools. This is for example the case of Taiwan.

The reflection by Cathy demonstrates an open attitude to partner-teachers' alternative pedagogical beliefs due to contextual differences, one of the telecollaborative teachers' competences as outlined by O'Dowd (2015). Interestingly, the same issue helped a Taiwanese participant in another group (Peter, Group 1) to better understand his own cultural context: "In addition to the points discussed in the meeting, I found that we have more and more immigrant students in Taiwan (mostly one of the parents from South-East Asia)." This reflection made him depart from his existing knowledge of language teaching and learning, and to contend the following: "How should we incorporate the cultural elements into our teaching is something we should consider."

There was also no shortage of evidence in the reflections indicating that the participants viewed successful intercultural telecollaboration as allowing each of the group members to have his/her own voice and contribute equally. Observe the following examples:

> Each group member chose one or more elements to incorporate into our collage. We collaborated together as a whole and had the same vision where no one person dominated the group. (Lily, Group 3)

> We just shared our own opinions and if our visions varied, we tried to analyze whether it actually made sense. Even though the ideas, opinions, and experiences varied from each of us, they are all be cherished. (Tammy, Group 2)

As seen in the two reflections, teachers made deliberate efforts to make use of their different cultural positions to negotiate better understandings that reduced any power differentials that existed among them.

Analyses of the multimodal ensembles on the finalized collages revealed further information of the participants' decentering from their individual pre-conceptions of language teaching to an intercultural "third space" (Bhabha, 1994) in which deeper understandings of each member's pedagogical beliefs and aims were represented and respected. Figures 6a–c present the finalized collages constructed by the three groups.

The collage by Group 1 consisted of different modalities: one webcam screen capture of their introductory Skype meeting, a YouTube video of a group member's teaching practice, two screen captures of the YouTube video, and one multi-image diagram depicting main characteristics of 21st-century teachers. The characteristics, including knowledge, collaboration, technology, culture, motivation, positive learning environment, and the four Cs of teachers' skills were placed at the center of their collage. By comparing the elements of the collage to what has been discussed and posted on Google Docs, it was evident that the group members had reached a consensus of focusing on teachers' required competencies. At the same time, the fact of having posted a video of a personal experience and screenshots of the whole group working and communicating on Skype implied that this

136 *Understanding Attitude in Intercultural Virtual Communication*

Figure 6a. The finalized collage of Group 1

Figure 6b. The finalized collage of Group 2

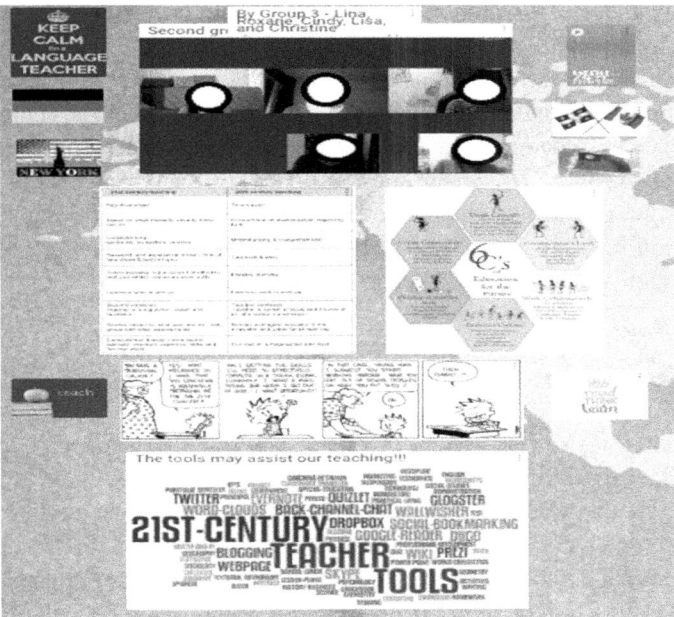

Figure 6c. The finalized collage of Group 3

consensus was the result of a deliberate process of mutual learning and decentering.

The collage composed by Group 2 also consisted of multimodal postings. A written summary of the ideas being discussed on Google Docs is situated in the center and surrounded by five YouTube videos of speeches and demonstrations of classroom activities, as well as one multi-image diagram. The concepts in the collage included: pedagogical change, challenges for teachers, active learning, qualities of a good teacher, and 21st-century skills in the language classroom; all were brought up by individual members of the group during Google Doc discussions. Giving their co-writing the center stage sends a clear message that joint efforts were crucial in constructing new knowledge.

The participants of Group 3 posted twelve items. Situated at the top of the collage are a Skype screenshot and the voice recording of their Skype meeting, surrounded by the four participants' respective national flags. Giving the screenshot with images of group members and national flags a prominent space on the collage foregrounds the intercultural dynamics of the group. Then, the diagram of six Cs of education for the future, the table contrasting the 21st-century teaching with teaching in the past, the comic strip alluding to students' required skills in the 21st century, and the word cloud, gave information on what they commonly agreed as essential in teaching language in the 21st century.

By examining the selections of multimodal resources representing the co-constructed knowledge on language teaching in the 21st century and how they were positioned in the finalized collages, there appeared to be deliberate "designs" (Bezemer & Kress, 2008) by each group. These deliberate designs connected the diverse elements that transpired during the communication into cohesive and coherent intercultural and intellectual "third spaces" that were co-created and commonly shared.

5 Conclusion

This chapter has focused on L2 teachers' use of multimodal resources in a telecollaborative project as well as on the extent to which their use facilitated their ability to decenter from pre-existing notions of language learning and teaching. Overall, it was found that the multimodal design of the project provided participants with opportunities for intercultural dialoguing of pedagogical issues, and thus for epistemological and cultural decentering. This has been exemplified with evidence from the participants' written discussions on Google Docs, from one of the groups' Skype discussions, and from their joint written reflections. In addition, it was found that the final multimodal collages represented the participants' intercultural "third space," as the selection of multimodal resources resulted from of a consensus achieved either by their common epistemological representations or because of their ability to decenter from their original representations. As such, this study, despite being small in scale, responds to the need for research to elucidate the effects of multimodality and to focus on the social production of representation (Kaplan, 1995, cited in Bezemer & Kress, 2008).

At a methodological level, results from this study suggest that the four-level social semiotic discourse analysis provides a valuable framework for analyzing how students used multimodal resources for intercultural dialoguing of pedagogical issues. By analyzing the participants' online discussions, joint reflections, and multimodal collages, we have come to understand how the multimodal resources have facilitated the development of L2 teachers' ability to "decenter" (Byram, 1989) from pre-existing notions of language learning and teaching.

At a pedagogical level, our findings demonstrate the importance of incorporating this type of project in L2 teacher education courses. First, the findings have allowed us to contend that telecollaboration gave students the chance to express their ideas, share their experiences, and find commonalities of teaching an L2 in different parts of the world. This also shows that this telecollaborative project has helped participants to build a sense of community among teachers from different countries. Second, the activities used in this project allowed participants to explore the use of multimodal resources to share, communicate, and grow professionally. Lastly, our results underscore the potential of telecollaboration to enhance students' awareness of the importance of multimodal pedagogy, crucial for teaching in the 21st century.

Multimodal communication is a reality of our daily life. Multimodal communication skills are thus useful in teaching and learning. Given that multimodal telecollaboration is a new territory for research, further studies need to be conducted in L2 teacher education courses in order to investigate the impact of telecollaborative projects through platforms allowing for multimodality on L2 teachers' attitude.

References

Altstaedter, L. L., & Falasca, M. (2015). Exploring foreign language pre-service teacher beliefs: An international exchange experience. *Global Partners in Education Journal*, 5(1), 38–50.

Archer, A., & Newfield, D. (2014). Challenges and opportunities of multimodal approaches to education in South Africa. In A. Archer & D. Newfield (eds.) *Multimodal Approaches to Research and Pedagogy: Recognition, Resources and Access* (pp. 1–16). London and New York: Routledge. https://doi.org/10.4324/9781315879475

Avgousti, M. I. (2018). Intercultural communicative competence and online exchanges: A systematic review. *Computer Assisted Language Learning*, 31(8), 819–853. https://doi.org/10.1080/09588221.2018.1455713

Berglund, T. O. (2009). Multimodal student interaction online: an ecological perspective. *ReCALL*, 21(2), 186–205. https://doi.org/10.1017/S0958344009000184

Bezemer, J., & Kress, G. (2008). Writing in multimodal texts: A social semiotic account of designs for learning, *Written Communication*, 25(2), 166–195. https://doi.org/10.1177/0741088307313177

Bezemer, J., & Kress, G. (2016). *Multimodality, Learning and Communication: A Social Semiotic Frame*. New York, NY: Routledge. https://doi.org/10.4324/9781315687537

Bhabha, H. (1994). *Location of Culture*. London: Routledge.

Byram, M. (1989). *Cultural Studies in Foreign Language Education*. Clevedon: Multilingual Matters Ltd.

Byram, M., & Feng, A. (2004). Culture and language learning: Teaching, research and scholarship. *Language Teaching*, 37, 149–168. https://doi.org/10.1017/S0261444804002289

Byram, M., Gribkova, B., & Starkey, H. (2002). *Developing the Intercultural Dimension in Language Teaching: A Practical Introduction for Teachers*. Strasbourg: Language Policy Division, Directorate of School, Out-of-School and Higher Education, Council of Europe.

Byram, M., & Zarate, G. (1997). Defining and assessing intercultural competence: Some principles and proposals for the European context. *Language Teaching*, 29, 239–243.https://doi.org/10.1017/S0261444800008557

Bush, M., & Roberts, T. (eds.). (1997). *Technology-enhanced Language Learning*. National Textbook Company: Illinois.

Chandler, P. D. (2017). To what extent are teachers well prepared to teach multimodal authoring? *Cogent Education*, 4: 1266820. https://doi.org/10.1080/2331186X.2016.1266820

Dooly, M. (2010). The teacher 2.0. In S. Guth & F. Helm (eds.), *Telecollaboration 2.0: Language, Literacies and Intercultural Learning in the 21st Century* (pp. 277–303). Bern: Peter Lang.

Dooly, M. (2011). Crossing the intercultural borders into 3rd space culture(s): Implications for teacher education in the twenty-first century. *Language and Intercultural Communication*, 11(4), 319–337. https://doi.org/10.1080/14708477.2011.599390

Dooly, M., & Hauck, M. (2012). Researching multimodal communicative competence in video and audio telecollaborative encounters. In M. Dooly & R. O'Dowd (eds). *Researching Online Interaction and Exchange in Foreign Language Education* (pp. 135–162). Bern: Peter Lang.

Dooly, M., & O'Dowd, R. (2018). Telecollaboration in the foreign language classroom: A review of its origins and its application to language teaching practices. In M. Dooly & R. O'Dowd (eds.), *In This Together: Teachers' Experiences with Transnational, Telecollaborative Language Learning Projects* (pp. 11–34). New York/Bern: Peter Lang.

Dooly, M., & Sadler, R. (2013). Filling in the gaps: Linking theory and practice through telecollaboration in teacher education. *ReCALL*, 25(1), 4–29. https://doi.org/10.1017/S0958344012000237

Durham, C. (2018). Teacher interculturality in an English as a second language elementary pull-out program: Teacher as broker in the school's community of practice. *The Qualitative Report*, 23(3), 677–695. Retrieved from https://nsuworks.nova.edu/tqr/vol23/ iss3/13

Early, M., Kendrick, M., & Potts, D. (2015). Multimodality: Out from the margins of English language teaching. *TESOL Quarterly*, 49(3), 447–622. https://doi.org/10.1002/tesq.246

Farías, M., Obilinovic, K., & Orrego, R. (2007). Implications of multimodal learning models for foreign language teaching and learning. *Columbia Applied Linguistics Journal*, 9, 174–199. https://doi.org/10.14483/22487085.3150

Gill, M., Ashton, P., & Algina, J. (2004). Changing preservice teachers' epistemological beliefs about teaching and learning in mathematics: An intervention study. *Contemporary Educational Psychology*, 29, 164–185. https://doi.org/10.1016/j.cedpsych.2004.01.003

Haley, M. H. (2012). An online cultural exchange in pre-service language teacher education: A dialogic approach to understanding. *US-China Education Review*, B5, 528–533.

Halliday, M. A. K. (1989). *Spoken and Written Language*. Oxford: Oxford University Press.

Hampel, R. (2006). Rethinking task design for the digital age: A framework for language teaching and learning in a synchronous online environment. *ReCALL*, 18(1), 105–121. https://doi.org/10.1017/S0958344006000711

Hauck, M., & Kurek, M. (2017). Digital literacies in teacher preparation. In S. Thorne & M. Stephen (eds.), *Language, Education and Technology, Encyclopedia of Language and Education* (3rd edition) (pp. 1–13). New York: Springer International Publishing. https://doi.org/10.1007/978-3-319-02237-6_22

Hauck, M., & Youngs, B. L. (2008). Telecollaboration in multimodal environments: The impact on task design and learner interaction. *Computer Assisted Language Learning*, 21(2), 87–124. https://doi.org/10.1080/09588220801943510

Hubbard, P. (2007). Critical issues: Professional development, in J. Egbert & E. Hanson Smith (eds.), *CALL Environments* (2nd edition) (pp. 272–292). Alexandria, VA: TESOL.

Jaipal, K. (2009). Meaning making through multiple modalities in a Biology classroom: A multimodal semiotics discourse analysis. *Science Education*, 94(1), 48–72. https://doi.org/10.1002/sce.20359

Jaipal Jamani, K. (2011). A semiotics discourse analysis framework: Understanding meaning making in science education contexts. In S. C. Hamel (ed.), *Semiotics Theory and Applications* (pp. 191–208). Hauppauge, NY: Nova Science Publishers, Inc.

Jewitt, C. (2017). Multimodal discourse across curriculum. In S. L. Thorne & S. May (eds.), *Language, Education and Technology, Encyclopedia of Language and Education* (pp. 31–43). New York: Springer International Publishing. https://doi.org/10.1007/978-3-319-02237-6_4

Jones, R. H. (2013). Multimodal discourse analysis. In C. A. Chapelle (ed.), *The Encyclopedia of Applied Linguistics* (pp. 1–4). Blackwell Publishing Ltd. https://doi.org/10.1002/9781405198431.wbeal0813

Kaplan, N. (1995). Politexts, hypertexts, and other cultural formations in the late age of print. *Computer-Mediated Communication Magazine*, 2(3), 3–10. http://www.ibiblio.org/cmc/mag/1995/mar/kaplan.html

Kelly, M., Grenfell, M., Allan, R., Kriza, C., & McEvoy, W. (2004). *European Profile for Language Teacher Education – A Frame of Reference*. A Report submitted to the European Commission Directorate General for Education and Culture.

Keranen, N., & Bayyurt, Y. (2006). Intercultural telecollaboration: In-service EFL teachers in Mexico and pre-service EFL teachers in Turkey, *TESL-EJ*, 10(3). https://files.eric.ed.gov/fulltext/EJ1065007.pdf

Kessler, G. (2006). Assessing CALL teacher training: What are we doing and what could we do better? In P. Hubbard & M. Levy (eds.), *Teacher Education in CALL* (pp. 23–42). Amsterdam/Philadelphia: John Benjamins. https://doi.org/10.1075/lllt.14.05kes

Kramsch, C. (2013). Culture in foreign language teaching. *Iranian Journal of Language Teaching Research*, 1(1), 57–78.
Kress, G. (2009). *Multimodality: A Social Semiotic Approach to Contemporary Communication*. London: Routledge. https://doi.org/10.4324/9780203970034
Kress, G. (2011). Discourse analysis and education: A multimodal social semiotic approach. *An Introduction to Critical Discourse Analysis in Education* (pp. 205–226). New York, NY: Routledge.
Kress, G., & van Leeuwen, T. (1996). *Reading Images*. London: Routledge.
Kress, G., & van Leeuwen, T. (2001). *Multimodal Discourse: The Modes and Media of Contemporary Communication*. Oxford: Oxford University Press.
Lemke, J. L. (1998). Analysing verbal data: Principles, methods, and problems. In B. J. Fraser & K. Toblin (eds.), *International Handbook of Science Education* (pp. 1175–1199). Dordrecht: Kluwer. https://doi.org/10.1007/978-94-011-4940-2_68
Lemke, J. L. (2002). Travelers in hypermodality. *Visual Communication*, 1(3), 299–325. https://doi.org/10.1177/147035720200100303
Malinowski, D., & Nelson, E. (2010). Reflexibility in motion in language and literacy learning. In J. S. Byrd Clark & F. Dervin (eds.), *Reflexibility in Language and Intercultural Education: Rethinking Multilingualism and Interculturality* (pp. 138–157). New York: Routledge.
Menard-Warwick, J. (2008). The cultural and intercultural identities of transnational English teachers: Two case studies from the Americas. *TESOL*, 42(4), 617–640. https://doi.org/10.1002/j.1545-7249.2008.tb00151.x
Müller-Hartmann, A. (2006). Learning how to teach intercultural communicative competence via telecollaboration: A model for language teacher education. In J. Belz & S. Thorne (eds.), *Internet Mediated Intercultural Foreign Language Education* (pp. 63–84). Boston: Heinle & Heinle.
O'Dowd, R. (2015). The competences of the telecollaborative teacher. *The Language Learning Journal*, 43(2), 194–207. https://doi.org/10.1080/09571736.2013.853374
O'Dowd, R. (2016). Emerging trends and new directions in telecollaborative learning. *CALICO Journal*, 33(3), 291–310. https://doi.org/10.1558/cj.v33i3.30747
Patel, D. S. (2015). Significance of technology enhanced language learning (TELL) in language classes. *Journal of Technology for ELT*, 7(2), Retrieved from https://sites.google.com/site/journaloftechnologyforelt/archive/vol-4-no-2-1/2
Quebec Education Ministry (2001). *Teacher Training: Orientations, Professional Competencies*. Gouvernement du Québec: Québec. http://www.education.gouv.qc.ca/fileadmin/site_web/documents/dpse/formation_ens_a.pdf
Ryan, J., Scott, A., & Walsh, M. (2010) Pedagogy in the multimodal classroom: An analysis of the challenges and opportunities for teachers. *Teachers and Teaching*, 16(4), 477–489. https://doi.org/10.1080/13540601003754871
Sadler, R., & Dooly, M. (2016). Twelve years of telecollaboration: What we have learnt. *ELT Journal*, 70(4), 401–413. https://doi.org/10.1093/elt/ccw041
Stein, P. (2008). *Multimodal Pedagogies in Diverse Classrooms*. London/New York: Routledge. https://doi.org/10.4324/9780203935804

Sun, Y.-C. (2017). Following the heart or the crowd: Epistemological beliefs and actual practices of in-service language teachers in Taiwan. *Taiwan Journal of TESOL*, 14(1), 119–144.

Taiwan Ministry of Education (2016). *Taiwan's 2016–2020 Masterplan for ICT in Eeducation*. http://english.moe.gov.tw/public/Attachment/610515505671.pdf

White, B. C. (2000). Pre-service teachers' epistemology viewed through perspectives on problematic classroom situations. *Journal of Education for Teaching: International Research and Pedagogy*, 26(3), 279–305. https://doi.org/10.1080/713676891

Yi, Y., & Angay-Crowder, T. (2016). Multimodal pedagogies for teacher education in TESOL. *TESOL Quarterly*, 50(4), 988–998. https://doi.org/10.1002/tesq.326

About the Authors

Meei-Ling Liaw is a professor in the English Department at the National Taichung University of Education in Taiwan. As a two-time Fulbright Scholar, she visited UC Berkeley in 2000 and UC Irvine in 2008. Her research focuses on intercultural learning, teacher education, and CALL. Her publications have appeared in professional journals including *System*, *Foreign Language Annals*, *Computer-Assisted Language Learning*, *ReCALL*, and *Language Learning & Technology*. She has been Associate Editor of *Language Learning & Technology* since 2016, and is on the editorial board of other international journals, including *Journal of Virtual Exchanges* and *Journal of Intercultural Communication Education*.

Sabrina Priego is an Associate Professor of the Department of Languages, Linguistics and Translation at Université Laval in Quebec, Canada where she teaches undergraduate and graduate courses in second language (L2) teacher education. Her research focuses on multilingual digital storytelling, telecollaboration, Virtual Reality, Tandem language learning, and L2 teacher education. She has published on the role of telecollaboration in language learning and on Tandem language learning in refereed journals and given talks at several international conferences. In collaboration with Dr Liaw, she has designed and implemented several telecollaborative projects involving L2/FL learners, and pre- and in-service L2/FL teachers.

6   What's with the Attitude? Exploring Attitudinal Resources in Telecollaboration for Teacher Education

D. Joseph Cunningham and Marianna Ryshina-Pankova

1   Introduction

As Internet-based communication technologies have become anchored in our day-to-day lives – extending into both educational and professional spheres – their reach has prompted a reconsideration of the fundamental skills and competences needed by foreign language teachers in a rapidly shifting pedagogical and technological landscape. These "techno-pedagogical competences" include, at a minimum, the ability to (1) assess the potential of technologies for language and culture learning, (2) use and troubleshoot basic tools and applications, and (3) design appropriate tasks and interactions in light of the technologies' affordances (Guichon & Hauck, 2011: 191). In the specific context of virtual exchange/telecollaboration (henceforth, telecollaboration), a number of studies (e.g., Cunningham, 2013; Müller-Hartmann; 2016; O'Dowd, 2015) have focused on the broad range of competences and skills needed by foreign language teachers. Nevertheless, the question bears asking: How can we ensure the development of these teaching competences and to what extent is it possible to document this development?

A possible answer to these questions can be found by turning to the construct of Attitude, a "framework for mapping feelings as they are construed in … texts" (Martin & White, 2005: 42). By examining the attitudes on display during synchronous computer-mediated communication (SCMC) in the context of a telecollaboration for teacher education, the current study attempts to show the development of specific pedagogical abilities related to materials and task development for a text-based and content- and language-integrated foreign language curriculum.

2 Literature Review

This section reviews relevant research findings, beginning with studies investigating teacher development as tied to literacy and multiliteracy. The focus then shifts to research of teacher competences in the telecollaborative context. To conclude, we review previous work relating discourse in telecollaboration to the construct of Attitude as part of the Appraisal system (Martin & White, 2005).

2.1 Teacher Education and Literacy

Recognizing that models of teacher education based purely on knowledge transmission do not automatically translate into meaningful pedagogical action (Rankin & Becker, 2006), teacher educators are increasingly looking toward literacy-based pedagogy as a means to prepare student teachers (Allen, 2011; Allen & Dupuy, 2011; Paesani, 2011; Ryshina-Pankova, 2011). In the context of foreign language education, literacy can be viewed as a multidimensional construct that encompasses linguistic, cognitive, and sociocultural aspects and is grounded in seven principles that give rise to literacy development: language use, cultural knowledge, conventions, interpretation, collaboration, problem solving, and reflection (Kern, 2000). From this understanding flow four pedagogical acts integral to literacy-based instruction: situated practice, overt instruction, critical framing, and transformed practice, each of which can "help instructors teach in a way that facilitates students' access to the language, conventions, [and] cultural content" (Paesani, Allen, & Dupuy, 2015: 37).

As regards a literacy-based framework for teacher education, conceptual knowledge and pedagogical awareness are seen to emerge gradually and over time (Allen, 2011; Allen & Dupuy, 2011). For example, Allen reports on the case of two PhD student teachers who tended to focus more on practical matters during their initial semesters of student teaching; however, in subsequent semesters and in the context of a literacy-based teaching seminar, both student teachers showed evidence of developing conceptual knowledge as a result of "their participation in dialogic mediation, scaffolded learning, and assisted performance with others" (Allen, 2011: 100). Further reinforcing the link between formal coursework and literacy-based teacher education, Paesani (2011) notes the opportunity for student teacher involvement in curricular and pedagogical decision-making. Nevertheless, she calls for additional research focused on the "development of literacy-based teaching materials to more clearly establish links between course concepts and their practical applications" (2011: 77). Menke & Paesani

(2019: 13) issue a similar call in their review of literacy-based teaching materials, noting, "It is particularly important to investigate instructors' understandings of literacy ... and then to create tools, resources, and professional development experiences ... that enhance those understandings and facilitate classroom application." In this regard, the current study seeks to link student teachers' pedagogical abilities to their participation in a professional development opportunity (i.e., telecollaboration) that affords in-depth discussion of teaching materials.

2.2 Teacher Education in Telecollaboration

As a complex endeavor with overlapping technological, logistical, and pedagogical demands, telecollaboration requires of its practitioners a commensurately broad set of skills. Accordingly, a concerted effort has been made to describe the various skills, competences, and attitudes necessary for telecollaborative teaching. Dooly (2010: 294) lists a set of 13 abilities ranging from purely pedagogical (e.g., "help students determine their own learning goals and plans") to those that more intentionally foreground the role of technology (e.g., "coordinate and manage Web 2.0 resources effectively as a means of reaching learning goals"). While acknowledging the contributions of Dooly (2010) and other practitioners in describing the abilities of the telecollaborative teacher, O'Dowd (2015: 201) nonetheless sees the "need for a reliable and comprehensive model of telecollaborative competences for teachers." Using a three-stage iterative process and drawing on the input of 60+ experts, he has developed a model of telecollaborative teacher competence containing over 40 descriptors organized into four different sections: organizational competences, pedagogical competences, digital competences, and attitudes/beliefs.

In order to cultivate necessary telecollaborative competences among their student teachers, teacher educators frequently opt to use the situated experience of participating in a telecollaboration. Documenting two iterations of a two-semester project between student teachers in the USA and Spain, Dooly & Sadler (2013) note several benefits that can emerge from the situated learning context of telecollaboration, including the opportunity to participate in and internalize elements of pedagogical discourse(s), as well as integrate technology into teacher practice, thereby linking theoretical and practical aspects of coursework and learning. Also in reference to situated learning, and pointing towards Hampel & Stickler's (2005) skills pyramid, Fuchs, Hauck, & Müller-Hartmann (2012) show how a well-articulated series of telecollaborative tasks can not only foster student teacher autonomy, but can also afford opportunity for the development of multimodal competence and professional literacy.

From the above studies, it is clear that a concerted effort has been made to describe the various skills, competences, and attitudes of the telecollaborative teacher. Moreover, the situated experience of participating in a telecollaboration can be foundational in developing this broad and varied set of abilities. Nevertheless, the field could benefit from an increased understanding of how these competences related to materials development and task design are actually displayed by student teachers who participate in telecollaboration. The present study aims to do so by implementing a qualitative, discourse-based analysis of attitude in telecollaborative interaction.

2.3   Attitude and Appraisal Theory

Before proceeding further, it is necessary to explain what is meant by "attitude" and how this construct has been treated previously in the literature. Although O'Dowd (2015) does not provide a specific definition of attitude, he describes seven "socio-affective" factors grounded in "openness," "willingness," and "interest" (p. 204) that are characteristic of effective and experienced telecollaborative practitioners. In contrast, Turula (2016: 248) ties the notion of attitude to the personality traits of deference and demeanor, noting that effective collaborators should display "a balance between other-orientation and self-orientation." Such descriptions are informative, but they do not equip researchers with specific tools for investigating how attitude is displayed in telecollaborative discourse, and how these attitudes might inform our understanding of how teacher competences are enacted via situated participation in telecollaboration. To gain such insights, we turn to the system of Appraisal, "one of three major discourse semantic resources for construing interpersonal meaning" (Martin & White, 2005: 34) in the Systemic Functional Linguistic (SFL) tradition.

Appraisal is comprised of three interrelated domains: Attitude, Engagement, and Graduation, whereby Attitude can be further subdivided into three regions of feeling: Affect (i.e., resources for construing emotion), Judgment (i.e., resources for assessing behavior), and Appreciation (i.e., resources for construing the value of things). To date, just a handful of studies have examined the linguistic realization of Attitude in telecollaborative discourse vis-à-vis Appraisal and SFL. Belz (2003) investigated the language used by L2 learners of German and English as regards "developing attitudes toward both the other and the self" (p. 70). Finding that the two groups displayed different patterns of linguistic realizations of attitude, Belz (2003) calls not for a relativization of how learners interact in telecollaboration, but instead promotes the need for participants to develop a better awareness of interactional patterns in the respective languages (e.g., directness in German vs. indirectness in English) and the meanings that these patterns encode. Also drawing on the system of Attitude, Oskoz & Pérez-Broncano (2016) investigated what specific linguistic markers American learners of Spanish used in online discussions to construe attitudes towards the first culture (C1) and the second culture (C2). Their analysis showed that learners displayed a more positive orientation towards the C2 than towards the C1, with criticism often framed through notions of the C1's cultural imperialism towards the C2. Lastly, the work of Vinagre & Corral (2018) shows how the email communication of telecollaborative partners was most often characterized by expressions of Affect that aimed to build rapport. In other words, participants were more inclined to express their own feelings towards a topic, rather than judge the responses of their partners.

Taken together, this group of studies shows the usefulness of linguistically based analysis of attitude in telecollaborative discourse. At the same time, because the studies focus on the student participants in telecollaboration, they do not shed light on the linguistic realization of attitude in telecollaborative discourse among student teachers. Furthermore, the studies discussed are based in asynchronous, text-based (i.e., written) interaction. In contrast, the current research focuses on synchronous audiovisual interaction between two student teachers of German. By examining this interaction, the study seeks to answer the following questions:

1. What attitudes are on display as two student teachers negotiate the selection of a text and the development of a corresponding task?
2. How can these attitudes be related to student teachers' abilities to select and develop pedagogical materials?

3 Methodology

3.1 Pedagogical Context

The study took place in a graduate-level seminar ("Foreign Language Teaching and Literacy") at a private, medium-sized research university in the United States. The course aims to prepare students to teach foreign languages at the postsecondary level within a multiliteracies framework (Cope & Kalantzis, 2009), where texts and tasks are linked to an understanding of genre as "staged, goal-oriented, purposeful activity in which speakers engage as members of culture" (Martin, 1984: 25). Accordingly, a central goal of the course is for students to develop pedagogical competences related to text selection, materials development, and instructional sequencing for a language- and content-integrated foreign language program. Also with an eye towards developing competences for telecollaborative teaching (Dooly, 2010; O'Dowd, 2015), the course featured an integrated 10-week telecollaboration with students at a German university who wish to teach German as a Foreign/Second Language. For the duration of the exchange, participants from the USA (N = 10) were partnered with participants from Germany (N = 12), resulting in eight dyads and two triads. The groups worked through a series of tasks that culminated in the joint selection of a text and the development of pedagogical materials in relation to that text (Table 1). Participants were free to use either German or English, but were encouraged to seek a balance between both languages. Participants were also free to select which technologies they would use to communicate with their partners during the task cycle, with the agreement that any communication was to be recorded and shared with the researchers. Instructor-provided

Table 1. Timeline and task cycle of telecollaboration

Timeline	Task
Weeks 1–2	**Task #1: Group selection/Getting to know your partner(s)** • Participants create a profile and post it to StudIP • Participants browse profiles of partner class and select three potential partners to work with • Newly created working groups arrange synchronous online meeting in order to get to know one another
Week 3	**Task #2: Virtual lecture** • Participants listen to and comment on an asynchronous lecture ("The generic stages and sequencing of narrative texts") delivered via VoiceThread • Lecturer responds to student questions and comments
Weeks 4–5	**Task #3: Discussion of research** • Working groups arrange two synchronous online meetings in order to discuss assigned readings (i.e., Byrnes, 2005; Cope & Kalantzis, 2009; Crane, 2006; Liamkina & Ryshina-Pankova, 2012)
Week 6–8	**Task #4: Text selection and materials creation** • Participants select text appropriate to specific curricular level • Participants work to develop instructional materials • Participants post the results to StudIP and view/comment on one another's work
Week 9	**Wrap up: Video conference** • Participants conduct class-to-class synchronous video conference, sharing reflections and evaluations regarding the exchange

materials (e.g., articles for discussion during Task #3) and student-produced materials (e.g., results of Task #4) were shared via the course management system "StudIP" hosted by the German university.

Bearing in mind that the final task in the cycle, Task #4 ("Text selection and materials creation"), is the locus for the study's data collection, it is important to describe it in more detail. Guided by principles including genre typicality and text as cultural product, working groups had to select a text that would form the core of an instructional sequence. Following text selection, participants had to conduct a thorough analysis of the text in order to ascertain its generic purpose, audience, and how relevant meanings are created in the text. In creating materials for the text and determining an instructional sequence, participants had to work with explicit reference to the pedagogical acts of *situated practice*, *overt instruction*, and *critical framing* (Paesani et al., 2015) to determine language and content learning outcomes. As a final step, and in keeping with *transformed practice* (Paesani et al., 2015), participants had to design a speaking or writing task linked to a particular genre and reflective of the cultural themes in the original text.

3.2 Study Participants and Data Collection

Data for the study come from one dyad consisting of two speakers of German as a first language (L1). The participant in the USA was an exchange student from the partner university in Germany, studying for one year at the American university, and did not know the participant in Germany prior to the exchange. Neither of the participants had experience teaching within a multiliteracies framework, nor had they previously taken part in a telecollaboration. In this regard, we can say that the student teachers were exposed to a novel teaching approach and provided a unique forum in which to operationalize new pedagogical knowledge. This dyad was selected because it was of interest to see how educated L1 speakers of German would display attitude as related to pedagogical materials selection and development. The data examined in this study come from an hour-long discussion during Task #4 of the task cycle (see Table 1), as the participants considered the merits of two different texts that could form the basis for a short instructional sequence. The discussion took place and was recorded via Zoom, a synchronous audiovisual communication tool. The data were then transcribed and entered into a small corpus to facilitate analysis (see the Procedure section below).

3.3 Analytical Framework

The system of Attitude as part of the Appraisal framework (Martin & White, 2005) was used for the analysis. Figure 1, based on Martin & White (2005), presents a taxonomy of attitudinal meanings that guided the coding. The exchange was coded with regard to four independent systems: Attitude **type**, Attitude **target**, Attitudinal **explicitness**, and Attitudinal **polarity**.[1] Attitude type (Table 2) included: **Affect** as encoding of feelings; **Judgment** as encoding of ethical values, differentiated further into judgments related to *social esteem* and *social sanction*; and **Appreciation** as evaluation of things and semiotic entities, further divided into *reaction quality, reaction impact, composition balance, composition complexity*, and *valuation*.

Table 2. Types of Attitude

Affect	Judgment	Appreciation
also da waren wir alle richtig geschockt/ so we were all really shocked	**Social esteem** *sonst komme ich mir so dumm vor/otherwise I feel so stupid* **Social sanction** *Das hilft uns noch nicht/That does not help us*	**Reaction quality** *dafür ist der Text hier nicht geeignet/for that the text here is not suitable* **Reaction impact** *die haben alle traumatische Dinge erlebt/they have all experienced traumatizing things* **Composition balance** *die Kurse sind nicht so gross/the courses are not very big* **Composition complexity** *dein Textvorschlag geht mehr in die Tiefe/your text suggestion goes more into depth* **Valuation** *wichtiger Aspekt/important aspect*

In the process of coding, the following **targets** of attitude were identified in the analysis (Table 3): *instructional materials, aspects of texts within the materials* (e.g., characters, historical circumstances), *instructional tasks, process of task completion, instructors in general, learners, instructors of the course*, and *self* (i.e., the participants themselves).

---

1 The exchange was also coded for attitude **source**. We do not report on it in this study, as it did not play a significant role in the current analysis. The two exchange participants were the most frequent sources of evaluation, and differentiating between the two did not yield results that were particularly interesting.

Table 3. Targets of Attitude

Instructional materials	*dann gibt der einfach nicht genug her/then it just doesn't offer enough* (in reference to a text)
Aspects of texts within the materials	*Und dann passieren auch total blöde Sachen wie eben Immobilien, die keinen Wert haben/and then completely stupid things also happen like property that has no value* (in reference to the content of the song under discussion)
Instructional tasks	*das kann man ruhig machen/one can easily do it*
Process of task completion	*Und dass wir schreiben warum der Text gut passt und dass es nochnicht ganz ausgefeilt sein soll/and that we write why the text fits well and that it does not have to be completely polished*
Instructors in general	*Wenn man sich damit jetzt so ganz vertieft auseinandersetzen will/if one wants to grapple with it in a very serious way*
Learners	*womit sie sich sehr gut identifizieren können/something with which they can identify very well*
Instructors of the course	*der ist halt ganz interessiert/he is very interested*
Self	*Ich bin nicht so richtig zufrieden/I am not completely satisfied*

Attitudinal **explicitness** (Table 4) was differentiated with regard to being directly realized through explicitly attitudinal lexis (i.e., *ascribed*) or indirectly realized (i.e., *invoked*) through implication and association.

Table 4. Attitudinal explicitness[2]

Ascribed	Invoked
nicht so gut lesen kann/cannot read very well	*können ja auch schon in Level II nen Roman lesen/can already read a novel at Level II*

Attitudinal **polarity** (Table 5) was differentiated into *positive* and *negative*.

Table 5. Polarity

Positive	Negative
das ist gut/this is good	*ich finde es schwierig/I find it hard*

2   *Nicht so gut lesen/cannot read very well* – contains *nicht so gut/not very well* as an explicit marker of attitude, whereas *können ja auch schon lesen/ can already read* can initially be read as a statement about the ability of the students to read because there is no explicit attitudinal marker used.

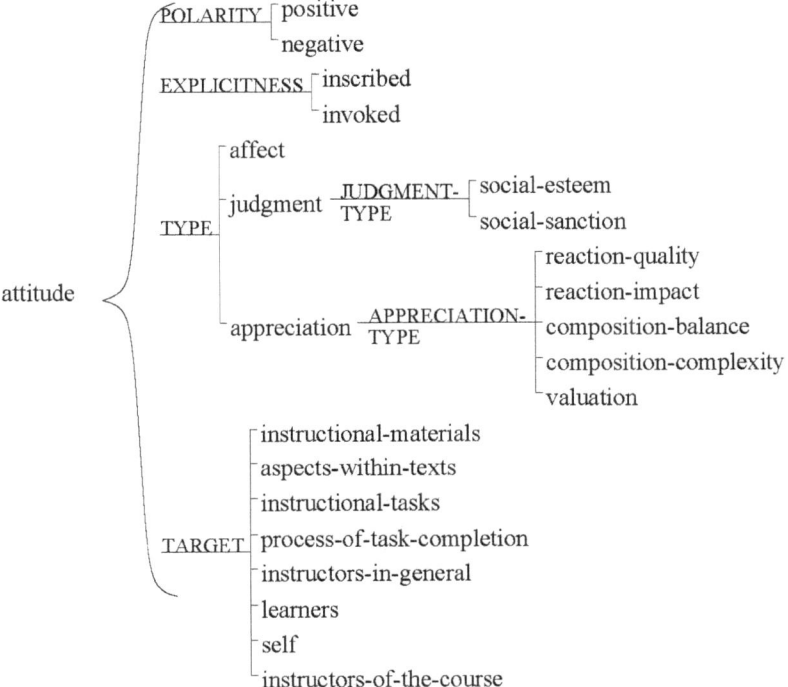

Figure 1. Attitude Framework

3.4 Procedure

The Corpus Tool for linguistic annotation of texts, developed by Mick O'Donnell at the Universidad Autónoma de Madrid (henceforth, UAM-Corpus Tool), is specifically designed to facilitate Appraisal analysis (O'Donnell, 2014) and was used for coding the exchange. The UAM-Corpus Tool enables one to code tokens of various length, search for the co-occurrence of various features (e.g., all instances of Appreciation and positive polarity or Appreciation and instructional materials as attitudinal targets), and enables retrieval of attitudinal tokens in context through a concordancer. After being transformed into an appropriate format, the file was coded for C-units that are defined as main clauses with all subordinate clauses (Crookes, 1990). Unlike T-units, which refer to complete main clauses and any attached subordinate clauses, C-units allow for including sentence fragments in the analysis. One C-unit could contain more than one instance of attitude. The program allowed us to count all C-units containing at least one or more instances of attitude. The following example, drawn from Excerpt 1, illustrates that the division into C-units in the oral data was based both on formal and semantic features. For example, the insertion of the full main clause in *zum Beispiel eben die sollen einen Liedtext produzieren/for example they have to produce a song text* was considered part of the subordinate *wenn/if* clause; the next clause that started with *das/that* which contradicts the rules of the German word order in a typical subordinate-main clause sequence was considered to start the main independent clause on the semantic basis; the subordinate conjunction *weil/because* in 3* was interpreted as the German coordinate *denn* both on the semantic basis – there is no real causation involved, and on the basis of the formal word order that is typical of a main clause, not a subordinate clause. Such use of *weil/because* to open independent clauses is well described as a feature of German oral discourse (e.g., Bendig, Betz, & Huth, 2016).

> Excerpt 1
> *1* Dafür wenn man die Task hätte die sollen so nen Task produzieren zum Beispiel eben die sollen einen Liedtext produzieren das kann man ja durchaus machen natürlich ... 2* aber dafür ist der Text hier halt nicht geeignet 3* sondern weil dafür bräuchte man halt einen genretypischen Text und keinen genreuntypischen Text.*
> *1* For that if one had the task they have to produce for example they have to produce a song text one can do that of course ... 2* but for that the text here is just not suitable 3* but because for that one would need a text that is typical of the genre and not an atypical text.*

Based on the above understanding, a research assistant coded the entire file for C-units. The C-unit coding was then checked by both researchers, and all disagreements were resolved. The coding of the attitudinal meanings in the exchange was conducted by both researchers on 30% of the data, with the rest of the exchange coded by one researcher. All disagreements about attitudinal coding were resolved by discussion.

4   Results: Attitudinal Analysis

This section presents the results of the analysis of attitudinal meanings, with a particular focus on attitude type and explicitness, attitude target and type, and attitudinal polarity in the telecollaborative exchange. As such, it is oriented toward answering the first research question.

Attitudinal meanings play a significant role in the exchange, appearing in 30.89% of all C-units, as evident from Table 6.

Table 6. Number of C-units

Total # of C-Units	683
# of C-Units with Attitude	211 (30.89% of all C-units)

Table 7 shows that Appreciation (60.23%) is the most frequent type of attitudinal meaning used in the exchange, followed by Judgment (31.44%) and Affect (8.33%). Furthermore, while Affect and Appreciation are most often explicitly encoded, (86.36% and 77.35%, respectively) Judgment is more often expressed indirectly (i.e., 68.67% of it is invoked).

Table 7. Attitude type and explicitness

	Total	Inscribed	Invoked
Affect	8.33%	86.36%	13.63%
Judgment	31.44%	31.32%	68.67%
Appreciation	60.23%	77.35%	22.64%

Table 8 presents targets of attitude in the order of frequency, as well as in terms of how they were evaluated, with regard to attitude type. The most frequent targets of evaluation in the materials development task were instructional materials, with 44.69% of all evaluation instances, followed by the evaluations of the aspects inside these materials (20.83%), including attitudes towards characters and events within the texts. Tasks were the third most frequent attitudinal target, with 12.87% of instances in this category. The process of telecollaborative task completion was evaluated in 9.09% of all instances. The participants of the exchange also evaluated both themselves (5.68%) and potential learners (4.16%). The least frequently evaluated targets were instructors in general (1.51%), as well as the two instructors of the course (0.75%). With regard to the type of attitude used with the targets, except for the attitude toward self, toward learners, and toward instructors, most of which were instances of Judgment (86.66%, 81.81%, and 100% respectively), all other targets were most frequently evaluated through Appreciation.

As Table 9 reveals, within the attitude of Appreciation, by far the most frequent evaluation encoded a reaction toward the target's quality (52.83%) followed by the target's significance (i.e., valuation, 18.24%), its complexity (15.72%), impact (11.95%), and, least frequently, balance (0.63%). Within Judgment, most evaluations were in reference to the target's propriety and veracity (56.63%) followed by their capacity and normality (43.37%), as seen in Table 10. And according to Table 11, most Attitudinal meanings (68.56%) are characterized by positive polarity as a salient feature of the exchange.

As evident from Table 12, positive polarity was mostly used when discussing instructional materials (93 instances) and instructional tasks (26 instances). Negative evaluations were mostly used in connection with the happenings within the texts (30 instances), but also in reference to some aspects of instructional materials (25 instances). The process of task

Table 8. Target and Attitude type

Target	Total	Affect	Judgment	Appreciation
Instructional materials	44.69%	3.38%	11.86%	84.74%
Aspects inside the texts	20.83%	23.63%	34.54%	41.81%
Tasks	12.87%	2.94%	35.29%	61.76%
Process of task completion	9.09%	8.33%	41.66%	50%
Self	5.68%	13.33%	86.66%	0%
Learners	4.16%	0%	81.81%	18.18%
Instructors (in general)	1.51%	0%	100%	0%
Instructors of the FL Teaching and Literacy course	0.75%	0%	50%	50%

Table 9. Appreciation type

Reaction/quality	52.83%
Reaction/valuation	18.24%
Composition/complexity	15.72%
Reaction/impact	11.95%
Composition/balance	0.63%

Table 10. Judgment type

Social esteem (capacity, normality)	43.37%
Social sanction (propriety, veracity)	56.63%

Table 11. Attitude polarity

Positive Attitude	68.56%
Negative Attitude	31.44%

Table 12. Polarity and target type

Target	Negative polarity	Positive polarity
Instructional materials	25	93
Aspects inside texts	30	25
Tasks	8	26
Process of task completion	9	15
Self	7	8
Instructors in general	2	2
Learners	2	9
Instructors of the course	0	2

completion that the exchange participants were engaged in was more often evaluated as positive (15 instances), rather than negative (9 instances). And the positive and negative evaluations of the participants themselves are almost equal in number (i.e., *Self:* 7 negative and 8 positive instances).

5 Discussion

While the results presented above reveal various types and targets of attitude expressed in the telecollaborative exchange, the discussion that follows is oriented towards the second research question and aims to connect these attitudes to the discourse evidence of student teachers' pedagogical competences in the areas of materials selection and didacticization, task design, as well as telecollaborative interaction with the goal of completing the materials development task.

5.1 Materials Selection and Didacticization

The predominance of instructional materials as a target of evaluation suggests that materials selection and didacticization constitute the most salient focus of the telecollaborative discussion, which is in line with the focus of the tasks that teachers had to complete (Table 1). Justifying the selection of texts from the perspective of emotions (Affect) or assessing their capacity or propriety (Judgment) is not prominent in the exchange. Expressing one's feelings about the texts might appear too subjective, personal, and not sufficiently academic, while judgment that is oriented to moral values of right and wrong may be perceived as too direct and face-threatening. Student negotiation and reasoning about the selection of authentic texts for instruction are thus mostly based on Appreciation or feelings institutionalized in terms of certain criteria of quality (e.g., *ausschmückend/decorative; original/original*), potential impact on the learner (e.g., *befremdlich/disconcerting; interessant/interesting; langweilig/boring; traumatisch/traumatic; voll Gänsehaut/giving one goose bumps*), complexity (e.g., *klar/clear*), and cultural significance (e.g., *authentisch/authentic; wichtig/important*).

Importantly, when appraising the texts, the participants consider their quality in terms of being typical or not typical of a particular genre, which is a central consideration for developing materials in a literacy-oriented and genre-based instructional framework (Crane, 2006). Excerpt 2 shows, for example, how a genre atypical text can be problematic (*nicht geeignet/not suitable*) as a model for the construction of an instructional task based on the text.

> Excerpt 2
> *Dafür wenn man die Task hätte die sollen so nen Task produzieren zum Beispiel eben die sollen einen Liedtext produzieren das kann man ja durchaus machen natürlich ... aber dafür ist der Text hier halt nicht geeignet sondern weil dafür bräuchte man halt einen genretypischen Text und keinen genreuntypischen Text.*
> *For that if one had the task they have to produce for example they have to produce a song text one can do that of course ... but for that the text here is just not suitable but because for that one would need a text that is typical of the genre and not an atypical text.*

In line with the guidelines for the materials development task (Table 1), the student teachers further evaluate the texts under consideration with regard to the cultural or historical importance of the aspects that each text highlights (*historischen Bezug/historical connection*) or the complexity of their overarching theme (*geht mehr in die Tiefe/goes into more depth*), as in Excerpt 3. The salience of the historical aspects forms the basis for selecting the second text centered on the fall of the Berlin Wall, rather than a wine advertisement that the student evaluates as *süss/nice*, but not thematically substantive (*gibt nicht genug her/does not offer enough*).

> Excerpt 3
> *Ja aber ich finde deins trotzdem besser weil ich mir überlegt hab dass also dein Textvorschlag hat ja so nen historischen Bezug und geht mehr in die Tiefe also ich find hier das ist so ein ganz süsses Beispiel aber ich glaub wenn man sich damit jetzt so ganz vertieft auseinandersetzen will dann gibt der einfach nicht genug her.*
> *Yes but I find your text still better because I thought that your text suggestion has a historical connection and goes more into depth*

so I find that this is a nice example but I think if one wants to discuss it in depth then it does not offer enough.

Excerpt 4 provides an additional illustration of the significance of the thematic elements inside texts (the second evaluation target with regard to frequency) that are discussed in detail throughout the exchange. In this example, the nominalized emotions of *Erwartung/expectation* and *Enttäuschung/ disappointment* that the student teachers ascribe to the characters in their text are appreciated as *wichtig/important* aspects of that moment in history that need to be emphasized in instruction.

Excerpt 4
Diese Aspekte die wir gerade besprochen haben ... dass man als wichtigen Aspekt rausarbeitet, dann das äh[3] vielleicht mit Erwartung und Enttäuschung und diesem Symbolcharakter für Freiheit. These aspects that we have just discussed ... that one shows it to be an important aspect, then that uh perhaps with expectation and disappointment and that symbol for freedom.

This analysis shows that, in addition to the question of genre, the cultural or historical themes that the texts represent, as well as considerations of impact on the learner, also play a prominent role in the discussion. The awareness of and attention to these issues provide evidence of the student teachers' expertise as material developers in a content-based curriculum where texts are used not only to entertain students (i.e., interesting vs. boring), but also to teach form-function connections within clearly defined genres, as well as explore salient cultural content through form-function links in texts that center on historically significant themes.

5.2 Tasks

Most often instructional tasks in this dataset are evaluated through Appreciation. Task design is discussed with regard to task originality or lack thereof and task complexity. For example, in Excerpt 5, the task of creating an advertisement is negatively appraised as *null acht fünfzehn/run-of-the mill*, while Excerpt 6 shows that asking students to produce a story based on the original narrative runs the risk of designing an assignment that is too close to the original (*zu nah, nicht genug Transfer/too close, not enough transfer*).

3   Interjection.

Excerpt 5
Weil das ist halt ja eigentlich ... null acht fünfzehn die Task die die meisten halt machen werden oder die eigentlich die ganze Zeit gemacht wird.
Because this is actually ... run-of-the-mill the task that most will do or that actually is done all the time.

Excerpt 6
Man könnte halt auch sagen die sollen genau das als Text schreiben ... als Erzählung schreiben. Aber andererseits wär das halt wahrscheinlich auch einfach zu nahan dem was halt hier schon da ist. Ich glaub auch das ist nicht genug Transfer.
One could just say they should write this as text ... as a story. But on the other hand that would be probably simply too close to what is here. I also think that this is not enough transfer.

These excerpts demonstrate, on the one hand, the student teachers' awareness of the importance of modelling tasks on texts in order to scaffold learner independent genre production (Byrnes, Crane, Maxim, & Sprang, 2006) and, on the other hand, their differentiated understanding that such tasks should not be too common or too close to the models. Constructing tasks that enable learners to do both – that is, draw on the model texts and create new meanings for a new context – is one of the key challenges for material developers (Ryshina-Pankova, 2016).

As regards Appreciation **quality,** the most frequent evaluating term for activities and tasks is the general *gut/good*, suggesting that while the student teachers know what tasks not to design, they might still be hesitant about what exactly a good task looks like. In Excerpt 7, the initial intent to ask learners to produce a dialogue is evaluated as a good idea (*sehr gut find/find very good*), but it is not clear to the student teacher what exactly this task entails and how one would scaffold its production (*müsste man das noch irgendwie unterfüttern/one would have to somehow prepare them*).

Excerpt 7
Wenn man die große Aufgabe haben will dass die nen Dialog schreiben was ich sehr gut find muss ich sagen ähm müsste man das noch irgendwie unterfüttern.
If one wants to have a big task that they write a dialogue that I find very good I have to say um one would have to somehow prepare them.

From the results it is also evident that tasks are frequently evaluated through Judgment. Typically such evaluations concern the ability of the student teachers to design tasks and are often negatively colored (*immer*

Exploring Attitudinal Resources in Telecollaboration 161

schwierig finde mit der Task/I always find it difficult with the task; mir fällt keine endgültige Task ein, die ich ja gut finde/I can think of no final task that I find good). On the other hand, evaluations of the ability of the student teachers to do the task with the learners are often positively colored (*das kann man ja durchaus machen/one can certainly do it; könnte man ja ruhig machen/one could easily do it*).

5.3   Telecollaborative Interaction for Task Completion

The two participants were successful in building a productive interaction in the telecollaborative activity where their goal was to select a text, justify their selection, and brainstorm about potential instructional tasks. The rapport that the student teachers built can be attributed to the predominance of positive polarity in the attitudinal meanings expressed by the telecollaboration partners across the various targets of evaluation. They were also specifically positive with regard to the process of task completion itself, as shown in Excerpt 8, and with regard to the attitude attributed to the two instructors of the course – for example, to the one in Germany, as in Excerpt 9:

> Excerpt 8
> *Also ich find das was wir p-per WhatsApp schon besprochen haben eigentlich ganz gut.*
> So I find that what we've already discussed via WhatsApp is actually quite good.

> Excerpt 9
> *Ich glaube die (Frau ...) hat den Optimismus aller auf ihrer Seite und das machen wir schon gut.*
> I think that the (instructor of the course) has the optimism of everyone on her side and we will do it well.

Furthermore, the prevalence of Appreciation vis-à-vis the spare use of Affect as potentially too subjective and emotional, on the one hand, and the tendency to use the less face-threatening invoked Judgment, on the other, helped the telecollaboration participants maintain the objective stance necessary for the completion of the academic task with which they were charged and not to call into question their partners' pedagogical competences, thereby ultimately contributing to the constructive and positive nature of the exchange. Bearing in mind teaching competences in the telecollaborative context (O'Dowd, 2015), we see evidence of the partner teachers' willingness to look for compromise and an openness to alternative pedagogical beliefs and aims.

Finally, the telecollaborative interaction included some instances of the student teachers' self-evaluation which appear balanced. Negative evaluations reflect that students can share their own lack of knowledge and thereby build a connection with their partner "in distress" (Excerpt 10), while positive evaluations reinforce the optimistic outlook on the task at hand (Excerpt 11).

Excerpt 10
Ich habe das falsch verstanden weil ich war voll verwirrt.
I understood it incorrectly because I was totally confused.

Excerpt 11
Ja genau da so einen Text brauchen wir und den werden wir auch finden.
Yes exactly we need such a text and we will also find it.

6 Conclusion

The goal of this study was to understand better how the attitudes on display during SCMC-based interaction between two student teachers can contribute to an understanding of teacher competences within a literacy-based pedagogical framework. During their interaction, the participants expressed a range of attitudes towards a variety of targets, thereby offering insight into decisions regarding text selection and task development. As regards text selection, the participants focused variously on quality, complexity, cultural significance, and impact on learner as important factors. Tasks, in contrast, were evaluated in terms of their originality and complexity, either through Appreciation (i.e., assessing the value of things) or Judgment (i.e., assessing the correctness of actions and the capacity of actors) (Martin & White, 2005), enabling the participants to offer and respond to potential ideas in an objective and non-threatening manner. In other words, through a process of dialogic mediation that afforded mutual assistance (Allen, 2011), participants were able to display their abilities to select appropriate pedagogical texts and develop related materials. Additionally, the study also showed the linguistic instantiation of beliefs and attitudes that are core to telecollaborative teaching, including readiness to compromise and willingness to consider pedagogical beliefs that may differ from the partner teacher's (O'Dowd, 2015). In sum, by evaluating themselves and their own ideas, as well as those of their partner, the participants could negotiate and co-construct a mutual understanding of text selection, materials development, and factors governing related pedagogical decisions.

It must be noted, however, that the study is essentially a snapshot of interaction between two student teachers *in situ*, and it should therefore not be considered as evidence of development in relation to an earlier state of knowledge. This limitation suggests, in turn, the need for longitudinal investigation of the phenomena observed in this study, so as to give insight into the *process* of pedagogical competence development via telecollaborative task completion (Müller-Hartmann, 2016).

References

Allen, H. W. (2011). Embracing literacy-based teaching: A longitudinal study of the conceptual development of novice foreign language teachers. In K. E. Johnson & P. E. Golombek (eds.), *Sociocultural Research on Second Language Teacher Education: Exploring the Complexities of Professional Development* (pp. 86–101). New York: Routledge.

Allen, H. W., & Dupuy, B. (2011). Evolving notions of literacy-based language teaching: A qualitative study of graduate student instructors. In H. W. Allen & H. H. Maxim (eds.), *Educating the Future Foreign Language Professoriate for the 21st Century* (pp. 171–191). Boston: Heinle.

Belz, J. A. (2003). Linguistic perspectives on the development of intercultural competence in telecollaboration. *Language Learning & Technology*, 7(2), 68–117.

Bendig, I., Betz, E., & Huth, T. (2016). "weil – das ist eben doch richtig so" Teaching variant types of *weil*- and *obwohl*-structures in German. *Die Unterrichtspraxis/Teaching German*, 49(2), 214–227. https://doi.org/10.1111/tger.12013

Byrnes, H. (2005). Literacy as a framework for advanced language acquisition. *ADFL Bulletin*, 37(1), 85–110. https://doi.org/10.1632/adfl.37.1.11

Byrnes, H., Crane, C., Maxim, H., & Sprang, C. (2006). Taking text to task: Issues and choice in curriculum construction. *International Journal of Applied Linguistics*, 52(1), 85–109. https://doi.org/10.2143/ITL.152.0.2017864

Cope, B., & Kalantzis, M. (2009). "Multiliteracies": New literacies, new learning. *Pedagogies: An International Journal*, 4(3), 164–195. https://doi.org/10.1080/15544800903076044

Crane, C. (2006). Modelling a genre-based foreign language curriculum: Staging advanced L2 learning. In H. Byrnes (ed.), *Advanced Language Learning: The Contribution of Halliday and Vygotsky*. London: Continuum.

Crookes, G. (1990). The utterance, and other basic units for second language discourse analysis. *Applied Linguistics*, 11(2), 183–199. https://doi.org/10.1093/applin/11.2.183

Cunningham, D. J. (2013). Teacher competences in telecollaboration: The case of Web conferencing and German for professional purposes. In J. Aitken (ed.), *Cases on Communication Technology for Second Language Acquisition and Cultural Learning* (pp. 173–205). Hershey, PA: IGI Global. https://doi.org/10.4018/978-1-4666-4482-3.ch012

Dooly, M. (2010). Teacher 2.0. In S. Guth & F. Helm (eds.), *Telecollaboration 2.0: Language, Literacies and Intercultural Learning in the 21st Century* (pp. 277–304). Bern, Switzerland: Peter Lang.

Dooly, M., & Sadler, R. (2013). Filling in the gaps: Linking theory and practice through telecollaboration in teacher education. *ReCALL*, 25(1), 4–29. https://doi.org/10.1017/S0958344012000237

Fuchs, C., Hauck, M., & Müller-Hartmann, A. (2012). Promoting learner autonomy through multiliteracy skills development in cross-institutional exchanges. *Language Learning & Technology*, 16(3), 82–102.

Guichon, N., & Hauck, M. (2011). Teacher education research in CALL and CMC: More in demand than ever. *ReCALL*, 23(3), 187–199. https://doi.org/10.1017/S0958344011000139

Hampel, R., & Stickler, U. (2005). New skills for new classrooms: Training tutors to teach languages online. *Computer Assisted Language Learning*, 18(4), 311–326. https://doi.org/10.1080/09588220500335455

Kern, R. (2000). *Literacy and Language Teaching*. Oxford: Oxford University Press.

Liamkina, O., & Ryshina-Pankova, M. (2012). Grammar dilemma: Teaching grammar as a resource for making meaning. *The Modern Language Journal*, 96(2), pp. 270–289. https://doi.org/10.1111/j.1540-4781.2012.01333_1.x

Martin, J. R. (1984). Language, register and genre. In F. Christie (ed.), *Children Writing: Reader* (pp. 21–29). Geelong, Victoria, Australia: Deakin University Press.

Martin, J. R., & White, P. R. R. (2005). *The Language of Evaluation: Appraisal in English*. New York: Palgrave Macmillan. https://doi.org/10.1057/9780230511910

Menke, M. R., & Paesani, K. (2019). Analysing foreign language instructional materials through the lens of the multiliteracies framework. *Language, Culture and Curriculum*, 32(1), 34–49. https://doi.org/10.1080/07908318.2018.1461898

Müller-Hartmann, A. (2016). A task is a task is a task is a task ... or is it? Researching telecollaborative teacher competence development – the need for more qualitative research. In S. Jager, M. Kurek, & B. O'Rourke (eds.), *New Directions in Telecollaborative Research and Practice: Selected Papers from the Second Conference on Telecollaboration in Higher Education* (pp. 31–43). Researchpublishing.net. https://doi.org/10.14705/rpnet.2016.telecollab2016.488

O'Donnell, M. (2014). Exploring identity through Appraisal analysis: A corpus annotation methodology. *Linguistics and the Human Sciences*, 9(1). https://doi.org/10.1558/lhs.v9i1.95

O'Dowd, R. (2015). The competences of the telecollaborative teacher. *The Language Learning Journal*, 43(2), 194–207. https://doi.org/10.1080/09571736.2013.853374

Oskoz, A., & Pérez-Broncano, O. (2016). What did you say? How did you say it? Linguistics choices in online discussions. *Foreign Language Annals*, 49(4), 772–788. https://doi.org/10.1111/flan.12240

Paesani, K. (2011). A literacy-based approach to foreign language teacher development. In H. W. Allen & H. H. Maxim (eds.), *Educating the Future Foreign Language Professoriate for the 21st Century* (pp. 60–81). Boston, MA: Heinle.

Paesani, K., Allen, H. W., & Dupuy, B. (2015). *A Multiliteracies Framework for Collegiate Foreign Language Teaching*. Boston: Pearson.

Rankin, J., & Becker, F. (2006). Does reading the research make a difference? A case study of teacher growth in FL German. *The Modern Language Journal*, 90(3), 353–372. https://doi.org/10.1111/j.1540-4781.2006.00429.x

Ryshina-Pankova, M. (2011). A literacy-based approach to foreign language teacher development. In H. W. Allen & H. H. Maxim (eds.), *Educating the Future Foreign Language Professoriate for the 21st Century* (pp. 82–103). Boston: Heinle.

Ryshina-Pankova, M. (2016). Scaffolding advanced literacy in the FL classroom: Implementing a genre-driven content-based approach. In L. Cammarata (ed.), *Content-based Foreign Language Teaching: Curriculum and Pedagogy for Developing Advanced Thinking and Literacy Skills* (pp. 51–70). New York: Routledge.

Turula, A. (2016). Designing pro-telecollaboration teacher training: Some insights based on the OCEAN personality measures. In L. Bradley & S. Thouësny (eds.), *20 Years of EUROCALL: Learning from the Past, Looking to the Future. Proceedings of the 2013 EUROCALL Conference, Évora, Portugal* (pp. 244–249). Dublin: Research-publishing.net. https://doi.org/10.14705/rpnet.2013.000168

Vinagre, M., & Corral Esteban, A. (2018). Evaluative language for rapport building in virtual collaboration: An analysis of appraisal in computer-mediated interaction. *Language and Intercultural Communication*, 18(3), 335–350. https://doi.org/10.1080/14708477.2017.1378227

About the Authors

D. Joseph Cunningham is Assistant Professor of German at Georgetown University in Washington, DC, where he is also Director of the undergraduate curriculum. Situated at the intersection of technology-mediated second language pedagogy and instructed pragmatic development, his research has appeared in peer-reviewed journals such as *CALICO Journal* and *Language Learning & Technology*. In addition to studying the benefits of virtual exchange for second language learning and teacher education, Dr Cunningham is interested in the role of telecollaboration at the curricular level.

Marianna Ryshina-Pankova is Associate Professor of German and Director of Graduate Studies at Georgetown University in Washington, DC. In collaboration with her colleagues she is actively involved in the maintenance, revision, and evaluation of the undergraduate curriculum and in mentoring graduate students in the program. Her research involves application of systemic functional theory in language pedagogy and content- and language-integrated curriculum design, development of advanced second language literacy and intercultural communicative competence through telecollaboration, and foreign language teacher education.

7 Researching Emotions and Attitude through Student Teachers' Reflections on Virtual Exchange

Francesca Helm and Alice Baroni

1 Introduction

In foreign language education and pre-service teacher education, the telecollaborative model of virtual exchange[1] (henceforth referred to as virtual exchange, or VE) is increasingly being implemented (Avgousti, 2018; Dooly, 2016; Dooly & Sadler, 2013; Vinagre, 2015) in order to enhance participants' language skills and intercultural competence. In this chapter we focus on attitude, and in particular the emotional dimension of language and intercultural learning. It has been explored in the literature on foreign language learning (Krashen, 1981; Pavlenko, 2013; Swain, 2013) and also intergroup relations (Paolini, Harwood, Hewstone, & Neumann, 2018), but to a much lesser extent in the telecollaboration literature (Vinagre & Corral, 2018). We start with a brief literature review of emotions in foreign language learning, also drawing links to recent research in the field of social psychology on the theme of intergroup contact. This is followed by a presentation of the context of this study, the EVALUATE[2] project, a large-scale virtual exchange project involving over 1,000 future teachers. The mixed methods approach adopted for this study draws on a dataset of reflective journal entries, and adopts content analysis based on principles of grounded theory as its main methodological approach, supported by sentiment analysis. First of all, the emotional journey of participants in this

---

[1] There are various models of virtual exchange; the telecollaborative model refers to the task-based approach to telecollaboration which was developed and is commonly used in foreign language education.
[2] Evaluating and Upscaling Telecollaborative Teacher Education (EVALUATE) is a European policy experimentation (http://www.evaluateproject.eu) led by Robert O'Dowd.

virtual exchange is explored, and the emotional impact of the challenges they faced. The focus then turns to participants' attitudes towards difference as expressed in their journal entries.

2 Literature Review

2.1 Early Research on Emotions and Language Learning

The field of language learning and second language acquisition (SLA) has been dominated by cognitivist theories, but emotions were first recognized as playing an important role in the 1970s. Dulay & Burt (1977) and Krashen (1981) conceptualized the influence of a learner's emotional state as a "filter," through which linguistic input has to pass. When this "affective filter" is low, language can be acquired, but when the filter is elevated – by factors such as high anxiety, or low self-esteem and motivation, then it is much more difficult for language acquisition to take place. Krashen's theories fell out of favor within the scientific community for being "unverifiable" and over-simplistic (Swain, 2013), focusing on the individual, and failing to take into consideration the importance of interaction, broader societal factors, and power relations (Norton, 2000). Nonetheless, together with other theories of SLA which foreground communication, such as Swain's (1995) output hypothesis and interactionist theories of language learning (Long, 1996), Krashen's affective filter hypothesis has remained influential in communicative language teaching (Liddicoat & Scarino, 2013) and also virtual exchange, which is centered around the engagement of students in interaction with distant peers.

Emotions also emerge in Gardner & Lambert's (1972) work on motivation with its focus on attitudes, affect, and intergroup relations, which opened the field of second language learning to a social psychological perspective. The concept of integrative motivation was developed from theories of intergroup contact, and linked motivation to how learners viewed the "target language community" and their desire to integrate within that community. The original model of integrative motivation has been criticized for the focus on the individual and ignoring societal factors (Taie & Afshari, 2015). Taking a sociocultural perspective, Ushioda (2007) contrasts the psychometric tradition which has explored motivation from the "individual differences" point of view and argues that our understanding of motivation should be recognized as "socially distributed, created with cultural systems of activities involving the mediation of others" (p. 23). Furthermore, the original concept of integrative motivation could be seen as presenting a somewhat narrow, essentialist conceptualization of the "target community."

Nonetheless the relevance of integrative motivation to the field of telecollaboration lies in its linking language and intergroup theory, which relates to intercultural learning. The field of intergroup relations has continued to grow in the disciplinary field of social psychology around Gordon Allport's "contact hypothesis" (Allport, 1954; Pettigrew, 1986), according to which contact between people from diverse groups is expected to result in positive intergroup relations and the reduction of prejudice if certain conditions are met. These conditions are that members of the group should have similar status, should work together on a common goal without competition, and some authority should support the contact and interactions between the groups.

In this early literature on emotions in language learning there was a strong focus on negative emotions such as anxiety, and different triggers have been identified, often linked to classroom contexts – such as harsh error correction (Gregersen, 2003), test scores, and attitude towards the target language (Horwitz, 2017). Likewise, negative emotions such as anxiety and anger were for a long time the focus in the social psychology research, with anxiety found to be associated with outgroup avoidance and anger associated with greater support for hostile action (Paolini et al. 2018).

2.2 The Emotional Turn

There has been a recent increase of interest in exploring emotion in the field of foreign language learning, which has been labelled as "the emotional turn" in SLA (Pavlenko, 2013). Although, as mentioned above, emotions have been explored in SLA, the cognitive dimension has tended to be prioritized over the emotional. Swain (2013) attributes this to socio-historical reasons and the birth of rationalism which separated cognition, associated with intelligence, from emotion – seen as more primitive and even bestial. She also links it to the difficulties perceived in defining and measuring emotions – with the exception of anxiety which was seen as more readily measurable and hence the focus of the early research on emotions.

The renewed attention to emotions in language learning this decade is characterized by a shift from focusing predominantly on negative emotions and anxiety to a more holistic analysis of both negative and positive emotions (Dewaele & MacIntyre, 2014; Dewaele & Li, 2018; MacIntyre & Mercer, 2014) and their impact on motivation and on language learning. Dewaele & MacIntyre (2014) found, for example, that enjoyment and anxiety are related, but independent. That is, they do not represent opposite ends of the same dimension – which means, for example, that a person who is enjoying an interaction in a foreign language may also experience a degree of anxiety, or that lack of enjoyment does not mean anxiety is present. Enjoyment is seen to be an important factor facilitating language acquisition (Dewaele & MacIntyre, 2014), as it is associated with the urge to play, be creative, and expand one's limits, and can be stimulated by interpersonal relations.

Recent studies of intergroup relations have found that emotions play a more crucial role than cognitive processes in changing beliefs and reducing prejudice through intergroup contact (Paolini et al., 2018: 12). Information acquired through contact can change beliefs and reduce prejudice by dismantling negative and inaccurate stereotypes (Brown & Hewstone, 2005), but this process is mediated by emotions. It is thus important to take into consideration the emotional dimension when setting up encounters between groups.

2.3 Emotions, Motivation, and Telecollaboration

Researchers of motivation in language learning have acknowledged that the motivation literature is "lagging behind" developments in CALL (Al-Hoorie, 2017) as the focus has been very much on the traditional classroom. They have recognized an "authenticity gap" (Henry, 2013) that an increasing number of language learners are experiencing: they are exposed to the L2 both inside and outside the classroom, but their experiences outside the classroom are more stimulating than in the classroom. One of the reasons for this is that online spaces have opened up the doors to situations where language learners' can invoke other (transportable and imagined) identities (Darvin & Norton, 2015; Helm 2018; Ushioda, 2011) and become users of the target language in more authentic contexts, drawing on their multiple identities rather than the deficient language learner identity they are so often cast into in the language class. This, indeed, is one of the rationales for the increasing adoption of telecollaboration in foreign language education. However, emotions and attitudes have been studied less than the cognitive and behavioral components of language learning and intercultural competence in the telecollaboration literature. In Lewis & O'Dowd's (2016) meta-analysis, for example, the attitudinal component was the object of analysis in only a handful of studies and emotion was not explicitly addressed in any. Nonetheless, attitudes are touched upon in a relevant body of research, and this volume certainly provides an important contribution to this expanding field of study.

In the telecollaboration literature, different approaches have been adopted in studies which have looked at attitude and/or emotion. Ware & Kramsch (2005), for example, provide a detailed analysis of a five-turn episode of misunderstanding that occurred in the interactions of a group which comprised two American students and three German students. One of the aspects they explored was the affective stance and emotional intensity of the interlocutors as regards the issue they were talking about (in this case German reunification), how this was interpreted, and the impact this had on participation – the disengagement of her interlocutor. They concluded that incidents such as these cannot be prevented, which could be seen as one of the "risks" of telecollaboration; at the same time they see these episodes as providing one of the richest learning opportunities in communicatively oriented curricula.

Vinagre & Corral (2018) used appraisal theory to analyze evaluative language used in interactions between partners in a Spanish–American virtual exchange (Martin, 2000; Martin & White, 2005) in order to understand how emotional and interpersonal issues influenced interaction. They looked at how participants used evaluative language and whether there were differences or similarities in the tokens used by the Spanish and American partners. They found that there was a strong emphasis on Affect and greater use of positive rather than negative evaluative language, which was possibly a strategy to build rapport and solidarity with partners. Similar use of positive tokens by both groups of students suggested the adaptation to one another's communicative practices to favor the creation of a close and friendly collaborative atmosphere which would foster further interactions.

Rather than looking at interaction data, Negueruela-Azarola (2011) used a narrative approach, through an open-ended interview with a single learner, in order to explore how a sociocultural understanding of L2 classroom motivation as emotional experience can allow researchers to make sense of sometimes contradictory explanations students articulate regarding motivations. He sees "transformative understanding of second language classroom motivation as emotional significance [...]" (p. 188) which is changing, mediating, and historical. Emotional significance is seen as signaling what matters to individuals at a given moment and is a personal disposition towards taking part in an activity, which may be mediated by both social and personal reasons. He takes a narrative perspective in exploring motivation because, he argues, narrative accounts allow for the reconstruction of the changing motivation of language learners. The methodology used was an open-ended interview with a learner of Spanish as a foreign language who had participated in a telecollaboration project, after a series of challenging classes which led to strong feelings of anxiety and insecurity. The interview revealed both to the researcher and the student that it was the "shift from language learning to communicative engagement and cultural understanding with real students from Spain" that transformed her experience of L2 learning; the experience mattered to her as she found emotional significance through it.

These three studies which have explored emotional dimensions of language learning and intercultural engagement in telecollaboration are, like most other research studies in this field, small-scale studies which focus on a single telecollaboration exchange. The kinds of in-depth qualitative analysis that they offer are a rich contribution to our understanding of the impact of the field. The study in this chapter differs in that it aims to look at the emotional dimension across a large number of comparable exchanges and hence inevitably lacks the depth of a fine-grained analysis. On the other hand, it provides a bird's-eye view of the emotional journey that telecollaboration can trigger, a perspective which has so far been missing from the field (O'Dowd, 2017).

3 Context and Aims of This Study

This research study was carried out in the context of the EVALUATE project, which is a large-scale policy experimentation funded by the European Commission, exploring the impact of telecollaborative virtual exchange (VE) on students of initial teacher education and its contribution to the development of their intercultural, linguistic, and digital competences.[3] The project was based on principles of experiential learning, and the premise that experiencing innovative and inclusive uses of technology in their education will stimulate future teachers to do the same in their classrooms (O'Dowd, 2017: 38).

This project was one of the first large-scale research projects on telecollaborative virtual exchange, exploring multiple exchanges that involved different partnerships but which shared some similarities: all the exchanges were in the context of teacher education, and they all adopted the "Progressive Exchange Model" (O'Dowd & Ware, 2009; O'Dowd & Lewis, 2016). This entails participants undertaking three interrelated tasks that move from information exchange, to comparing and analyzing cultural practices, and finally working on a collaborative product. Teacher trainers

---

3   In the context of this large-scale project, 25 exchanges were carried out over two semesters, involving 34 institutions of teacher education in 16 different countries (The EVALUATE Group, 2019). The majority of partners were in European countries but teacher educators from Brazil, Canada, Israel, Macau, the United States, and Turkey also took part. A total of 1,018 students from 34 institutions participated in the EVALUATE study.

who were involved in the pilot project took part in a workshop and agreed to implement a virtual exchange following this model, though they were free to adapt it to their specific context and needs.

The project's overall research questions regarded the impact of virtual exchange on participants' intercultural, digital-pedagogical, and language competences.[4] In particular, we examined (1) How do students experience their telecollaboration in terms of emotions? and (2) How do participants express their attitudes towards difference? In this chapter we provide an in-depth study based on the qualitative part of the dataset. As reflection is seen to be a key component in making sense of experiences (Kolb, 2015; Mezirow, 1991), reflective journal entries were chosen as a data collecting tool to provide insights into students' affective responses to events as well as the cognitive processes. Student reflections have been used with different forms of experiential learning, for example study abroad and multicultural group assignments (Savicki & Price, 2015; Zhou & Pilcher, 2018).

3.1   Research Method

In this study, we focus on the 804 participants who took part in the first round of the EVALUATE project, which consisted of 17 virtual exchanges. These students were required to respond to questions promoting reflections on different aspects of their experience at four different points of the exchange (see Appendix): before it started, and then after each of the three main tasks they engaged in. The corpus of reflective responses to questions that we analyzed consisted of 162,228 words.

To analyze the data and address our research questions, we combined qualitative content analysis, which has affinities with constructivist grounded theory approach (Charmaz, 2005, 2006; Charmaz & Belgrave, 2018),[5] and sentiment analysis, using a quantitative tool called Linguistic

---

4   In the EVALUATE study, a mixed-methods approach was adopted with a semi-experimental pre- and post-exchange survey with a control group to measure intercultural competence and the Technological Pedagogical Content Knowledge (TPACK) and also participant reflections. In terms of intercultural competence, the quantitative part of the study used Portalla & Chen's (2010) scale of intercultural effectiveness for pre- and post-exchange tests. This showed some improvement over time on the overall scale, but was not significant when compared to the control group. Significant changes were found in the subscales of behavioral flexibility, interaction management, and message skills. (For the full report on the mixed methods study see The EVALUATE Group, 2019.)

5   This qualitative analysis was supported by the software Nvivo.

Inquiry and Word Count (LIWC).[6] LIWC is a content analysis software program that counts the words in a text according to specific dictionaries that have been developed to tap various assumed cognitive and emotional processes (Pennebaker, Boyd, Jordan, & Blackburn, 2015). For the purpose of this study we focused on the two broad categories LIWC has in its dictionary related to emotion: positive emotions (love, hope, sweet) and negative emotions (hurt, ugly, nasty).[7] This sort of analysis has been applied to the study of journals written by students having study abroad experiences (Savicki & Price, 2015) to explore the positive and negative emotions and cognitive processes associated with the different phases of the experience. Savicki & Price (2015) found a healthy ratio of positive to negative emotion, and significant changes in positive emotion over time, with a peak before departure and in preparation for coming home.

We adopted a mixed-methods approach in a spiral way, as we started with qualitative analysis by identifying patterns in students' diaries in a constant comparative process between different codes created through the initial analysis. Then we made links with the research literature which helped us to rethink and narrow down our initial coding of data and create specific categories, such as those related to challenges in virtual exchange. Subsequently, we ran the complete set of diaries through LIWC and also the text coded in some of the categories we had developed through grounded theory,[8] which gave us a different insight into students' emotional experiences in VE, in addition to validating our initial findings. This brought us back to the qualitative analysis in a constant process of comparison and re-reading of data and research enquiry.

3.2 Findings

As reported above, the content analysis software LIWC provides measures of positive and negative emotion in written texts. Figure 1 shows the intensity of these emotions in students' diaries at the different collection points, that is, it shows the percentage of words which fall into each of these categories at each collection point.[9] We can see from Figure 1 that there is a high

---

6   We used the 2015 version of LIWC.
7   It also provides three sub-categories of negative emotions which are anxiety (worried, fearful), anger (hate, annoyed), and sadness (crying, grief, sad). There are no sub-categories of positive emotions.
8   That is, the nodes created in NVivo were downloaded as Excel files, and these were then uploaded to LIWC for content analysis.
9   The data in this graph come from the first round of implementation of EVALUATE which involved 17 exchanges.

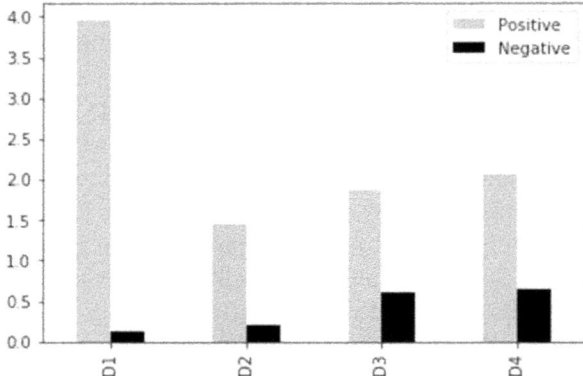

Figure 1. Scores on positive and negative emotions across data collection points

starting point in terms of positive emotions, which then dips quite dramatically as the students begin their exchanges, and gradually rises, together with an increase in negative emotions over the exchange. The use of the tool for sentiment analysis served above all to gauge the overall "emotional temperature" over time across a large body of data. It is important to point out that this is the pattern across data gathered from 17 different exchanges, and the graph does not show the difference between the exchanges. There was considerable variation in the scores on positive and negative emotion among the various exchanges, but virtually all showed the same pattern, that is, initial high emotion and virtually no negative emotion, followed by a dip in positive emotion, followed by a gradual rise in both positive and negative emotions. In the following sections we explore potential reasons for these changes in emotion through qualitative analysis of the students' texts.

3.2.1 High expectations and imagined selves

Analysis of the qualitative data revealed high expectations with many of the students motivated by the idea of learning skills and knowledges which they saw as being related to their future career as teachers, framed in terms of intercultural competence, language, and/or digital skills. There was a difference in terms of the degree to which respondents emphasized the relationship-building opportunities that the exchange offered, and the skills. Their positive emotions are linked to their talking about their imagined selves, what they see themselves becoming – across all exchanges. We can see this in the extract below where a Portuguese student writes about how she was motivated by the idea of building relations with people from "other cultures," and hoped to gain intercultural understanding and learn about the Brazilian educational system:

> I hope to improve my relationship with people from other cultures which is what motivates me in this project. I think the contact with people from other cultures, who study the same as me, is always important. I also hope to get to know the educational system of another culture as well as its educational project, and how the Brazilian students train themselves to become future teachers/educators. (Exchange 3, female, 23)

An Israeli student commented on his hopes in exchanging with German peers, again focusing on the relational dimension and getting to know his peers, but also on developing confidence in using technology:

> First, to learn more about my colleagues from Germany, not just about their journey as students but mostly about themselves, their lives, their passions, their interests. Second, I hope to gain more trust in the technological experience. (Exchange 10, male, 44)

On the other hand, a Polish student expected to acquire technological pedagogical competence that can be employed during her career, as well as improve her language skills, while exchanging with German students. As we see in the quote below there is less of an orientation towards relationship building and more emphasis on developing skills:

> I hope to learn more about the usage of new media and technology in the classroom. Exchanges with different countries are always fun, interesting and quite educational (language and culture). Therefore, I hope I will learn how I can use such projects in my further career as a teacher. Additionally, I hope I will improve my understanding of non-native English speakers. I think my understanding of spoken English is okay but I always struggle in understanding non-native speakers. (Exchange 1, female, 27)

The exchanges are seen as a means to becoming an imagined self, a teacher with connections to people from other cultures, with some knowledge of different educational systems, pedagogical approaches, language competence, and/or technical skills. Integrative motivation could thus be re-framed as a desire to become part of an imagined future community of practice, to learn the skills and competences and build relationships that will support them in this endeavour.

3.2.2 Facing challenges in virtual exchange

The initial enthusiasm and positive emotion in students' writing about their expectations dampened as the project evolved and participants began to interact with their transnational partners/groups and were required to collaborate in completing specific tasks. The slight increase in negative emotions and decrease in positive emotions overall could be attributed to the fact that they began to face the complications that communication and collaboration entail, not only when mediated through technology across borders, but also in classes with students of diverse backgrounds (Zhou & Pilcher 2018). Through our analysis using grounded theory we found that many of the participants' responses to the reflective diaries at collection points 2, 3 and 4 were concerned with the challenges they faced, and we categorized these into four broad groups: communication, cultural, technical, and finally language issues (see Figure 2).

These same issues have been abundantly documented in the telecollaboration literature over the last two decades (Basharina, 2007; Belz, 2002; Belz & Muller-Hartmann, 2003; Helm, 2015; O'Dowd & Ritter 2006; Ware, 2005). What we sought to explore in this study was the emotional impact of these challenges on the participants. Figure 3 shows students' use of words related to different emotions in their writing about the various issues they faced during the exchange. The graph illustrates the scores on positive and negative emotions generated in LIWC for the texts coded under each of the categories described in this section: communication (COMM), cultural

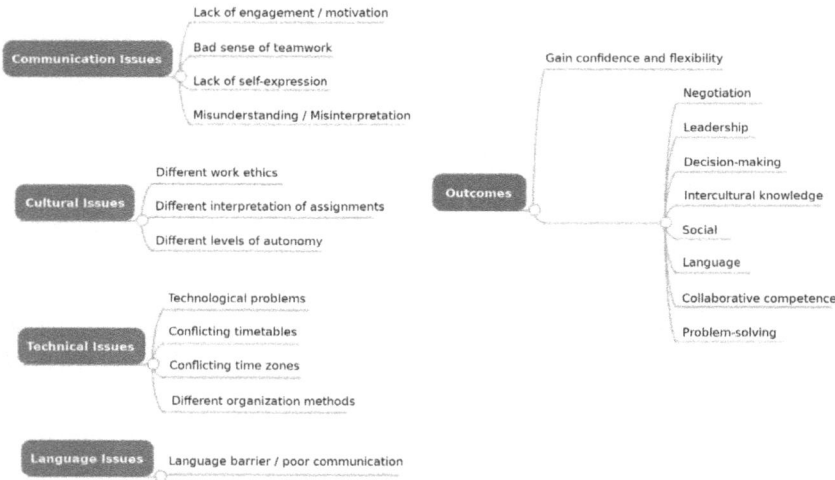

Figure 2. Intercultural issues in VE

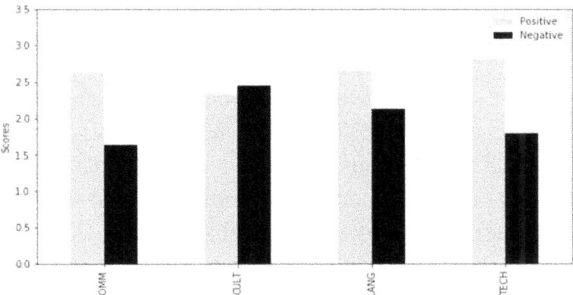

Figure 3. Emotions on challenges

(CULT), linguistic (LANG), and technical (TECH) issues. Predictably, we find that the percentage of words indicating negative emotion when students talk about the challenges they face is much higher than across the entire diaries overall.

3.2.3 Communication issues

The category "communication issues" describes students' difficulties in motivating themselves along the exchange; engaging in dialogue with their peers; working collaboratively as a team; and expressing their own ideas, making themselves understood, and understanding their counterparts. Students reported on the challenges of negotiating and coming to terms with partners in order to make decisions. This entailed finding compromises, or sometimes suppressing differences or desires:

> The biggest challenge was to come to similar conclusions as our Spanish friends. Sometimes their ideas were so much different than ours so it was difficult to find a common ground in our discussion. (Exchange 5, female, 22)

However, many of the students reported developing strategies to overcome the challenges they faced along the exchange and approached the issues from a positive viewpoint, presenting low levels of anxiety, anger, and sadness. One example is given by a group that decided to use visual materials to attract their peers' attention, thus putting into practice their multimodal competences (Hauck, 2010).

> The first task was a chaos because we did not know what to do, but when the time passed, we learnt how can we catch the attention of our students. We did a Voicethread and a Padlet with a lot of images that could attract them. Therefore, we could say that

images were the key for our communicative problems. (Exchange 16, male, 22)

In this case, the use of images was seen as helping the group to attract their partners' attention and keep the conversation going, overcoming prior communication issues. Other groups organized web-based video conferences, or used instant messaging to address their problems and were generally satisfied when they seemed to overcome the challenges.

In a different exchange involving Swedish, Spanish, and Israeli students, a participant reported on the challenges faced over time and the strategies used to overcome the difficulties. At the end of the citation we see that there is, nonetheless, an overall satisfaction with the exchange:

> Some of the challenges included lack of contribution, different priorities and lack of communication. Some of these could depend on that people were busy with other things that they prioritized more at the time. Another reason can also be cultural differences when it comes to performing and adapting to the group. We talked about contribution and the importance of the same already in the beginning of our project. Later, we also reminded each other of that during the various tasks. Finally, we managed to deal with the problems that occurred and I believe that we all were satisfied with the final outcome. (Exchange 17, no info on gender or age)

3.2.4 Technical issues

The text coded under the category "technical issues" presents emotional patterns very similar to those of "communication issues" both in the broad categories of positive and negative emotions, as well as the subcategories of negative emotions. This includes students' comments on both technical and logistic issues, such as the Internet connection, conflicting timetables, time management, and organization methods.

> In my opinion it was difficult that we all were on different schedules, so we worked on the project at different times. We could not check whether our Spanish colleagues had received our messages, so if they didn`t react for a longer time, we didn`t know why, or what was going on. The platform we used for communication nobody had known before. Maybe it would have been smoother if we had used a more popular community platform for (mandatory) cooperation. (Exchange 16, female, 22)

In an exchange involving Israeli and German students, participants expressed their satisfaction with the interaction, pointing out a few misunderstandings that were easily resolved, as the following quote states:

> Only tech issues, there weren't any disagreements, we all listened to each other and were very open to suggestions. The challenges we faced is mostly technological issues other than that I think we were dealing pretty much fine, we understood each other and most importantly respected each other, I think everything is fine as long as there is respect. (Exchange 10, male, 24)

What we found in the reflection diaries is that participants often sought to find ways to overcome the challenges rather than getting stuck on hurdles, and generally developed positive relations, as the following student's reflection shows:

> The group's rules were a good start. We also kept in touch, sharing a WhatsApp group. And yet, we had a few misunderstandings along the way. We always faced them, talked them over and moved on towards our common goal. I think the common denominators of those [snags] were: conflicting schedules and unclear, confusing correspondence. (Exchange 10, male, 44)

3.2.5 Language issues

In the category "language issues" students reported on how they dealt with participants' different proficiency levels of English.[10] Some students expressed frustration with their peers' lower competence levels, which were seen as the cause of miscommunications, hindrances to task completion in terms of slowing things down, imbalances in amount of work done, or poor quality work.

> I think we had some serious communication issues. I think this was caused partially by the fact that their English was not that great. Their sentences could sometimes sound very offensive "Do not work on the document without asking us first." In hindsight I think they did not mean it in a negative way, but just did not have the vocabulary to express themselves in a nice way. (Exchange 8, female, 21)

Others expressed frustration at their own struggles to express themselves but also satisfaction with the progress they made over time. A Spanish student commented on the challenges faced while interacting with Swedish partners:

10　The majority of exchanges in the project took place in English – though hardly any of the partner classes were located in anglophone contexts.

> One of the challenges was to write all the information in English, because sometimes you weren't able to say exactly what you meant, so you had to think the best way to explain, in little words, what you wanted. The first time took me lot of time to come up with the right ideas, but when time went by, I got used to writing faster and better. (Exchange 15, male, 28)

Technical, communication, and language issues all presented similar patterns in terms of positive and negative emotions. In their final reflections participants retrospectively framed the difficulties from a generally positive perspective; while acknowledging the challenges, they saw them as opportunities which allowed them to improve their skills and learn from the exchange and partners.

3.2.6 Cultural issues

In the text we coded as cultural issues, participants reported on the difficulties they faced in understanding their partners' different ways of thinking and behaving, and this was accompanied by negative emotions in some cases. Certain behaviors were read as impolite and rude, while others were ascribed to personality differences. Some students approached what they identified as cultural differences as opportunities to learn from their peers and their interactions with them, as in the quote below, while others engaged with difference from a polarizing perspective of "us" versus "them," which made the challenges difficult to overcome. In the following quote, a German student refers to differences as cultural gaps, but approaches them from a positive light in order to learn from the experience and have a good interaction with his/her Israeli partners:

> I faced some challenges when communicating in the group. Along with the technological difficulties (Internet connections and so on), there were many cultural gaps that were hard to ignore. I had to compromise about some of the ideas in the projects to maintain good manners and politeness. I had a different way of thinking then the group overseas but I guess that what makes the connection and the interaction more interesting. (Exchange 10, no info on gender or age)

The following reflection shows what appear to be different orientations to the project, but also a student recognizing that her own particular ways of behaving might not have been appreciated by her peers, demonstrating a degree of self-reflexivity and openness in her attempt to understand what went wrong:

> We did not really find a personal base. We just had a work relationship. I think that was a shame, but we tried sometimes and our relationship did not improve. I told them about my weekend for example and what I did with my friends but they were not really interested in it and just talked about work again. I guess we were just too different in personality. They seemed to be very shy and more reserved than I am. Moreover they seemed to be very dutiful and therefore always primarily concentrated on the tasks. And I guess I did some things too, that they did not like. (Exchange 1, female, 23)

However, in some cases, which we categorized as "blaming others," participants expressed frustration and anger because they felt alone and/or ignored by their peers and complained about the burden of having to meet deadlines and accomplish tasks that were supposed to be done collaboratively. In the following quote, a Polish student expressed strong negative feelings about the local partners with whom s/he was working in a group as well as the international ones:

> I am furious with all of my partners. I had to take responsibility for the project because if I hadn't done it, I wonder if somebody else would have remembered about meeting the deadlines. I had to nag people, especially my Polish partners, about doing the tasks. I was angry because most of them didn't contribute anything in our conversations on Facebook; they were just lurking and it was almost always me who consulted our Spanish partners. I was really angry, frustrated and ashamed that my Polish partners didn't respond but I didn't do anything about it because I think I was already secretly perceived by them as a nag. I'm furious that I had to nag people. I'm also furious about the fact that I'm probably the only person who completed every task. And yet everybody will probably get a certificate that they don't deserve. (Exchange 9, no info on gender or age)

3.3 Overall Learning Experience

With the exception of a few cases, it was found that whilst the challenges that students had to face led to negative emotions, they also served as opportunities for them to learn and search for creative ways to overcome the challenges and difficulties. Students' reflections report the difficulty of having to work collaboratively with transnational partners online – as well as working in local groups. In order to complete the tasks and meet deadlines, they had to improve their negotiation, problem-solving, and collaborative skills (in addition to other competencies shown in Figure 2), so as to make decisions regarding their assignments. The exchanges forced participants to leave their comfort zone, which was initially unsettling and challenging, but after the last main collaborative task that students engaged in, the majority reported on the positive contribution of VE to their learning experience. Many participants reported a greater acceptance of difference, and willingness to communicate and collaborate with others, though of course reporting certain attitudes such as openness to difference does not in itself constitute evidence for this.

3.3.1 Attitudes to difference

What seems to emerge in this first analysis of the data is that in order to meet course requirements and complete tasks the students focused on similarities and finding common ground in order to complete their assignments, but at times this meant suppressing personal opinions or deeper explorations and engagement with difference. In several of the student comments above we find a view of difference as something to be managed or tolerated in order to complete their tasks.

Students' attitudes to difference were thus further explored in the qualitative data analysis, which revealed a variety of attitudes towards difference – from the more frequent orientations to similarity and minimization of difference to engagement with difference at deeper levels and awareness of complexity.

3.3.2 Orientation to similarity

The majority of students' comments show an orientation to similarities and shared goals. The two quotes below refer to participants' reflections after the end of the completion of the first task, when they were required to respond to the question about their initial impressions of their virtual partners. The following reflection comes from a participant taking part in an exchange involving Israeli, Swedish, and Spanish students:

> Even coming from other countries, we are all the same. We all have obstacles, jobs and other challenges in life, but we are all looking for the same thing, which is to improve ourselves as professionals in the field of education. (Exchange 17, female, 30)

The following extract comes from the exchange involving Canadian and Israeli students:

> At the end of the day we are all people, with interests that are universal. Maybe the only significant differences are our age and the

fact that some of us are retraining students, heading for a second career as teachers. (Exchange 11, female, 46)

This focus on similarities was also found in later journal entries, when students responded to a question about their own and their partners' culture. The following quote comes from a Spanish student interacting with Swedish partners:

> There aren't many differences between our cultures as far as I could tell. They also like to have fun and get together with their friends every time they have the occasion, which is very Spanish too. (Exchange 16, no info on gender or age)

And also this quote:

> So far I could not see much difference, it was very interesting to read about their view and how it is in Portugal when reading their questionnaire. (Exchange 13, female, 24)

The recognition of shared interests may be important at the initial stage of a collaborative relationship, and indeed this project is framed in terms of a shared professional interest in education. However, the "assumption of similarity" can be problematic, it has been called a "stumbling block" in intercultural understanding as it can prevent students from cultivating curiosity and openness towards difference, and assumes mutual understanding in communication.

Some of the participants identify differences, but do not know what to do with them, as the recognition of difference might lead to conflict. In the comment below we see a participant who has noticed different perspectives on teaching and reports on the emotional impact this had on her – though the different views are not explained in the reflection, nor do they seem to have been explored.

> In my opinion, [participant] has different views on teaching. Sometimes it makes me a little angry but we should notice that we can learn something new from her and she can learn something from us. Despite this fact, our main life goal is to be a perfect teacher in the future and we want to achieve it by our experiences. (Exchange 1, female, 22)

We can feel the frustration of this student: while she recognizes her partner's different views on teaching, she sees a need to be open or tolerant so they can learn from each other.

3.3.3 Making cultural comparisons

Following the design of the virtual exchange and the second phase which entailed cultural comparisons about their educational systems, some of the students reflected on how the differences and similarities might shape their own views on education as well as their expectations and the challenges they faced in the exchange itself:

> We used the platform to talk about the education system and the schools that they have there. We compared these with our schools and saw the differences. We then asked questions and continued on in this way to keep the conversation going. (Exchange 15, male, 19)

There is some evidence of looking beyond static national culture categories, but there is often an us-them orientation, with respondents' own culture being the standard by which others are measured:

> I noticed that our (German) ideas of teaching is to teach the students the curriculum, but in an exciting way, to make it fun and also to keep inclusion in mind. The first thing the Israeli teacher said is that it is the most important to teach the students respect and values above all and also to teach them to be better persons before they teach them the curriculum. That is a different mindset for teaching, one that is not really brought to us in our education. (Exchange 10, female, 19)

The student comments on the different mindset, but does not reflect on or show evidence of having explored the possible historical, social, and/or political motivations behind these different orientations, though of course this is not to say that they were not discussed in class or with their partners, simply that they were not reported.

Students sometimes perceived particular behavioral responses as culturally motivated – and tended to define culture in terms of national cultures. There is also, as illustrated in the comment below, an awareness amongst some students of the negative cultural evaluation of stereotyping and making generalizations (Tusting, Crawshaw, & Callen, 2002). The diary prompts, however, can be seen to legitimate generalizations, and the students use their experience in the exchange, or information provided by their peers, to provide "evidence" for these generalizations:

> Well, since I am always trying to avoid prejudices I was not really thinking about my partners' culture a lot. However, I have to admit, that I was a little "shocked" when my partners told me that Polish

people can be very greedy due to their low wages. (Exchange 1, male, 23)

Regarding interculturality, students reflect on cultural differences in generic terms, or with respect to "others," yet only a few reflect on the origin of their own assumptions and beliefs, or present a view of culture as dynamic and creative.

3.3.4 Engaging with complexity

A small number of participants did demonstrate a higher level of self-reflexivity and openness towards difference as they compared cultures, habits, and ways of thinking and/or behaving, while reflecting on the collaboration with their international partners and how they could implement some ideas that come from their peers in their own educational contexts.

> I learned that we have a different way of thinking and acting. This does not mean that one is better than the other, just that they are different and I think it is really interesting to be able to learn and even experience the habits and ways of life, which change depending on what we are used to doing in our everyday lives. (Exchange 15, female, 23)

The use of inclusive "we" and "they" in the reflection above suggests that the participant is also reflecting on the cultural embeddedness of her own beliefs and values and how one's life experiences also affect these beliefs. In the following extract, a student is reflecting upon their differences and similarities when they are engaged in group tasks:

> I believe that we have similarities as well as differences in our approaches doing different tasks, especially group tasks. The similarities are for example avoiding too direct tone to each other, instead, we tended to have patience with each other and trying to avoid conflicts. The differences include various levels of effort and ambition, willingness to start conversations, and adaptation to deadlines. (Exchange 17, no info available)

Some of the participants reflect on the complexity that exists between different cultures and also within their own in a more abstract/theoretical way: "I think this experience will help us all to understand a little bit more about educational backgrounds around the world and how the culture of each country plays a fundamental role in the language learning-teaching process." There is an understanding of the many different dimensions of cultures, identities, and beliefs, and of the factors which can influence this. In this way of engaging with difference, students speculate about their differences and similarities, but leave the questions open for reflection. The language used for these reflections however is more cognitive and analytical than emotional.

> Differences and similarities I have noticed are difficult to put down as cultural so far. The strictness of deadlines might be a difference between Spanish and Dutch cultures, but it might have other reasons as well. Our group also has a gender divide (2 Dutch boys and 4 Spanish girls) so perhaps there are gender differences as well when dealing with these kind of assignments. For example, the Dutch (boys) are very result-driven and the Spanish (girls) are more focused on discussing as much as possible before finalizing a task. Whether that is cultural or not is difficult to say. (Exchange 8, male, 19)

4 Discussion

This study sought to examine first of all how students experienced their telecollaboration in terms of emotions. We found that participants' reflections revealed high expectations – linked to integrative motivation (Gardner & Lambert, 1972), which were accompanied by positive emotions at the outset of the exchanges, but also perhaps an unrealistic or idealized view of intercultural communication. As they began to engage with their peers in "real-life communication" and had to address linguistic, technical, and communication issues, some negative emotions began to appear in the reflections, such as frustration and anxiety. However, although they struggled, many participants reported on how they identified ways to overcome the difficulties they were facing, and by the end of the project reported being generally satisfied with their achievements. They saw the challenges as having provided a learning opportunity through which they were able to develop, for example, flexibility in communication and problem-solving skills. The participants' emotional "journey" confirms the importance of viewing emotions and attitudes not as unchangeable individual variables but rather as related to the activities learners engage in, and socially constructed through their interactions and collaboration with their peers (Ushioda, 2007; Negueruela-Azaruola, 2011).

Some of the tensions that several small-scale studies have found as regards the practice of telecollaboration (Ware & Kramsch, 2005) have been confirmed in this large-scale study, in particular the types of challenges that participants face in communicating and collaborating with their peers. These were primarily issues related to limited interaction with peers, language and technical problems, and different orientations to the exchange and the tasks they were supposed to do (Basharina, 2007; Belz, 2002; Belz & Muller-Hartmann, 2003; O'Dowd & Ritter, 2006; Helm, 2015; Ware, 2005). This study adds to the field an understanding of the emotional impact that these challenges might have on participants, in terms of positive/negative emotions, and on a broader level rather than individual. It could be suggested that careful planning of exchanges on the part of the partner teachers and more clearly defined and mutually agreed "rules of engagement" for students might lead to fewer problems and hence less negative emotions for students. On the other hand, having everything prepared for them would lead to a less authentic and "real-life" experience for the students, and fewer opportunities for problem-solving and team work. This is one of the long-standing tensions in telecollaboration research. At the turn of this century, Belz (2002) asked this same question in her conclusions of a study on a virtual exchange in which students had suggested that the main cultural learning came from the "epiphenomena which arose in the process of task completion" (p. 75) rather than the pedagogical goals of the tasks assigned. She concluded that cultural faultlines should not be smoothed over, but that participants could be sensitized to concepts of intercultural communication in order to prepare them to learn from these epiphenomena. Telecollaborative exchanges are valuable because indeed they can meet the "authenticity gap" that motivation researchers have identified in the language classroom (Henry, 2013), by giving participants the opportunity to engage as "users" of a foreign language (Darvin & Norton, 2015; Ushioda, 2011) which entails also grappling with the "messiness" and unpredictability of real-life communication.

The second research question regarded how participants' expressed their attitude towards difference. We found that many participants oriented towards similarity as this was seen to make their collaborations with their peers easier, and allowed them to complete the tasks they had been assigned by their teachers. This could be seen as a way of avoiding the risks of critical episodes that Ware & Kramsch (2005) identified, though as has been highlighted by Ware (2005), it can lead to missed opportunities for intercultural learning. Few reflections displayed evidence of curiosity and interest in exploring cultural diversity or divergences in opinion.

The students' attitudes reflect a functional orientation towards intercultural competence, which stems in part from the design of the model of virtual exchange and the underlying rationale. The main focus of this task-based model of virtual exchange was on developing future teachers' ability to use technology to exchange information, to communicate and collaborate with distant partners on specific activities so that in the future they themselves would be able to implement virtual exchange with their students

(O'Dowd, 2017). The need to collaborate and work together with their transnational partners was the main concern of many of the participants and led them to sometimes set aside or to "tolerate" differences in opinion so they could move forward with their tasks, find solutions to their problems. This model of virtual exchange responds to the employability orientation of European policy, where a functional view of competences – digital, linguistic, and intercultural – is seen to prepare young people for the workplace (Council of Europe, 2018). In terms of intercultural learning, it may be an opportunity for "intergroup contact" (Paolini et al., 2018) which, according to social psychologists, can lead to a reduction in prejudice and change beliefs. A positive experience might thus be an important step in arousing future teachers' curiosity to engage with people outside their regular sphere. Nonetheless, it may not equip them for the "confrontations with differences of all kinds" (Souza, 2011: 1) that social tensions and increasing social inequalities are bringing about.

Kramsch & Hua (2016: 48) argue that what is missing from task-based teaching is "a process- and context-oriented approach that is politically and ideologically sensitive, that goes beyond the here-and-now of problem-solving and the negotiation of immediate tasks, and that raises historical and political consciousness." This argument appears to be supported by our analysis of the student reflections which show a strong focus on the tasks and few reflections on the power dynamics behind the exchanges, for which historical and political awareness is required, what Kramsch defines as "symbolic competence" (2009).

Scholars who take a critical, decolonial stance on intercultural communication argue that relational and functional models of intercultural communication serve to maintain the status quo, to maintain the advantages and privileges of those who wield them (Andreotti & Souza, 2016). A more ethical engagement with the other would pose interculturality as a social project which looks more closely at the colonial, racial, and structural issues and seeks to transform structures and institutions. In emotional terms this would no doubt be more challenging for participants as a critical approach does not seek simple solutions to clear problems but rather "commands us to become comfortable with the discomfort of the uncertainties inherent in living the plurality of existence" (Andreotti, 2012: 26).

5 Conclusion

Dealing with such a large dataset has presented us with the opportunity to explore the impact of a certain model of virtual exchange on participants' emotions and attitudes to difference. This model is based on engaging partner classes in a series of tasks which go from introductions and exchange of information, to cultural comparisons and finally collaboration on the development of a final product (The EVALUATE Group, 2019). Adopting a large-scale approach in this study, which was part of a European policy experimentation, was seen as important because most of the research in the telecollaboration field has, until now, explored case studies and single exchanges and there was a need for research "that analyzes a greater number of student cohorts using the same study design" (Ware, 2005: 79). In this study we have identified some general trends across these multiple exchanges regarding the "emotional journey" of this model of virtual exchange, the impact of the challenges on participants, and also the different ways they engaged with difference in their reflections.

However this study also presents several limitations. The strength of a large-scale approach is that it can offer a kaleidoscopic view of emotions and engagement, but clearly it will not take into account the contingencies and specificities of the local classrooms and contexts from which the learners and teachers were interacting, or details regarding the tasks used, all of which have a strong impact on the outcomes of an exchange and would also offer explanatory power for an interpretation of the reflections (see The EVALUATE Group, 2019 for case studies focusing on specific exchanges). Secondly, the questions guiding the students' reflections were developed by the research team and not the teachers, and though they were related to the virtual exchange model, they may not always have been relevant to the discussions taking place in class. Also, the students were writing for the research team, not the teachers, though students could choose to send their reflections or adapt and share them with teachers. This was a deliberate part of the research design as the aim was for participants to feel free in sharing their honest opinions. However, the disadvantages of this include a possible lack of student investment in the reflections, and a lost opportunity for further learning if students' experiences and reflections on the exchanges were not also discussed in class. Reflection should be an integral part of the learning process.

Finally, the guiding questions for reflection were framed in terms of similarity and difference between national and educational cultures. Whilst this may support a sensitization to the institutional conditions that Belz (2002) recommends – and an awareness of how culture may influence the way we think – it may also contribute to participants' essentializing culture and perhaps may even legitimate generalizations. Future research could use different questions which lead students to reflect on diversity and heterogeneity within their own classes and societies as well as others', the multiple dimensions of their identities, and the socio-historical groundings of their own and educational discourses.

References

Al-Hoorie, A. H. (2017). Sixty years of language motivation research: Looking back and looking forward. *SAGE Open*, Jan.–March, 1–11. https://doi.org/10.1177/2158244017701976

Allport, G. W. (1954). *The Nature of Prejudice*. Reading, MA: Addison-Wesley.

Andreotti, V. (2012). Education, knowledge, and the righting of wrongs. *Other Education: The Journal of Educational Alternatives*, 1(1), 19–31.

Andreotti, V., & Souza, L. M. T. M. de. (2016). Critical education and postcolonialism. In M. A. Peters (ed.), *Encyclopedia of Educational Philosophy and Theory*. Singapore: Springer. https://doi.org/10.1007/978-981-287-532-7_182-1

Avgousti, M. I. (2018). Intercultural communicative competence and online exchanges: A systematic review. *Computer Assisted Language Learning*, 31(8), 819–853. https://doi.org/10.1080/09588221.2018.1455713

Basharina, O. K. (2007). An activity theory perspective on student-reported contradictions in international telecollaboration. *Language Learning & Technology*, 11(2), 82–103. http://dx.doi.org/10125/44105

Belz, J. A. (2002). Social dimensions of telecollaborative foreign language study [electronic version]. *Language Learning & Technology*, 6(1), 60–81.

Belz, J. A., & Muller-Hartmann, A. (2003). Teachers as intercultural learners: Negotiating German-American telecollaboration along the institutional fault line. *Modern Language Journal*, 87, 71–89. https://doi.org/10.1111/1540-4781.00179

Brown, R., & Hewstone, M. (2005). An integrative theory of intergroup contact. In M. P. Zanna (ed.), *Advances in Experimental Social Psychology*, Vol. 37 (pp. 255–343). San Diego, CA: Elsevier Academic Press.

Charmaz, K. (2005). Grounded theory in the 21st century: A qualitative method for advancing social justice research. *Handbook of Qualitative Research*, 3, 507–535.

Charmaz, K. (2006). *Constructing Grounded Theory: A Practical Guide through Qualitative Analysis*. London: SAGE.

Charmaz, K., & Belgrave, L. L. (2018). Thinking about data with grounded theory. *Qualitative Inquiry*. Online preprint https://doi.org/10.1177/1077800418809455

Council of Europe (2018). *Common European Framework of Reference for Languages: Learning, Teaching, Assessment. Companion Volume with New Descriptors*. Strasbourg: Council of Europe. https://rm.coe.int/cefr-companion-volume-with-new-descriptors-2018/1680787989

Darvin, R., & Norton, B. (2015). Identity and a model of investment in applied linguistics. *Annual Review of Applied Linguistics*, 35, 36–56. https://doi.org/10.1017/S0267190514000191

Dewaele, J.-M., & Li, C. (2018). Editorial. *SSLLT*, 8(1), 15–19. http://pressto.amu.edu.pl/index.php/ssllt. https://doi.org/10.14746/ssllt.2014.4.2.5 https://doi.org/10.14746/ssllt.2018.8.1.1

Dewaele, J.-M., & MacIntyre, P. D. (2014). The two faces of Janus? Anxiety and enjoyment in the foreign language classroom. *Studies in Second Language Learning and Teaching*, 4(2), 237–274. https://doi.org/10.14746/ssllt.2014.4.2.5

Dooly, M. (2016). "Please remove your avatar from my personal space": Competences of the telecollaboratively efficient person. In R. O'Dowd & T. Lewis (eds.), *Online Intercultural Exchange: Policy, Pedagogy, Practice* (pp. 192–208). New York: Routledge.

Dooly, M., & Sadler, R. (2013). Filling in the gaps: Linking theory and practice through telecollaboration in teacher education. *ReCALL*, 25(1), 4–29. https://doi.org/10.1017/S0958344012000237

Dulay, H., & Burt, A. (1977). Remarks on creativity in language acquisition. In M. Burt, H. Dulay, & M. Finnochiaro (eds.), *Viewpoints on English as a Second Language* (pp. 95–126). New York: Regents.

Gardner, R., & Lambert, W. (1972). *Attitude and Motivation in Second-language Learning*. Rowley, MA: Newbury House.

Gregersen, T. S. (2003). To err is human: A reminder to instructors of language-anxious students. *Foreign Language Annals*, 36(1): 25–32. https://doi.org/10.1111/j.1944-9720.2003.tb01929.x

Hauck, M. (2010). Telecollaboration: At the interface between multimodal and intercultural communicative competence. In S. Guth & F. Helm (eds.), *Telecollaboration 2.0: Language, Literacy and Intercultural Learning in the 21st Century* (pp. 219–248). Bern: Peter Lang

Helm, F. (2015). The practices and challenges of telecollaboration in higher education in Europe. *Language Learning & Technology*, 19(2), 197–217. http://dx.doi.org/10125/44424

Helm, F. (2018). *Emerging Identities in Virtual Exchange*. Research-publishing.net. https://doi.org/10.14705/rpnet.2018.25.9782490057191

Henry, A. (2013). Digital games and ELT: Bridging the authenticity gap. In E. Ushioda (ed.), *International Perspectives on Motivation: Language Learning and Professional Challenges* (pp. 133–155). Basingstoke, UK: Palgrave Macmillan. https://doi.org/10.1057/9781137000873_8

Horwitz, E. K. (2017). On the misreading of Horwitz, Horwitz, and Cope (1986) and the need to balance anxiety research and the experiences of anxious language learners. In C. Gkonou, M. Daubney, & J.-M. Dewaele (eds.), *New Insights into Language Anxiety*. Bristol: Multilingual Matters. https://doi.org/10.21832/9781783097722-004

Kolb, D. A. (2015). *Experiential Learning: Experience as the Source of Learning and Development* (2nd ed.). New York: Pearson Education, Inc.

Kramsch, C. (2009). *The Multilingual Subject*. Oxford: Oxford University Press.

Kramsch, C., & Zhu Hua (2016). Language, culture and language teaching. In G. Hall (ed.), *Routledge Handbook of English Language Teaching* (pp. 38–50). London: Routlege.

Krashen, S. (1981). *Second Language Acquisition and Second Language Learning*. Oxford: Pergamon Press (Internet edition 2002). Retrieved from http://www.sdkrashen.com/content/books/sl_acquisition_and_learning.pdf.

Lewis, T., & O'Dowd, R. (2016). Online intercultural exchange and foreign language learning: a systematic review. In R. O'Dowd & T. Lewis (eds.), *Online*

Intercultural Exchange: Policy, Pedagogy, Practice (pp. 21–66). London: Routledge. https://doi.org/10.4324/9781315678931

Liddicoat, D., & Scarino, A. (2013). *Intercultural Language Teaching and Learning*. Oxford: Wiley-Blackwell. https://doi.org/10.1002/9781118482070

Long, M. (1996). The role of the linguistic environment in second language acquisition. In William Ritchie & Tej Bhatia (eds.), *Handbook of Second Language Acquisition* (pp. 413–468). San Diego: Academic Press. https://doi.org/10.1016/B978-012589042-7/50015-3

MacIntyre, P. D., & Mercer, S. (2014). Introducing positive psychology to SLA. *Studies in Second Language Learning and Teaching*, 4(2), 153–172. https://doi.org/10.14746/ssllt.2014.4.2.2

Martin, J. R. (2000). Beyond exchange: Appraisal systems in English. In S. Hunston & G. Thompson (eds.), *Evaluation in Text: Authorial Stance and the Construction of Discourse* (pp. 142–175). Oxford: Oxford University Press.

Martin, J. R., & White, P. R. R. (2005). *The Language of Evaluation: Appraisal in English*. London: Palgrave.

Mezirow, J. (1991). *Transformative Dimensions of Adult Learning*. San Francisco: Jossey Bass.

Negueruela-Azarola, E. (2011). Changing reasons as reasoning changes: A narrative interview on second language classroom motivation, telecollaboration, and the learning of foreign languages. *Language Awareness*, 20(3), 183–201. https://doi.org/10.1080/09658416.2011.570348

Norton, B. (2000). *Identity and Language Learning*. London: Pearson Education.

O'Dowd, R. (2017). Exploring the impact of telecollaboration in initial teacher education: The EVALUATE project. *The EUROCALL Review*, 25(2), 38–42. https://doi.org/10.4995/eurocall.2017.7636

O'Dowd, R., & Lewis, T. (eds). (2016). *Online Intercultural Exchange: Policy, Pedagogy, Practice*. London: Routledge. https://doi.org/10.4324/9781315678931

O'Dowd, R., & Ritter, M. (2006). Understanding and working with "failed communication" in telecollaborative exchanges. *CALICO Journal*, 23(3), 623–642. https://doi.org/10.1558/cj.v23i3.623-642

O'Dowd, R., & Ware, P. (2009). Critical issues in telecollaborative task design. *Computer Assisted Language Learning*, 22(2), 173–188.

Paolini, S., Harwood, J., Hewstone, M., & Neumann, D. L. (2018). Seeking and avoiding intergroup contact: Future frontiers of research on building social integration. *Social and Personality Psychology Compass*. Retrieved from https://www.researchgate.net/publication/328741781_Seeking_and_avoiding_intergroup_contact_Future_frontiers_of_research_on_building_social_integration. https://doi.org/10.1111/spc3.12422

Pavlenko, A. (2013). The affective turn in SLA: From "affective factors" to "language desire" and "commodification of affect." In D. Gabryś-Barker & J. Bielska (eds.), *The Affective Dimension in Second Language Acquisition* (pp. 3–28). Bristol, UK: Multilingual Matters.

Pennebaker, J. W., Boyd, R. L., Jordan, K., & Blackburn, K. (2015). *The Development and Psychometric Properties of LIWC 2015*. Austin, TX: University of Texas at Austin.

Pettigrew, T. F. (1986). The intergroup contact hypothesis reconsidered. In M. Hewstone & R. Brown (eds.), *Contact and Conflict in Intergroup Encounters* (pp. 169–195). Oxford: Blackwell.

Portalla, T., & Chen, G.-M. (2010). The development and validation of the intercultural effectiveness scale. *Intercultural Communication Studies*, 19(3), 21–37.

Savicki, V., & Price, M. V. (2015). Student reflective writing: Cognition and affect before, during, and after study abroad. *Journal of College Student Development*, 56(6), 587–601. https://doi.org/10.1353/csd.2015.0063

Souza, L. M. T. M. de. (2011). Towards a redefinition of critical literacy: Conflict and meaning making. Translation of "Para uma redefinição de letramento crítico: conflito e produção de significação" in R. F. Maciel & V. A. Araújo (eds.), *Formação de Professores de Línguas: Ampliando Perspectiva* (pp. 128–140). Jundiaí, São Paolo: Paco Editorial.

Swain, M. (1995). Three functions of output in second language learning. In G. Cook & B. Seidlhofer (eds.), *Principle and Practice in Applied Linguistics: Studies in Honor of H. G. Widdowson* (pp. 125–144). Oxford University Press, Oxford.

Swain, M. (2013). The inseparability of cognition and emotion in second language learning. *Language Teaching*, 46, 195–207. https://doi.org/10.1017/S0261444811000486

Taie, M., & Afshari, A. (2015). A critical review on the socio-educational model of SLA. *Theory and Practice in Language Studies*, 5(3), 605–612. https://doi.org/10.17507/tpls.0503.21

The EVALUATE Group (2019). *Evaluating the Impact of Virtual Exchange on Initial Teacher Education: A European Policy Experiment*. Retrieved from https://doi.org/10.14705/rpnet.2019.29.9782490057337

Tusting, K., Crawshaw, R., & Callen, B. (2002). "I know, 'cos I was there": How residence abroad students use personal experience to legitimate cultural generalizations. *Discourse & Society*, 13(5), 651–672. https://doi.org/10.1177/0957926502013005278

Ushioda, E. (2007). Motivation, autonomy and sociocultural theory. In P. Benson (ed.), *Learner Autonomy 8: Teacher and Learner Perspectives* (pp. 5–24). Dublin: Authentik.

Ushioda, E. (2011). Language learning motivation, self and identity: Current theoretical perspectives. *Computer Assisted Language Learning*, 24, 199–210. https://doi.org/10.1080/09588221.2010.538701

Vinagre, M. (2015). Training teachers for virtual collaboration: A case study. *British Journal of Educational Technology*, 47(4), 787–802. https://doi.org/10.1111/bjet.12363

Vinagre, M., & Corral, A. (2018). Evaluative language for rapport building in virtual collaboration: An analysis of appraisal in computer-mediated interaction. *Language and Intercultural Communication*, 18(3), 335–350. https://doi.org/10.1080/14708477.2017.1378227

Ware, P. (2005). "Missed" communication in online communication: Tensions in a German-American telecollaboration. *Language Learning & Technology*, 9(2), 64–89. https://scholarspace.manoa.hawaii.edu/bitstream/10125/44020/1/09_02_ware.pdf

Ware, P., & Kramsch, C. (2005). Toward an intercultural stance: Teaching German and English through telecollaboration. *Modern Language Journal*, 89, 190–205. https://doi.org/10.1111/j.1540-4781.2005.00274.x

Zhou, V., & Pilcher, N. (2018). Tapping the thirdness in the intercultural space of dialogue, *Language and Intercultural Communication*, 19(1), 23–37. https://doi.org/10.1080/14708477.2018.1545025

Appendix: Prompts for Reflective Journals

D1
How would you describe your cultural background?
What do you hope to achieve or learn from this virtual exchange?

D2
What do you feel you have learnt about your own and your partners' national and educational cultures?
Do you think you or your partners have any stereotyped views of each other's cultures? If so, describe them. Have you discussed them or just noticed them? What do you think lies behind these stereotypes?
After working together on this first task, what are your initial impressions of your virtual partners?

D3
How do you feel about the interactions with your virtual partners so far? What are you finding easy or difficult? What steps do you think you could take to improve the interactions?
What have you learnt about the topics that you investigated? What cultural differences and similarities did you notice between the way your topic is dealt with in the two contexts?
Have you learned anything about your own or your partners' culture that you didn't expect?

D4
How do you feel about working in an intercultural team?
Describe any challenges you faced in your group work. What do you think the causes were? How did you try to solve them?
Is there anything that has positively affected your telecollaborative exchange experience?
Is there anything that has negatively affected your experience?

About the Authors

Francesca Helm is Assistant Professor of English at the Department of Political Science, Law and International Studies, University of Padova, Italy. Her research interests are in the fields of identity, intercultural learning, virtual exchange, and internationalization of education. She currently leads the Monitoring and Evaluation of the European Commission's recently launched Erasmus+Virtual Exchange project. Recent publications include the 2018 volume *Emerging Identities in Virtual Exchange*, https://research-publishing.net/book?10.14705/rpnet.2018.25.9782490057191.

Alice Baroni is a postdoctoral researcher at the Department of Political Science, Law and International Studies, University of Padova, Italy. Her main interests are in (visual) ethnographic and participatory research in the contexts of urban violence; the relationships between conventional and new media; policies on media and gender equality; and the role of media as a tool for conflict resolution and social justice.

Index

ability to decenter: 3, 117, 121, 123, 127, 133, 134, 135, 137, 138
acceptance: 11, 15, 21, 122, 182
anxiety: 17, 32, 33, 34, 36, 39, 45, 49, 167, 168, 169, 170, 173, 177, 186
appraisal theory: 2, 4, 5, 65, 66, 67, 68, 71, 72, 73, 74, 76, 81, 82, 86, 87, 88, 145, 147, 151, 170

computer-mediated communication: 34, 35, 95, 121, 144
corpus: 71, 96, 150, 153, 172
culture: 2, 9, 10, 11, 12, 13, 14, 15, 16, 17, 18, 23, 24, 25, 30, 31, 35, 38, 40, 41, 46, 47, 51, 53, 61, 67, 68, 69, 70, 76, 82, 87, 92, 94, 95, 96, 104, 109, 112, 121, 122, 133, 135, 144, 148, 175, 183, 184, 185, 186, 189, 194
curiosity: 4, 9, 10, 13, 16, 22, 92, 183, 187, 188

emotions: 4, 17, 18, 65, 66, 72, 157, 159, 166, 167, 168, 169, 172, 173, 174, 176, 177, 180, 181, 186, 187, 188, 189
engagement: 2, 4, 11, 22, 35, 65, 66, 97, 108, 147, 167, 170, 171, 182, 187, 188, 189
ethnographic approach: 3, 97, 99
evaluative language: 67, 170

identity: 31, 33, 36, 48, 52, 169
instructional materials: 149, 151, 152, 153, 155, 156, 157
intercultural communication: 1, 4, 9, 10, 15, 18, 31, 32, 34, 35, 36, 40, 45, 47, 48, 52, 54, 94, 121, 122, 126, 134, 187

intercultural communicative competence: 2, 10, 12, 13, 23, 24, 119, 121

learner beliefs: 33, 35
literacy: 13, 24, 118, 120, 145, 146, 147, 148, 158

mixed methods: 166, 172
motivation: 2, 13, 16, 18, 33, 39, 43, 49, 50, 51, 62, 95, 97, 102, 112, 135, 167, 168, 169, 170, 175, 184, 186, 187
multimodality: 3, 24, 118, 119, 124, 139

negotiation: 3, 5, 15, 16, 23, 51, 52, 92, 93, 94, 96, 97, 98, 100, 104, 107, 108, 110, 111, 112, 157, 181, 188
novice learner: 30, 31, 32, 34, 36, 41, 45, 46, 47, 50, 51, 56

openness: 2, 4, 9, 10, 11, 16, 17, 21, 92, 112, 133, 147, 161, 180, 182, 183, 185

perceptions: 3, 4, 21, 23, 31, 32, 33, 34, 35, 36, 39, 40, 41, 42, 45, 47, 50, 54, 55, 56

reflection/reflective: 3, 4, 11, 14, 23, 31, 37, 39, 40, 50, 65, 71, 112, 125, 127, 133, 134, 135, 138, 145, 149, 166, 172, 176, 179, 180, 181, 182, 183, 184, 185, 186, 187, 188, 189, 194
respect: 16, 24, 135, 179

social media: 12, 30, 95, 97, 98, 99
social semiotic discourse: 4, 125, 128
sociocognitive theory: 9, 11, 12, 15, 16, 17, 19, 22, 94, 169, 173, 186

sociocultural perspective: 19, 92, 145, 167, 170

task-based teaching: 95, 158, 166, 188
task design: 2, 21, 147, 157, 159
teacher education: 5, 117, 118, 119, 120, 121, 122, 123, 139, 144, 145, 146, 166, 171
telecollaboration: 2, 3, 9, 12, 13, 14, 15, 18, 20, 21, 22, 23, 24, 25, 30, 36, 92, 93, 94, 95, 96, 97, 98, 102, 112, 117, 118, 119, 120, 121, 122, 123, 135, 138, 139, 144, 145, 146, 147, 149, 150, 161, 166, 168, 169, 170, 171, 172, 176, 186, 187, 189
text selection: 149, 150, 162

virtual exchange: 1, 2, 4, 5, 6, 30, 31, 32, 36, 37, 38, 41, 42, 45, 47, 50, 51, 53, 54, 55, 56, 64, 73, 87, 144, 166, 167, 170, 171, 172, 173, 176, 184, 187, 188, 189, 194
virtual interaction: 2, 3, 4, 5, 65, 68, 86, 122

Milton Keynes UK
Ingram Content Group UK Ltd.
UKHW030009010324
438477UK00004B/62